Building Practice

Introduction

Continual States of Becoming

Shrinking demand for new office and commercial space, rising building-material costs, and a weakened housing sector effectively left the United States without a market for architectural services during the global economic downturn of the late aughts.[1] On the heels of this so-called Great Recession, many recent graduates of architecture schools and aspiring practitioners confronted unplanned pathways: leave architecture for steadier job markets, enter conventional settings for professional practice (often with less compensation and job security), or attempt to practice alone (or with a small group of collaborators). Those who chose to weather the storm on their own ended up facing a decade of uncertainty and, in most cases, added responsibilities associated with teaching jobs they took on to ensure a relatively stable source of income. Perhaps unexpectedly, these designers, because of their comfort with risk as well as the privilege of prac-

[1] C. J. Hughes, "Architects Hit Hard by Financial Crisis," Architectural Record, October 15, 2008, https://www.architecturalrecord.com/articles/4613-architects-hit-hard-by-financial-crisis.

ticing with a leisurely approach to finding commercial success, have positioned themselves among the most interesting individuals in architectural culture in the United States today. Evidence for this claim includes both the imaginative aesthetic and formal territories these designers explore as well as the ways in which they continue to demonstrate the value of architecture in relation to today's most pressing societal concerns.

As a result of the lack of meaningful opportunities to practice architecture through building, the aesthetic and formal experiments of the late aughts were characterized by enthusiasm for novelty and a loose allegiance to the practical and financial concerns that accompany providing professional architectural services. Spanning from the formal exuberance present in artifacts shown in the exhibition *Matters of Sensation* (Artists Space, 2008) to the promiscuity and playfulness of works amassed in the book *Possible Mediums* (Actar, 2018), these investigations were seemingly unsusceptible—problematically so—to social and political forces that existed outside of academic environments.[2] The intensity of this decade of sustained isolation concluded a thirty-year period of experimentation initially sponsored by the introduction of computers and digital design software into architecture studios in the 1990s, most notably at Columbia University's GSAPP.[3]

On the front end of this coming-of-age period for today's emerging designers and thinkers, the world was suffering from the effects of the financial crisis, and the status of the discipline of architecture was being called into question by leading scholars. The introspective endeavors of

[2] *Matters of Sensation* was curated by Georgina Huljich and Marcelo Spina and included artifacts created by David Erdman and Clover Lee (davidclovers), Tom Wiscombe (Emergent), Mark Foster Gage and Marc Clemenceau Bailly (Gage Clemenceau), Heather Roberge and Jason Payne (Gnuform), Jason Payne (Hirsuta), Eric Höweler and Meejin Yoon (Höweler + Yoon), Lisa Iwamoto and Craig Scott (IwamotoScott Architecture), Florencia Pita (FPmod), Michael Meredith and Hilary Sample (MOS), Karel Klein and David Ruy (Ruy Klein), Kivi Sotamaa (Sotamaa Architecture and Design), Ferda Kolatan (SU11), and Hernán Díaz Alonso (Xefirotarch). *Possible Mediums* was edited by Kelly Bair, Kristy Balliet, Adam Fure, and Kyle Miller, and includes contributions from Ellie Abrons, Andrew Atwood, Kutan Ayata, Kelly Bair, Kristy Balliet, Jennifer Bonner, Laurel Broughton, Brennan Buck, Brandon Clifford, McLain Clutter, Angela Co, Greg Corso, Justin Diles, Dora Epstein Jones, David Freeland, Benjamin Freyinger, Adam Fure, Joanna Grant, Stewart Hicks, Andrew Holder, Molly Hunker, Thomas Kelley, Andrew Kovacs, Jimenez Lai, Michael Loverich, Alex Maymind, Wes McGee, John McMorrough, Jeff Mikolajewski, Kyle Miller, Meredith Miller, Whitney Moon, Thom Moran, Anna Neimark, Allison Newmeyer, Carrie Norman, William O'Brien Jr., Kyle Reynolds, Bryony Roberts, Michael Szivos, James Michael Tate, Clark Thenhaus, Antonio Torres, and Michael Young. Of note, fifteen of the forty-four contributors to *Possible Mediums* also appear in this book.

[3] Joan Ockman, ed., *Architecture School: Three Centuries of Educating Architects in North America* (Cambridge, MA: MIT Press), 214–16.

successive generations of architects entertained the possibility that architecture could be pursued as an autonomous project, with the expectation that their efforts would determine the conditions or output of the marketplace, not be determined by it. With a desire to advance contemporary discourse, these individuals dove deep into disciplinary explorations of aesthetics and form in search of unprecedented qualities and effects, in part as a response to the perceived regressive, populist tilt of postmodernism. In a piece titled "Transdisciplinarity," the theorist Mark Linder provided new insight into this reactionary endeavor. After a prosperous decade for architecture with respect to economic growth and increased cultural value, Linder observed a conservative turn toward recuperating disciplinary identity. Finding this nostalgic turn equally as problematic as calls for interdisciplinarity that diminished the specificity of architectural knowledge, Linder offered transdisciplinarity as a third approach to advancing architectural production: "Transdisciplinarity scrutinizes architecture's *appearance* and seeks its significance in the forms of other disciplines, or in the spaces in between disciplines, but it in no way abandons the specific modes of the architectural discipline."[4]

In the essay, Linder defines a division between forms of architectural production. On the side affiliated with "institutionalized modes of production and reception," he explains, one can ask how "architecture make[s] its appearance as *architecture*." But another kind of work, the side where Linder finds more purchase, prompts one to ask, "How, when, or where, does, did, or could architecture make its appearance *other than as architecture*?" In considering architecture in relation to its outward expression, Linder situates transdisciplinarity on the edges of traditional disciplines, a space between centric disciplinarity and interdisciplinarity. One side faces inward for reassurance and the

[4] Mark Linder, "Transdisciplinarity," in "Disciplines," Hunch 9 (2005): 14.

Troy Schaum:

Practice is a process of continual reflection on the entanglements that produce the built environment. Those entanglements can be engaged in real and meaningful ways, but any practice is formulated with a necessarily incomplete set of tools. Sensitively confronting the gaps between your tools and the world is something that starts to generate a unique kind of knowledge—built up over time.

other glances outward for unexpected alliances and unconventional manifestations. Ultimately, Linder called for a simultaneous intensification and expansion of architecture's "tools, techniques, and technologies" as a means of demonstrating the flexibility of the identity of architecture as a discipline and practice.[5]

The years following the publication of Linder's essay coincided with the wave of alternative forms of architectural production described above. In place of buildings: immersive drawings, tactile objects, cartoonish forms, kinetic models, interactive projections, spatially active public artworks … the list goes on. A combination of the slow economic recovery and increased allure of advancing architectural production in academic environments resulted in a generation of architects who formulated new approaches to practice through research and teaching. This phenomenon was especially present in the American Midwest at

[5] Linder, 14, 15.

the time because of new academic leaders with opportunities to hire full-time tenure-track faculty. Between 2007 and 2010, John McMorrough, Monica Ponce de Leon, Bob Somol, and Michael Speaks became academic administrators at architecture schools in Ohio, Michigan, Illinois, and Kentucky, respectively.[6] Outside of the Midwest, Preston Scott Cohen was appointed chair at Harvard GSD in 2008; Sarah Whiting, dean at Rice University School of Architecture in 2009; Nader Tehrani, head of architecture at MIT in 2010; and Amale Andraos, dean at Columbia University GSAPP in 2014. Shared across the unique approaches of these eight individuals at their respective schools was an attempt to define alternative forms of engaging with the marketplace and resituate architecture as a form of cultural production. More importantly, they created space for their new hires to initiate unique approaches

[6] Bob Somol was named director of the School of Architecture at the University of Illinois Chicago in August 2007; Michael Speaks, dean of the University of Kentucky College of Design in January 2008; Monica Ponce de Leon, dean of the University of Michigan Taubman College in April 2008; and John McMorrough, architecture section head at Ohio State University's Knowlton School in July 2009, and chair at the University of Michigan Taubman College in June 2010. Nearly one quarter of the contributors to this publication had or continue to have a direct affiliation to one of these four institutions.

to contributing to the culture of architecture, individually and collectively. One manifestation of this support came in the form of *Possible Mediums*, a three-day summit hosted by Ohio State University's Knowlton School of Architecture in 2013. The event featured new faculty at the Midwestern schools and included lectures, workshops, panel discussions, and an exhibition, all broadly focused on the emergence of new conceptual supports upon which emerging designers were advancing ideas about aesthetics and form in architecture. This event marked an important early opportunity for organized conversation among several new academics born into a field of architecture shaped by the economic and disciplinary circumstances of the mid-to-late aughts.

In the following years, conversations like the ones enabled at *Possible Mediums* expanded to more schools and involved an even greater number of young designers. Perhaps most significant is the tangible separation these new academic architects established from the previous generation. The excitement surrounding digital production that concretized during the mid-aughts was loosened up as digital modeling and fabrication became commonplace in most schools of architecture in the United States. Additionally, the preference for intellectual and aesthetic esoterica—and with it, limited accessibility by and engagement with broader audiences—began to take a back seat to an increased comfort in engaging with the so-called *familiar:* geometric primitives, common architectural elements, anthropomorphic figures, and banal aspects of everyday life.

The honeymoon phase for the generation of architects included in this book extended well into the 2010s as a result of their successes as academics and recognition of their abilities as designers from notable institutions such as the Architectural League of New York and the Museum of Modern Art.[7] Concurrently, research sponsored by the Graham Foundation for Advanced Studies in the Fine Arts, contributions to well-regarded

Oana Stănescu:

I try not to define the practice of architecture for myself, and I rarely use the word architecture, for that matter. I am an architect and I have the skill set of an architect. However, for me, joy or reward comes from doing many other things that don't necessarily materialize as buildings. I've been thinking more about how the skill set that I have can be applied to many different disciplines.

Jess Myers:

The built environment is a stage on which human life unfolds. I consider my work to be a part of reframing the practice in those terms. If we are concerned with creating a staging ground for life to unfold, then we have to understand what lives are out there.

journals such as *Log* and *Project*, and residencies at the American Academy in Rome provided this group with prominent platforms for developing and disseminating their ideas.[8]

As much as the Great Recession sponsored alternative approaches to practice, another shift nearly ten years later was equally dramatic and impactful. In 2017, the beginning of the Trump presidency—and the Trump administration's regressive and destructive policies toward climate change and social justice—initiated a radical change in how individuals approached participating in architectural culture. These conditions were exaggerated at the end of the decade and into the beginning of the next with the increase in the murders of Black men and women at the hands of groups

[7] Among the contributors to this publication, Architectural League Prize winners include Tei Carpenter (2021), Ivi Diamantopoulou and Jaffer Kolb (2020), Jennifer Bonner (2019), Bryony Roberts (2018), Molly Hunker (with Greg Corso, 2017), Thom Moran (2015), Kutan Ayata and Michael Young, Benjamin Freyinger and Andrew Holder, and Adam Fure (2014), and Liam O'Brien Jr. (2011). MoMA PS1 Young Architects Program winners include Dream The Combine (2018), and finalists include Oana Stănescu (2019), Brennan Buck and David Freeland (2018), Troy Schaum and Rosalyne Shieh (2017), Vivian Lee and James MacGillivray and Anna Puigjaner / MAIO (2014), Liam O'Brien Jr. (with Collective-LOK, 2014 and 2010), and Anda French and Jenny French (2013).

[8] Contributors to *Log* include Ellie Abrons (issues 37 and 41), Shumi Bose (38), Brennan Buck (18, 23), Ivi Diamantopoulou (46), Adam Fure (36, 37), Jia Gu (48), Andrew Holder (38, 41), Elisa Iturbe (39, 47), Jaffer Kolb (41), Helen Leung and Elizabeth Timme (48), Kyle Miller (51, 52), Meredith Miller (37), Thom Moran (37), Jess Myers (48), Liam O'Brien Jr. (17, 26, 31), Bryony Roberts (26, 31, 32, 48), Jack Self (38), Rosalyne Shieh (41), and Michael Young (41). Contributors to *Project* include Kutan Ayata and Michael Young (issue 5), Brennan Buck and David Freeland (7), Adam Fure (3), Andrew Holder (4), Jaffer Kolb (7), Kyle Miller (4), and Troy Schaum and Rosalyne Shieh (7). Rome Prize winners include Michael Young (2019–20), Bryony Roberts (2015–16), and Liam O'Brien Jr. (2012–13).

that allege protection, senseless attacks on Asian Americans, and infringements on the rights of women and LGBTQIA+ individuals and communities. The increased urgency with which architects and architectural culture more broadly needed to confront conservatism and nationalism—and with it, racism, misogyny, white supremacy, and the destruction of the environment—encouraged a moment of self-reflection, one akin to the inward turn of the late aughts. For this *still*-emerging generation of architects, this pivotal moment made evident that their participation in constructing a more accessible, equitable, inspiring, and sustainable future was necessary. What followed the decade-long formative period, and what is captured in the interviews in this book, was the development of approaches to practice that critically interrogate how architecture makes its *appearance* and seeks *significance*.

...

Not only to thrive, but merely to exist, architects today are faced with a seemingly insurmountable array of challenges. *Building Practice* is an attempt to document continual states of becoming for a generation of architects born into architectural culture during a global recession and entering their most formative years during a pandemic and a time of heightened awareness of the climate crisis and pervasive racial injustice. The book convenes architects who construct forms of practice within and adjacent to architecture that increase the ability of design to demonstrate multiple types of value. Through conversations with architects, designers, educators, curators, fabricators, strategists, critics, and activists, this book captures critical and formative moments associated with building new forms of practice that challenge outdated models for conceiving of and producing architecture.

One objective of this publication—an objective with a philosophical tilt—is to reveal how an act of *beginning* initiates a body of work that seeks to produce new forms of architectural knowledge through various modes of production (building, curating, designing, teaching, and writing, to name a few). In the book *Beginnings*, Edward W. Said set out to answer a seemingly simple question: "What is a beginning?" Said scrutinized what one must do to *begin*, and what is special or unique about such a moment. He posited that the designation of *beginning* is also the designation of consequent intention: "The beginning … is the first step in the intentional production of meaning." Said unpacked the consequences of the act of beginning by suggesting that marking a beginning simultaneously marks a difference from preexisting traditions.[9] In *Building Practice*, a beginning also marks an end. In keeping with this provocation, the book is an occasion not only to assess the meanings produced in the first acts of these designers' and thinkers' careers, but also to open speculation on subsequent actions and the lim-

[9] Edward W. Said, *Beginnings: Intention and Method* (New York: Columbia University Press, 1985), 5.

David Freeland:

Practice allows us to translate our values and ideas about architecture that we develop through teaching, reading, and writing into built form and test their validity in three dimensions in a cultural, economic, and ecological context. It also is where our ideas about architecture can have an impact on the world. Building is the fullest realization or our ideas and values as a practice.

Emanuel Admassu:

We're extremely frustrated with the complicity of the discipline of architecture as it relates to the way cities are intensifying wealth disparities, the way cities are speeding up the dispossession and displacement of marginalized communities. Because of that, we have strategically positioned ourselves at the edge of architecture, and in some ways, we work against architecture.

itations of these practices given the territories and themes they operate within and on. With an ambition to uncover epistemological traits that are unique to this generation, *Building Practice* convenes a diverse group of individuals and prompts conversations that are as reflective as they are projective.

A second objective is to document the practical matters associated with running a business that interfaces with a variety of clients and assumes responsibilities inherent in operating within and on the built environment. As these architects move beyond private-gallery–hosted, do-it-yourself initiatives and earn or generate opportunities to develop larger projects in the public realm, new challenges emerge and practical questions demand answers. How does an office get clients? Are there employees? How are employees paid, and what amount is fair? Do they have office space? How much is rent, and how is that paid? How are contracts structured to protect the office? How are good contractors found in places where the office has never worked before? What kind of insurance is needed and how much does it cost? How much should the practice spend on marketing? Does the office hire a professional for this or do it themselves? These questions and more are often met with frustration at how much a young architect is somehow supposed to know—design, law, code, policy, marketing, and promotion, among other areas of expertise—despite the small amount of professional-practice preparation provided by a single required course in architecture school.

With independent research and guidance from peers and more experienced professionals, architects can navigate their way through legal and logistical aspects of developing a practice, but are then confronted with conceptually oriented questions that present additional challenges. How can the intellectual rigor of research-oriented approaches to practice be maintained when architecture is provided as a service? How can ongoing speculative efforts conceived in academic and professional environments mature and be made more accessible and meaningful through engagement with broader audiences? Similarly, how can theoretical forms of knowledge enhance and enliven practical forms of knowledge through building? How can the aesthetic and formal affinities of the design team persist when confronted with the demands of the client, equipped with their own aesthetic sensibilities? When compromise is required, what is lost? On the other end, how can conversations with clients and collaborators bring unexpected benefits to or enhance the conceptual agenda of a project?

Perhaps most importantly, additional questions arise when the forms of practice an architect pursues are unconventional: What are legitimate alternative structures for practicing architecture? How are these alternative structures made accessible to those in need, and how do they challenge the exclusionary, elitist history of the profession? Lastly, how can cultural, economic, environmental, and social value be assessed in modes of practice that are without precedent?

While many of the questions above became fodder for conversations with the contributors to this book, an equal number were unaddressed and remain unanswered, or are in the process of being answered. An aspect of conducting these interviews was to ask questions that encourage reflection on the initial phase of building a practice. The hope is that many of these questions arise again and again, ensuring that these practices and others continue to make meaningful and lasting contributions to the discipline and beyond. Collectively, the interviews reveal the complexity of practice today and the increased burden on design to produce sophisticated and thoughtful responses to the challenges of this time. Moreso than ever before, architects face growing responsibility to operate not only as architects, but also as responsible and forward-thinking citizens.

. . .

To ensure coherence, criteria were established for selecting individuals and offices to interview. Broadly, the book's interest is in the impact younger designers and thinkers have on critical practice and academia in the United States. Of equal importance was an interest in the disobedient dispositions of these individuals with respect to conforming to conventional modes of practice and maintaining the status quo in architecture and beyond. Every individual or office interviewed is either based in the United States or has produced work that has been, and continues to be, impactful within the United States. Finally, there is an intentionally narrow age range of contributors to this publication, which follows an assertion that shared lived experiences condition the way that generations of architects operate in the world as a loosely affiliated collective. The vast majority of contributors were born between 1974 and 1988; graduated with a degree in archi-

Jaffer Kolb:

We're drawn to architecture's expansiveness—that is, the openness of architecture's possibilities. For us, practice can mean designing a building, developing a program, or collaborating with an artist. It can also mean advocacy, invention, curation, and writing. In other words, it can take many forms. But ultimately, it involves some form of engagement: a way of relating, or of communicating. We never shy away from architecture's implications as a service industry, but at the same time, we never accept practice as totally determined or fixed.

Wei-Han Vivian Lee:

It is important to us that to practice architecture is to navigate between our experimental interests, be considerate of our clients' desires, be empathetic to the trades that have to build our designs, and be conscious of materials and detailing choices so that we are responsible stewards of the environment.

tecture between 2002 and 2016; and, for those who have their own practices, formed their practice between 2004 and 2018.

The ambition of sharing these transcribed conversations is to capture the variety of types of practices that are in the process of being built. Among the fifty-three individuals (representing thirty-two practices) included in this book, patterns emerged with respect to how they situate themselves as protagonists within the culture of architecture, how their efforts relate (or don't) to more conventional modes of architectural production, and how their work both challenges and brings distinction to the discipline and practice of architecture.

One way in which these individuals and offices manifest their abilities as trained architects is through designing at a variety of scales and in diverse contexts, including within other disciplinary realms. With projects such as *We Know How to Order* (Chicago, 2015) and *Corpo Estraneo* (Rome, 2016), Bryony Roberts considers the spatial capacity of choreography and dance. Tei Carpenter's New Public Hydrant (New York, 2018) convenes small-scale water infrastructure and public-space design. Tom Carruthers and Jennifer Newsom of Dream The Combine create public art installations, such as *Clearing* (Minneapolis, 2017) and *Columbus Columbia Colombo Colón* (Columbus, Indiana, 2021), that encourage aesthetic engagement with the natural environment and awareness of histories of the places in which their works are situated. At the smallest scale, New Affiliates' Gnomes (2016) and Spinagu's Other Turns (2016) investigate figure and form through beloved, quotidian artifacts such as garden furniture and chess pieces, respectively. At a similar size, LAMAS investigates the architectural effects of thinness in Perfection Pantheon (2015), a prototype for a light fixture. On the other end of the spectrum of scale, Oana Stănescu brings together recreation and environmental renewal in Plus Pool (with Dong-Ping Wong; New York, ongoing), a plus-shaped, water-filtering, floating swimming pool in the East River. More notable acts of transdisciplinarity come from Justin Rice and Kagan Taylor of Knowhow Shop, and Jonathan Jackson (with Sarah Nelson Jackson) of WeShouldDoItAll. Trained as architects, these individuals venture into fabrication and graphic design, respectively, to test the limits of design thinking and craft.

Alongside these design investigations are advances in criticism and curating by individuals who first studied architecture. With The World Around, a conference series and global networking platform initiated in 2020, Beatrice Galilee advocates for the value of architecture in all forms by connecting progressive designers and thinkers to industry professionals to speculate on how design can address a broad range of global issues.[10] Through more intimate conversations, Jess Myers's podcast *Here There Be Dragons*, which she started in 2016, assesses

[10] *The World Around* was founded in New York in 2020 by Diego Marroquin and Beatrice Galilee. Their global platform seeks to connect and create a diverse and international network of designers and thinkers with wider industry professionals through educational initiatives. More information can be found at https://theworldaround.com.

how architecture and planning play a role in how residents of cities like New York, Paris, and Stockholm navigate fear in urban space.[11] In the realm of criticism, in 2016, Jack Self started *Real Review*, a culture magazine dedicated to unpacking in a very broad sense "what it means to live today."[12] Now in its twelfth issue (Spring 2022), *Real Review* critically interrogates the role that architecture plays in economics, fashion, politics, technology, and beyond.

Another way in which the individuals highlighted in this book contribute to architectural culture is through assuming the role of author and editor. Felipe Correa of Somatic Collaborative is prolific in this realm. As an extension of the books *A Line in the Andes* (Applied Research & Design, 2013), *Beyond the City: Resource Extraction Urbanism in South America* (University of Texas Press, 2016), and *São Paulo:*

[11] *Here There Be Dragons* is a podcast by Jess Myers on urban residents' experiences with fear and identity. More information can be found at https://www.htbdpodcast.com.

[12] *Real Review* is a contemporary culture magazine dedicated to "what it means to live today." It is a creative partnership between REAL and OK-RM. More information can be found at https://real-review.org.

Paul Andersen:

Generally speaking, I think that to practice architecture is to contribute something to the discourse—in the form of models, essays, drawings, gossip, or buildings. The goal is to open up new ways of thinking and designing, which is different than, say, practicing piano, which is more geared toward refinement.

Adam Frampton:

Practice, by definition, is related to the implementation of ideas or methods, not just their theorization, and is performed regularly and repetitively, hopefully toward greater skill and proficiency. In this sense, we really appreciate "practice" as a description of our own work that is hands-on, ongoing, open-ended, and hopefully always getting better.

A Graphic Biography (University of Texas Press, 2018), Somatic Collaborative's architectural and infrastructural design demonstrates the potential for urban research to inspire projective speculations. Other recent publications by contributors eschew contextual specificity in favor of reflecting on histories and potential futures of disciplinary issues such as image-making and materiality. In *Reality Modeled After Images: Architecture and Aesthetics after the Digital Image* (Routledge, 2021), Michael Young unpacks the interrelation of architecture and contemporary image culture. In *Blank: Speculations on CLT* (Applied Research & Design, 2022), Jennifer Bonner (with Hanif Kara) examines cross-laminated timber as it pertains to architectural experimentation and, more specifically, the material's potential aesthetic and spatial effects.

Perhaps most impactful among many modes of architectural production pursued by the contributors to this book are alternative models of real estate development. Previously working together as LA Más, Helen Leung and Elizabeth Timme conceptualized an architecture office as a resource center that serves the community through knowledge building. As advocates for their community's residents, LA Más initiates projects that support housing stability and economic security. Similarly, Outside Development, led by Elisa Iturbe, pursues new landownership models, government subsidies, and infrastructure- and energy-distribution strategies to counter traditional real estate processes and support local communities. These efforts most clearly manifest in Document 03 (2021), a project that explores the possibility of the community land trust as a catalyst for economic and social transformation in San Ysidro, California. As an alternative form of community empowerment, Mollie Claypool and Gilles Retsin, cofounders of AUAR (Automated Architecture), create sustainable homes using localized, automated production that enables community participation in the design and development process. As strategists, Iben Falconer (with SOM) and Julia Gamolina (with Ennead Architects) instigate innovative methods of project acquisition, client management, and expansion into new markets, ensuring continual, progressive evolution of some of the world's largest architecture offices.

Collectives—both formal and informal, academic and professional—are another means to cultivate alternative modes of architectural production. Emanuel Admassu (of AD–WO) is a contributor to the Black Reconstruction Collective, Bryony Roberts to WIP Collaborative, and Jennifer Newsom to Dark Matter University.[13] Each of these collaboratives acknowledges the systemic way in which women or racial

[13] The Black Reconstruction Collective (BRC) provides funding, design, and intellectual support to the ongoing and incomplete project of emancipation for the African Diaspora. The BRC is committed to multidisciplinary work dedicated to dismantling systemic white supremacy and hegemonic whiteness within art, design, and academia. Founded by a group of Black architects, artists, designers, and scholars, the BRC aims to amplify knowledge production and spatial practices by individuals and organizations that further the reconstruction project. More information can be found at https://www.blackreconstructioncollective.org. WIP is Work In Progress | Women In Practice, a design collective founded on the in-progress nature of practice and the collaborative power of women engaged in it. WIP Collaborative is a shared feminist practice of independent design professionals focused on research and design projects that improve the public realm. More information can be found at https://wip-designcollective.com. Dark Matter University is a democratic network with the following principles guiding its actions: New Forms of… 1) Knowledge and Knowledge Production; 2) Institutions; 3) Collectivity and Practice; 4) Community and Culture; and 5) Design. More information can be found at https://darkmatteruniversity.org.

minorities in the United States have been marginalized in the field of architecture and beyond, and use architectural design and pedagogy to speculate on more diverse, equitable, and inclusive futures. Equally notable, Julia Gamolina started the online magazine *Madame Architect* in 2018 and Shumi Bose formed the nonprofit Hold Space in 2021.[14] These five initiatives incorporate advocacy for design, community engagement, mentorship, and professional collaboration.

Finally, many of the contributors make an appearance as architects in the most expected way—they design buildings. Some of those buildings have been built. Among the notable accomplishments of this generation is the award-winning Transart House, a formally expressive residence and private gallery designed by SCHAUM/SHIEH and built in Houston in 2018.[15] Several other new-construction residential projects were also com-

[14] *Madame Architect* is an online magazine celebrating women that shape our world. It is designed to show young women entering the industry the choices they have in crafting a dynamic, meaningful, and interesting career. More information can be found at https://www.madamearchitect.org. Hold Space is an organization dedicated to reading, thinking, and talking about things that don't seem to fit in architecture school. More information can be found at https://holdspacearc.com.

Elisa Iturbe:

Architecture is a mode of knowledge—it's a way of seeing the world. It has a cultural and a symbolic power. There are modes of architectural production that are fully embedded in a capitalist system where practice means serving that system and creating value for it, but there are also modes of practice that engage with the broader history of the discipline of architecture. I am resistant to the idea that practice is necessarily divorced from theory, and I am reluctant to say that practice is just about the profession and not the discipline. The multiplicity of possibilities of what practice means is something that all practitioners have to navigate today.

pleted around this time, many of which represented the first built work for these offices. In 2017, Ajay Manthripragada completed construction of the Page House and Gallery in Berkeley, New Affiliates finished the Tunbridge Winter Cabin in Vermont, and the LAMAS-designed Townships Farmhouse was built in Quebec. In 2018, MALL's Haus Gables, a playful speculation on the spatial capacity of the gabled roof, was built in Atlanta, and FreelandBuck's geometrically intricate Second House—which was actually their first house—was built in Los Angeles. In 2019, Independent Architecture's Motherhouse (House with Qualities) was built in Denver, and Spinagu completed Piaggio House in Rosario, Argentina. Residential projects very recently completed (or nearing completion) include The LADG's House in Los Angeles I (…in Los Angeles); T+E+A+M's Northwood ADU, in Ann Arbor, Michigan; Only If's

[15] In 2018, Transart House, designed by SCHAUM/SHIEH and built in Houston, was awarded Building of the Year by the *Architect's Newspaper*. "Presenting the 2018 Best of Design Awards Winner for Building of the Year," *Architect's Newspaper*, December 5, 2018, https://www.archpaper.com/2018/12/2018-best-of-design-awards-winner-for-building-of-the-year/.

Narrow House, in Brooklyn; and WOJR's House of Horns, in Los Altos, California. Additionally, multi-residential housing projects designed by MAIO (110 Rooms, 2016), French 2D (Outlier Lofts, 2018), and Young & Ayata (DL1310 Apartments, with Michan Architecture, 2021) were completed in Boston, Barcelona, and Mexico City, respectively. Each of the projects listed above presented opportunities for designers to translate conceptually oriented endeavors into built form at full scale while being mindful of constructability, environmental impact, market demand, resident well-being, and—perhaps most importantly—the ability of the building to enhance and enliven the activities taking place within.

...

This book is organized into two sections: Interviews and Issues. Collectively, the interviews reveal strategies for linking practical and theoretical forms of knowledge and uncover how this generation of practitioners is advancing speculative design through the culture and politics of building. Certain questions—such as "What is the responsibility of the architect?" and "What does it mean to practice architecture?"—recur across interviews, with varied answers that nonetheless point to a generational approach to participating in architectural culture today. Issues are short reports that address topics that surfaced repeatedly during the conversations: academia, aesthetics, clients, collaboration, community, communication, construction, context, finance, identity, influence, and politics. Each report aspires to convene aspects of the individual interviews, reveal significant findings with respect to each issue and how they shape the interviewees' approaches, and articulate the collaborative construction of unique and unprecedented forms of practice.

Building Practice updates the narrative around a generation of architects more commonly associated with "speculative" or "academic" work, repositioning these designers and thinkers as able and eager to make genuine contributions to the built environment while mending unnecessary divides between image-making and activism, design and politics, and academics and practice. The contents of this book reveal how these thinkers and designers claim unique conceptual territory regarding aesthetics, form, materiality, space, and order, and convey urgency for design to acquire meaning in relation to cultural, environmental, political, and social concerns. These practices quietly partition themselves off from previous generations of experimentally motivated practices while individually exemplifying their inimitable affinities, techniques, and sensibilities. In drawing out the concerns that shaped the first acts of an emerging generation of designers and thinkers, *Building Practice* also reveals the peripheral yet pivotal aspects of building a practice today.

Acknowledgements:

Without support from Michael Speaks, Professor and Dean at Syracuse University School of Architecture, this book simply would not exist. Thank you, Michael.

In September 2019, Michael invited us to curate an exhibition for display in Slocum Hall in the spring of 2020. With an opportunity to make a statement about the status of architectural design at that time, the two of us entertained a range of themes that could bring together the work of academic architects across the country. Ultimately, we focused on what we understood to be a significant transitional moment in the maturation process of an up-and-coming generation of designers: finally, after a decade of self-initiated conceptual projects with a limited reach, our peers were being provided with and generating opportunities to make an impact on the built environment through building. We settled on collecting and exhibiting the first built works of many of these practices, as well as tangential, sometimes curious artifacts that evidence the act of building a practice. As educators, we also considered the impact this effort could have on our students and offered a class that involved interviews with the architects whose work would be exhibited. Because of COVID-19 restrictions, we were unable to mount the show as planned, but we did offer the course for a second time, in the fall of 2020. We conducted twenty-three of the thirty-two interviews collected in this book in the seminars offered in 2019 and 2020. We're incredibly grateful to the students who enrolled in our courses and contributed to our understanding of this generation of architects: David Acevedo, Vasundhra Aggarwal, Maria Daniela Andino, Ella Arne, Sachio Badham, Kelsey Benitez, Isabella Calidonio, Aaron Cass, Kristabel Chung, Dylan Crean, Sanat Dangol, Genevieve Dominiak, Dhvani Doshi, Zain Elwalkil, Demitri Gadzios, Rachael Gaydos, Emmei Yun Gootnick, Tianyi Hang, Jack Hymowitz, Aditya Jain, Coumba Kante, Dana Kelly, Kate Kini, Anna Korneeva, MaryKate Krege, Alise Lamothe, Ching Huen Leung, Jessica Libby, Yifei Luo, Peter Maffei, Stephen Marinelli, Hannah Michaelson, Jason Moline, Kayleen O'Brien, Julia Ocejo Vivanco, Ishita Parmar, Oswal Perez, Chay Phelps, Vanessa Poe, Jamely Ramos, Tanvi Rao, Alec Rovensky, Felix Samo, Zach Samuel, Heather Skinner, Lawrence Sprague, Jay Suriyanarayanan, Tirta Teguh, Stewart Tillyer, Irmak Turanli, Jesse Valgora, Hanneke van Deursen, Yuqian Tommy Wang, Eliza Williamson, Iris Yee, Eryn Young, Biyun Zhang, Hao Zheng, Hao Zhou, and Elise Zilius. We're also thankful for financial support from Syracuse University and Syracuse University School of Architecture. Additionally, we want to acknowledge Jayne Kelley and Cat Wentworth, who, respectively, provided invaluable support with editing the text and assembling the book graphically. Lastly, we want to express gratitude to *The Architect's Newspaper*, which first brought attention to this project when publishing the first fourteen interviews as a weekly series in early 2020. To everyone who has contributed to this project, thank you.

Issues

Academia

Rarely does an architect achieve the status of cultural figure without some academic affiliation. Conducting research and teaching in academic environments complements the service-oriented aspects of professional practice, which are often driven by finance. Research supported by academic institutions is a way for architects to enhance or extend their professional efforts without concern for profitability. Likewise, teaching, in addition to carrying the responsibility of educating future generations of architects, offers possibilities to work collaboratively with students on new ideas or technical investigations that do not have a place in commissioned professional projects constrained by budgets and defined timelines.

Typically, architects who teach regularly can practice architecture in a more idealized way—as a sociocultural act rather than only to earn money. In the United States in particular, long-term and permanent positions within academia come with a tremendous degree of freedom and financial support. In opposition to their counterparts in Asia and Europe, the youngest architects in American academia have freedom from the beginning of their teaching careers to determine the content of their courses and research, often with little oversight or direction from senior colleagues. This freedom sometimes results in architects using academic environments as testing grounds to construct their identities. This isn't necessarily a good thing, for two reasons. Exposed to preferred aesthetic sensibilities and methods of design, students may be left with less opportunity to cultivate their own aesthetic sensibilities. Additionally, academic architects may feel less urgency to make names for themselves through professional practice. This latter effect may explain why younger architects in the United States lag behind their peers in other countries with respect to recognition received beyond academia and the number of built projects in the first decade of practice.

Though many emerging architects in this group have teaching positions, they are conscious of and pushing back against these potential risks, especially by separating teaching from practice and working actively to materialize their ideas in the public realm. To be seen is how this group of architects achieve at a high level in academia and practice simultaneously. While some embrace academic affiliation and situate practice as a secondary endeavor, others are slowly distancing themselves from academia with an understanding that a successful commercial and cultural practice requires an elevated level of commitment.

Adam Frampton:

We have mixed feelings about the role of teaching and academia in our practice. On one hand, teaching and being connected to and supported by an academic environment facilitates and enables research. But on the other hand, teaching takes a lot of time. It's rewarding on many levels, but it sometimes feels difficult to devote enough time to both ends, as a teacher and scholar in the academic world and as an architect striving to make significant contributions to the built environment.

Jia Gu:

I like to think of practicing, teaching, and research not as separate activities, but as different modes of production that engage with similar sets of issues in architecture. So, some activities, like teaching, are opportunities to provide, share, and reflect on certain forms of foundational knowledge—however that is defined within a pedagogical practice. Other activities, like curating, are about bringing architecture and public audiences closer together. Both are opportunities to reframe what we think we know in architecture.

James Macgillivray:

There is an economic relationship between practicing and teaching. I think people who teach and practice are more willing to take risks with competitions and even with private clients. You can present things that are more conceptual because you always know that it's not the only job. It also creates opportunities to apply our academic research in our professional work from time to time, effectively allowing us to transcend simply providing a service. We can test design concepts in a client-based situation, and if they don't land, they can be offloaded to our academic research.

Aesthetics

In addition to form, formal organization, spatial relationships, and spatial volume, aesthetics—the principles underlying the visual qualities of a particular architect or architectural movement—are among the primary drivers of experience of the built environment. Aesthetics condition the reception of an individual work or a body of work. Occasionally, distinctive aesthetics typify entire generations of architects who confront similar social and cultural circumstances.

Two decades ago, during a moment of relative economic and political stability, many architects in the United States were obsessed with aesthetic paradigms supported by the skilled use of software and defined by complex three-dimensional curvilinearity, immateriality, and seamlessness. Unbridled enthusiasm for computer-aided design and image-making was paired with a pursuit of intangible elegance. On the heels of this digital turn, ushered in by an unfavorable economy for architects, a DIY culture emerged and, with it, an interest in novel material and visual effects enabled by digital fabrication. Many architects turned their attention away from formal expression toward sensual effects produced by clever combinations of color, texture, and translucency. An interest in affect and sensation broadened the ambitions of digital formalism. Today, when digital design and fabrication have become commonplace, and perhaps inspired by unprecedented attention to issues of public health and social justice, not only is there an absence of a shared, ideologically driven aesthetic sensibility among experimentally minded architects, but there is also an intentional lack of strict aesthetic coherence within individual bodies of work. There are some features common to emerging practices: geometric primitives, composite figures, misalignments, bold colors, rich textures, and off-the-shelf materials, for example. But the aesthetics of today's emerging architects vary, revealing a lack of interest in privileging something like brand legibility over demonstrating range and reflecting the collaborative nature of working with clients, consultants, and existing conditions, enabling aesthetics to develop naturally over time.

What will be the effect of the disconnected, almost democratic aesthetic pursuits of these architects on their abilities to remain culturally relevant, find commercial success, and sustain intellectual engagement? What do today's aesthetics say about how society perceives the role and value of architects? Rather than impose fixed aesthetics, architects building practices today understand the need for their aesthetic ambitions to simultaneously broaden architectural discourse and reflect the social and cultural conditions in which their work is situated. The geographic and racial diversity of these architects animates equally diverse aesthetic arrays that sponsor inspiring forms of inclusivity.

Anna Puigjaner:

The aesthetics of our projects evolve as we evolve as an office. The four of us are quite diverse. We have different interests and different backgrounds. So, our aesthetic predilections are different as well. That's positive. The outcomes that we achieve in our projects are the result of long conversations and debates between the four of us. For us, it's important to take time to evaluate the status and evolution of cultural constructions and aesthetics, which are always changing. If we do not also evolve, our identity will become fixed and we will be left behind.

Wei-Han Vivan Lee:

To be honest, I'm not sure we even have a game plan when we start working on a project. Sometimes it's liberating to know that we don't have to force certain interests or aesthetic ambitions into each project. We let the defining features of each project emerge naturally and over time.

Clients

Many young architects are not receiving the types of conventional commissions that past generations did. Is it because architecture's cultural value has diminished over the past century? Or is it that the median family income in the United States today is only $67,521, putting architectural services out of reach for many potential clients? Despite, or maybe because of, the portrayals of renovations and home-building on popular media outlets like HGTV, the already-small client base of young architects is shrinking. And while income from teaching and sponsored research may enable emerging practitioners some financial flexibility, there are numerous reasons why an architect may not want (or be able) to wait around for the perfect commission. Many new practices certainly don't. Design competitions, self-funded work, spec homes, grants, alternative funding models, and developer partnerships, among other strategies, all play important roles in architectural practices' first projects. Emerging architects still design single-family houses and small commercial projects, but it's more typical for them to be working on projects that redefine or rethink the meaning of "client" entirely. Communities, nonprofit organizations, and cities can be considered some of the most important—and even common—clients that newly formed architecture firms seek out and connect with.

There are (at least) three different aspects related to clients worth considering: the architect-client relationship, the commissioned project, and the compensation. Developing and maintaining relationships with clients takes work; how an architect communicates, how confident they are, and how knowledgeable they are all factor into the labor of client relations. Architects today—especially those who teach to support themselves and their professional endeavors—often feel strongly about working with clients whose social and political values align with their own. They may prioritize this above compensation as they determine whom to work for and with. That decision, however, also affects business growth and profitability. The clients architects choose may not have a lot of capital to spare; at the same time, the architects who want to work on projects with these clients also care very deeply about paying their employees well, for example. So, what spans this gap? As practices move from research-oriented activities to operating as registered businesses, what is emerging is a complex convergence of sociopolitical values and strategic development. These intersections yield to calls by business strategists to create pipelines to manage future work and cultivate greater agency and control over the act of building the practice, or risk going under.

Troy Schaum:

[When we started], we didn't say no to a lot of requests, because you never know where certain journeys are going to take you. In 2012 or 2013, we were asked by some relatively young people in Houston if we were interested in designing a music venue. We made some sketches and renderings for a very small amount of money. We just assumed these people would go away and we'd never hear from them again. What actually happened was that they took those renderings all over town and raised significant capital to build the music venue. What also happened was that lots of people who build things in Houston saw the renderings. They didn't necessarily want to invest in a music venue, but were very curious about us as architects. Developers would contact us and request a portfolio of built work. The problem was that we hadn't actually built anything! That said, some of them hired us anyway.

Bryony Roberts:

[I try to be] very particular about partnerships, whether with a client or a collaborator or an institution. There's a moment before you enter into a relationship where you can ask critically, "Is this really in alignment with my values?" There are also challenges once you enter into a relationship. You find out that what you want from the project is not necessarily what they want from the project. It's a constant tension.

Collaboration

A half century ago, a building *may* have been able to be designed by one person, but today architecture is (almost exclusively) a team sport. Collaborations are necessary for a project to be attentive and responsive to its sociopolitical context, sensitive to its environment, sustainable in its construction and ongoing maintenance, accessible to diverse constituents, (sometimes) less expensive, and (often) more joyful—all qualities that many younger architects are increasingly dedicated to pursuing.

In the process of building an architecture practice today, architects in the United States are facing a tedious licensure process, enormous financial pressure, growing oversight from local and national governing bodies, and a client base that may not recognize or value the role of the architect (or perhaps architects are just out of reach financially). Collaboration in numerous forms offers a way forward. Increasingly, newly established offices are seeking out and nurturing unique partnerships between designer and client, architect and developer, curator and audience, designer and contractor, activist and community, business strategist and employees ... and on and on, all as means to address issues related to aesthetics, culture, finance, politics, society, and sustainability.

Singular design visions and ideological agendas are not the driving forces in many of these collaborations. Regardless of their outputs (buildings, exhibitions, podcasts, business relationships), these collaborations focus more on the processes of exchange and interface among the voices and views of all contributors—architecture as a new kind of exquisite corpse. The role of the architect today is more curator, or even mediator, than individual genius. Over time, these unique collaborations are likely to yield innovative strategies for architecture firms to establish and sustain themselves, creating new financial models, forms of cultural activity and community engagement, fabrication systems, and, most importantly, inspiring and lasting contributions to the built environment.

Shumi Bose:

In my role as a curator, one of my responsibilities is to manage conversations between authors, exhibitors, gallery managers, contractors, budget holders, sponsors, etc. Exhibitions can be showcases; they can be commercially motivated; they can be critical; they can be all sorts of different things. So, my job as a curator is not necessarily to impose anything upon my collaborators, but to discern what in the conversation is necessary and fulfilling for the institution, for the exhibitors, for the sponsors ... and for who we understand to be our audience. Ultimately, the conversation that I care most about is between the exhibition and the audience.

Meredith Miller:

Critique is much more collaborative today. There's an awareness and a willingness to work across different fields, acknowledging that executing a building design isn't the work of a singular author. There are so many people involved, and the responsibilities associated with building are distributed across an ecology of different disciplines. A successful architect can assert a vision while acknowledging the different roles and contributions of many other individuals.

Communication

The question of whom architects are talking to through their work becomes a critical one as an office develops and grows. Is communication with clients most important because it enables a project to get built? Or is the builder more important, so that the project is executed with the highest possible level of craft and care? Or is it communication with the community, so a project is most useful over the course of its life? Or are architects ultimately communicating with other architects, contributing new knowledge? Of course, architects communicate to and with all these parties, and many others, in the processes of design and construction. It's how architects facilitate communication and how nimble architects are when communicating that facilitates growth in many facets of professional practice.

When architects work in academia, they often feel a responsibility (or are required) to produce critical disciplinary knowledge. Yet few among an emerging generation of architects feel this is the most important responsibility they have related to communication today. Instead, most younger architects building a practice today prioritize communication strategies that acknowledge and engage with broader audiences. These architects are experimenting with representational types, methods for dialogue earlier in the process, and channels for dissemination that embrace, and even leverage, a more inclusive set of voices. They are talking to more people along the way to ensure the project is economically, intellectually, and physically accessible to more people in the end. It's hard to know if this is a value that has grown out of a deeper, learned understanding of the importance of appealing to those outside of the discipline—an acknowldgement of the inherently political act of building a building—or if the pressure and exhilaration of amassing a following on social media requires this distributed approach. What remains to be seen is whether representational types that are allegedly more intellectually and visually accessible will have an impact on the value and advancement of architecture as an academic discipline and cultural practice. While an ambition to communicate more effectively with more people does seem to be common to many verbal and visual strategies today, the modest goal of a project being embraced by those who build it and use it is equally important and prioritized by many new architectural practices as a means of embracing stewardship of the built environment.

Jennifer Newsom:

The term audience implies directionality and passivity of reception. We are more interested in the work being a platform for an energetic exchange between us and other people. We're setting up a platform for things to happen. I don't think of it in a singular direction of experience or knowledge passing from one place or one person to another. Once we make the work... that's actually the beginning of the project. I get to observe how others engage with our work. That's when I feel like I'm then the audience. I get to learn about what we've made.

Jennifer Bonner:

I'm interested in using devices that already have a broad appeal—like the image of a gable or the medium of a guidebook—to draw people in, to educate them by making them feel included in a discussion about architecture.

Jonathan Jackson:

In our work, we are trying to embed ourselves in many different cultures. If we're designing an exhibition about past events, we have to understand our role as storytellers. It's important to get things right. We're working on a project right now centered around immigration. The idea of a legal or illegal immigrant is totally offensive. This political way of confronting immigration is embedded in American culture and we're constantly looking for cues within dialogue and delivery of messaging and content to make sure that how we speak, whether it be neutral or taking a stance, is appropriate, contextual, and progressive.

Elisa Iturbe:

One of the representation strategies we developed was to create "portraits" of the place, imagining it in its process of transformation. It was really important to include people, to suggest that the architecture was a scenographic element, a set piece for the community. We looked at medieval painting because they often use architecture as a framing device. One of the things that we in architecture always struggle with is the idea that a design is an imposition. But we were imagining that the architecture is actually something through which people can connect. In the work of thinking about how architecture comes into being, there's a reciprocity between the life lived and the building itself.

Community

Historically architects saw themselves as experts (or at least able to contribute a certain expertise). Architects know how to build things, how to propose new ways of living, how to envision space, how to create compelling environments... But a perception of the architect as sole genius has long been out of date (despite what may endure in certain award and tenure systems), and has given way to many forms of collaboration and, perhaps more importantly, acknowledging and even celebrating that expertise resides within the community in which an architect is working. Many new architecture firms feel a significant sense of responsibility to build relationships based in trust so that a project truly supports the community it serves, addresses its needs, and contributes to positive change.

But these efforts raise important questions. How does one even define the community of a project? Is it the group of people who live in or near the space an architect is designing or intervening in? Is it the group of people most affected by the project (and affected in what sense)? Is it the client? Does it include the individuals building the project—the labor that brings it to fruition? Does the architect belong to the community?

Young architects are grappling with the implications of these questions. Doing meaningful work that contributes to well-being seems to be a common goal for this generation of thinkers and designers. Many set out to work with specific groups of people or in particular locations—individuals and spaces consistently denied good design, infrastructure, and investment. But how one works in and supports a community they're not a part of is a complex issue. Are they always an outsider? Will their good intentions be mistaken for exploitation, or even lead to harm?

Together, new frameworks for talking to people affected by a project (in earlier phases), post-occupancy surveys and analysis, and active attempts to define collaboratively what success means may ultimately atomize the understanding of expertise. This atomization will not undermine the architect's own expertise, but instead account for voices and perspectives that have not been heard and considered previously.

Jennifer Newsom:

The terms community and audience both have a kind of distancing effect. That parsing between community versus neighbors and audience versus publics or just people ... we don't need so much distance. We're all here in the world experiencing these things together.

Helen Leung:

If we proclaim to be of service and to be in partnership to whoever we're working with—whether they be middle-class people, veterans, seniors, those who are homeless—it's common sense that if you don't honor and listen to those lived experiences, whatever you're creating is not going to be aligned and it's not going to work. I grew up in northeast LA.
I share my story with the community. There's space to be personal, and to share parts of yourself. There are other elements of your life that allow people to connect and understand why you're doing the work. That's important as a way of building trust. Why are you here? What are your intentions? Vulnerability builds trust, and it's something that we're going to have to continue to do in terms of how we build trust in the communities we work in down the road.

Construction

Perhaps it's that many young architects today were trained by the digital avant-garde and witnessed their struggles (or lack of desire) to build their work; or perhaps it's that they want to start building things right out of school, with no money or contractor connections; or perhaps it's the cost of custom fabrication and an acceptance that they lack certain skills—whatever it is, many new practices today are turning away from the high-tech and machine-driven and choosing off-the-shelf, local, or inexpensive materials and processes. Their projects are built using conventional assembly systems, with regular materials and typical details, but they are anything but conventional, regular, or typical. These architects acknowledge the environmental impact of material extraction and waste, the economic and sociopolitical impact of labor systems, the expertise and intelligence of craft, and the power in partnering with a builder. This recognition sponsors an approach to construction that looks very little like approaches developed by previous generations.

What remains to be seen is whether and how the conceptual and experimental character of new architectural practices perseveres given the pressing environmental, economic, and social impacts of construction. Some projects constructed by today's emerging architects appear to be exact replicas of their original design counterparts, while others have met significant value-engineering or market-driven restrictions that render them unrecognizable. One reason for the increased popularity of accessible, everyday materials and construction processes, then, may be a desire to work with and even embrace a variety of constraints in a project from the beginning. If one does not have a wealthy client who supports a design with rare materials and complex geometry, then making budget-friendly choices, working within the systems of conventional and local construction, and cultivating special relationships with builders is a clever (and necessary) thing to do. Doing more with less is a design and construction strategy that not only responds to larger environmental and societal issues, but also makes a positive impact on individuals involved in the project, including how a client lives their life or how a builder considers their craft. To ensure continued positive change, the responsibility will fall on architects to prioritize sustainable design and construction, setting standards for everyone involved that consider the urgent need to offset the detrimental effects of the building industry on the built environment.

Ben Freyinger:

We are using materials that are readily available and, in some cases, kind of ugly. And yes, it's in the interface between the materials and how they respond to one another or how they coexist … it's where the invention is. The reality is that we have contractors that are looking at what we are producing. What they see is complicated or complex. We can break it down very logically, piece by piece, and explain why it isn't. But the reception of it is often "Oh, this is unusual … this is too complex to build." We can get somewhere by showing them that the parts are all familiar and we've just made small modifications to the way things are assembled … and these small adjustments add up to a big difference in appearance.

Troy Schaum:

We're very interested in creating projects for collectives. There's a democratizing idea that architecture is for everyone. It is. But one of the things that I underestimated was how powerful architecture can be for individuals—our individual clients and the contractors who build our projects. When we visit the house in Virginia that's under construction, I have to say, the contractor is really falling in love with it. I think it's changing him in a way that is powerful to see.

Jaffer Kolb:

Our reuse projects are in this really weird niche, where we're mostly looking at what architects make and how we produce waste—looking at what we produce that's superfluous, or excessive—and to treat that as inherited material. But this work is less about responsibility and more about methodology—investigations into local economies and material flows. I don't want to pretend that we're experts in reuse. We use these projects to think about detailing and assembly, but also to think about how architecture operates as a narrative within the city. In this sense, the second life might intersect with things like form or program as a means of perpetual reinvention.

Minujín
arta
PAU
THE

Context

Whether a designer intentionally sets them into dialogue or not, the physical context in which a project is situated is as much a part of that project as the designer's conceptual intentions and the representation of the project. The contexts of buildings, conferences, exhibitions, installations, lectures, and scholarly texts come prepackaged with specific circumstances that shape their conception and reception. These circumstances include the politics of a place and the funding mechanisms that enable a project to be realized, as well as the context's cultural affiliations, demographics, environmental conditions, historical narratives, and social relations, among other conditions.

Today, emerging architects whose work was previously confined to backyards, galleries, living rooms, office spaces, and websites, now have opportunities to develop projects that confront and are inspired by the aforementioned contextual circumstances, which grow only more complex as venues become more public. For the first time in their careers, these architects are creating, seeking out, and presented with opportunities to make permanent marks in the built environment. Ranging from almost surgical, small-scale interventions in the public realm to bold statements in the form of new cultural venues or housing developments, the first built works of this generation of architects exhibit a common trait: an attentiveness to place that, in part, sponsors design. There is a conversation between the conditions of a site—the culture and politics of a place—and the architectural ambitions of these designers. This engagement counters the dominant predilection many so-called starchitects have to impose personal ideology on a place without concern for its material and immaterial realities. Now, architecture is understood as a thoughtful backdrop for life rather than an autonomous object partitioned from its surroundings.

The work of this generation of designers and thinkers considers context as a set of circumstances that is advantageous to address and fold into a project rather than a series of conditions that interfere with the process of design. These architects are inspired by working collaboratively, suggesting that critical interrogation of place will produce an architectural result that is informed, intelligent, and projective.

Bryony Roberts:

I aim for a dialogical relationship to the city. My projects are always highly site-specific, responding to many layers of a place, from its existing architecture and landscape to its social histories and contemporary politics. But they are also open-ended—because the work is activated only when people use it and transform it.

Emanuel Admassu:

As architects and urban designers, when we enter unfamiliar environments, we need to make sure that we are collaborating with people who really, really, really know that environment; people who really understand the ways in which that environment has been misrepresented.

Devin Dobrowolski:

When we look closely at a place where we are designing, we try to understand the context and assemble the design project through the observations that we have made about that place. After that, it's a process of active negotiation and calibration, working on how each of those issues begins to inform the design.

WAFFL
HOUS

Finance

The conventional strategy of starting an architecture office by taking on small projects, like residential additions and renovations, that enable steady, low-risk growth may simply be unavailable to new practices given financial pressures and limited opportunities in the United States today. Earning supplemental income and building an identity through academic positions has long been the norm for experimentally oriented critical thinkers and designers, and that remains true for today's emerging practices. But there are other modes of practice (business strategy, community nonprofits, architects working as developers) and new venues (gift shops, podcasts, co-ops) that these individuals are exploring that will open new territory for architects moving into the profession. Moreso than ever, it appears that many architects are exploring alternative manifestations of practice as/and business to develop projects that are equitable and value driven.

Along with conventional systems, unique financial models of practice that new architecture firms employ today include (a) using their life's savings to design, develop, and construct a residential project, which (hopefully) begets the next project, and the next, and the next; (b) writing endless grant proposals so that their nonprofit can do important, value-driven work with their community; (c) renting a warehouse that community members buy into (and sustain) as a co-op fabrication space; and (d) establishing partnerships with developers to ensure profit on top of fees... and the list goes on. In many new collaborative, critical practices in the United States, at least one member has an additional job (in academia, as a strategist, as a consultant, etc.) to provide financial stability that offsets riskier decisions and uncompensated research projects, and supports employee salaries, rent for office space, and insurance, among other costs of running a business.

Beyond the financial models that practices are using to sustain themselves, some are also working within and developing new models for how others can access architecture, most of which take the form of co-ownership. Co-op housing, community-land-trust development projects, and nonprofit community initiatives aim at addressing architecture's (economic) inaccessibility and find collective labor-ownership structures that allow for more people to be involved, ensuring financial viability for architects and clients alike. Efforts to rethink financialization in architecture challenge the status quo and sponsor a future for professional practice that distributes agency and opportunities for wealth creation beyond the privileged constituencies who previously held it in excess.

Jack Self:

I want to offer a new ownership model to people who might normally be excluded from the housing market for different reasons. There is an idea about incremental ownership that I'm developing that will enable residents to build up shares in their building. I found that if you have a building of 100 apartments where everyone owns one apartment, if there's a leak on the roof, the people on the ground floor don't give a shit because it doesn't affect their property. Whereas if you own one percent of a building, a leak is everyone's problem. The ultimate ambition is to transition to an entirely new model of society, which is more just and more equitable, but I'm looking for opportunities within the existing system where you might be able to create modest and incremental change. We should not be discouraged by the amount of time that it will take to make substantive change. If you can find very small and incremental ways to improve the lives of the people around you, that, in itself, is already a step in the right direction.

Helen Leung:

Every organization has their own revenue model. We had some seed funding, and, after building our reputation, we slowly received larger foundation grants. It's important to think about having a diverse funding stream. Our foundation grant strategy was one strategy. Another strategy was individual donations. The third way was through fee for service which is a pretty common approach in the design field. We took on a lot of those projects [in the beginning] because it was something we could do despite the fact that it may not have been aligned with our mission.

Identity

Identity is a composite of factors such as race and ethnicity, gender, and lived experiences, as well as cultivated behaviors, beliefs, and social interests. For many, identity also incorporates educational experiences, professional endeavors, and professional responsibilities. As cultural figures and mediators who operate across private and public realms, architects actively construct identities that reflect broader societal circumstances as much as they anticipate and project change.

Today, because of seemingly unlimited access to one another through social media, there is decreasing separation between personal and professional identities. An architect's professional work has become affiliated with their personal identity as much as their hobbies and interests form a portion of their professional identity. Similarly, buildings designed by architects who are fixtures in academia are generally understood to be intellectual endeavors, while buildings designed by architects who privilege commercial success and popularity are often partitioned from their critically oriented counterparts as market-driven pursuits. Rather than privilege one side over the other, architects today seek legitimacy and influence in academia as often as they do in the global marketplace and communities in which they work. Accruing cultural capital through relationships with generally well-known and respected institutions, as well as through engagement with local organizations and constituencies, these architects understand their roles as stewards of a built environment that serves a wide variety of individuals, each with their own unique identities.

Because of a desire for broad appeal and acknowledgment of the multitude of individuals and organizations involved in even the smallest of projects, practice today is more collaborative than it is an act of self expression, more about distributed authorship than ownership of ideas. Moving beyond models of practice that positioned the architect as the singular genius who bestowed a vision on others, architects today are presenting themselves as members of collaboratives that collectively construct their ambitions and objectives. Evidence of this can be found in a multitude of new formal and informal professional collaborations—Black Reconstruction Collective, Design Advocates, WIP Collaborative—as well as in efforts to share recognition and credit employees. This mentality is also present in the names of offices, which commonly identify their founder(s), not to celebrate the individual, but to project the identity of the individual outward and claim responsibility. Today, architects pursue an extension of their own cultural, political, and social identities and values through their work. Their identities are synchronized with what is designed and how design performs in a variety of contexts.

Jack Self:

Through exposure to my words and design work, people constructed their own idea of who I was, which, since they've never met me, was completely divorced from my own idea. It became difficult to manage the gap between my public persona and my private persona. I've tried to make sure that those two things stay as close to each other as possible.

Oana Stănescu:

I happily surrender any illusion of control over my public persona. I'm not interested in putting my time into designing the way others perceive me. The work and who I work with is what matters to me.

Influence

Automation, Black life, chess sets, chewing gum, choreography, clip art, color blocking, computer science, economics, environmental justice, fashion, film, gabled roofs, garden parties, geometric primitives, grids, historical building types, marzipan, money, music, neurodiversity, ocean floors, off-the-shelf materials, optical illusions, other architects, painting, parades, planetary scars, photography, politics, pop culture, public health, race, rituals of professional practice, rocks, storytelling, waste, water infrastructure, weaving, and violence. Like an endless image feed, sources of influence for architects today are as unintentionally varied and commonplace as they are deliberately coherent and obscure. Each item on this curious list has the capacity to affect the development of architectural design and practice. Equally important, architects' relationships with and acknowledgments of these influences flavor their work and assist in constructing unique aesthetics and conceptual identities.

What explains such assorted influences? Efforts to cultivate a particular source pool of disciplinary issues, aspects of everyday life, and intellectual history are inevitably contaminated by the twenty-four-hour news cycle and a reliance on social media for communication. Before the rise of virtual communities and networks that facilitate creation and sharing of information, ideas, and interests, generations of architects carefully and consciously associated themselves with sources of inspiration and influence. Gatekeeping enabled by limited access to gallery spaces and publishing negated open participation and prohibited the creation of diverse disciplinary narratives. For example, many predecessors of today's emerging architects rallied around a limited combination of topics: affect theory, biological paradigms, and digital design. Today's emerging architects see themselves as outside the influence of technological positivism and its associated neoliberal agenda. Instead, they operate as alchemists, transforming the matter of contemporary life into designs that reflect the surrounding world as much as they inspire positive change. The reflection is not a concession to the status quo as much as it is a means of endearing oneself to a broader audience through engagement with familiar points of reference and salient sociocultural issues. What's more, the impulse to inspire positive change is not overly idealistic or disembodied; rather, it's rooted in a desire to demonstrate the value of design in a tangible way and in real time. The diverse inherited and chosen influences cited by architects today reveal a collective desire to be influential in an equally diverse range of contexts and for multiple audiences.

Jenny French:

We don't curtail the ways that we think or talk about things. We let our entire lives filter back into architecture. There are no boundaries for where our references can come from and there's no judgment about the origins of our ideas.

Jonathan Jackson:

We've done a disservice to everyone who has graduated from architecture school in the United States. It's shocking and sad to recognize that everything I know about design is through a white lens. There's so much more to celebrate.

Ajay Manthripragada:

Canonical references are always in the back of my mind, but they're not necessarily departure points. The projects I often refer to don't inform my design, but they act as corollaries to an approach.

Politics

Architecture is inherently political. Building is a political act. Buildings reflect and record needs and desires of human civilizations, and in doing so are an expression of abilities, beliefs, power structures, and values. Today, architecture in the United States is often an instrument of capital and serves to augment wealth. While many architecture practices are complicit in profit-driven development, some are finding alternative means of enabling the act of building to sponsor progress where it is most needed. From climate change and environmental degradation to homelessness and racial injustice, architecture today addresses a broad range of political issues that are socially and environmentally charged and, for many reasons, elude expeditious resolution. These issues are among the innumerable that directly intersect with the construction and maintenance of the built environment and have garnered the attention of up-and-coming academics and practitioners, who have in turn affirmed the urgent need to ameliorate the negative effects of building. As these designers and thinkers confront, for the first time, opportunities to make permanent marks, they also confront their capacity to act politically.

Previous generations of experimentally minded architects set up unproductive binaries with respect to aesthetic affiliations and political predilections: white versus gray, construction versus deconstruction, critical versus projective, and autonomy versus engagement. These fabricated divisions fractured the discipline of architecture, which led to internalized quarrels that prohibited architecture from projecting outward, to declare and demonstrate its ability to participate in the construction of an equitable, inclusive, and awe-inspiring built environment, and to be a protagonist in progressive political endeavors. Now fractured beyond repair, the discipline is being actively reimagined by a cohort of individuals with new motivations and value sets, and with an intentional lack of authority figures. This generation is less concerned with what architecture is and more concerned with what architecture can do. Equipped with and empowered by a collective belief that form is political, and that aesthetic pursuits and activist agendas are not mutually exclusive, these individuals take on an entanglement of issues—those inherent to the discipline of architecture and those well beyond its blurry boundary—and are especially eager and prepared to demonstrate the value of architectural design. What *can* architecture do? What can *architects* do? By creating new economic models of practice, critically interrogating development, resisting environmentally insensitive construction methods, and engaging with local culture and constituencies, architects today are increasing access to quality architectural design and embracing their roles as attendants of the urban realm.

Rosalyne Shieh:

If being political means seeing and engaging structural inequality, I can't live in a world where those two things can be separated, because it would mean willfully denying a part of reality—if not my own, then the reality of someone else with whom I share this world. It's not only an issue of what we believe, but also about lived realities.

Kutan Ayata:

I'd like to draw the line between citizen and architect. We have our politics, we have our interests, we know where we stand. There are always voices within the discipline who claim a broader reach and express an urgency to deal with political issues. We're more interested in central disciplinary questions that operate through aesthetics, which has its own political agency.

Thom Moran:

I have a romantic view about the architect's role in society, as a visionary or as a critic or as someone who offers a different worldview compared to dominant ideologies. We have an opportunity and responsibility to offer a critique of the world through buildings we design.

Jess Myers:

We already have a social place. Right now, architects are seen as a luxury expense rather than something that the middle and working classes need. I'd like to say that it's our fault that the general public understands the profession in that way. This condition has been created by privileging aesthetics over effect. We need to do a better job understanding the social impact of architecture. We need to rearticulate why the built environment and stewardship of the built environment is inherent to life.

MoMA PS1

Image Credits

Academia:

1. Only-If, Irregular Development, UABB Bi-City Biennale for Urbanism and Architecture, Shenzhen, China, 2017. Courtesy Only If.

Aesthetics:

2. MALL, Haus Gables, Atlanta, Georgia, 2018. Photography by NAARO. Courtesy MALL.

Clients:

3. Spinagu, Piaggio House, Rosario, Argentina, 2019. Photograph by Javier Agustin Rojas. Courtesy Spinagu.

Collaboration:

4. Young & Ayata, DL 1310 Apartments (with Michan Architecture), Mexico City, Mexico, 2020. Photograph by Rafael Gomez. Courtesy Young & Ayata.

Communication:

5. WOJR: Organization for Architecture, Mask House (Rendering), Ithaca, New York, 2017. Courtesy WOJR: Organization for Architecture.

Community:

6. Dream the Combine, Hide & Seek, MoMA PS1 2018 Young Architects Program, Long Island City, New York, 2018. Photograph by Brandon Polanco. Courtesy MoMA PS1 and Dream the Combine.

Construction:

7. New Affiliates, Drywall is Forever, Performa 19, New York, New York, 2019. Courtesy New Affiliates.

Context:

8. AD–WO, Immeasurability: Georgia Conifers, Reconstructions: Architecture and Blackness in America, MoMA. New York. New York, 2021. Courtesy AD–WO.

Finance:

9. FreelandBuck, Stack House, Los Angeles, California, 2018. Photography by Eric Staudenmaier. Courtesy FreelandBuck.

Identity:

10. T+E+A+M, Ghostbox (Model Photograph), 2017 Chicago Architecture Biennial, Chicago, Illinois, 2017. Courtesy T+E+A+M.

Influence:

11. Paul Andersen and Paul Preissner, American Framing, the Pavilion of the United States at the 17th International Architecture Biennale, Venice, Italy, 2021. Courtesy Paul Andersen and Paul Preissner.

Politics:

12. SCHAUM/ SHIEH, Blow Up the Wall (Rendering), 2017. Courtesy SCHAUM/ SHIEH.

Interviews

AD–WO
Emanuel Admassu and Jen Wood

What does it mean to practice architecture?

Emanuel Admassu: Practicing architecture is frustrating because you spend all of this time and energy to produce something that might not end up materializing. We're also extremely frustrated with the complicity of the discipline of architecture as it relates to the way cities are intensifying wealth disparities, the way cities are speeding up the dispossession and displacement of marginalized communities. Because of that, we have strategically positioned ourselves at the edge of architecture, and in some ways, we work against architecture.

Jen Wood: It does feel more fraught to practice architecture today. But also, over the last year, it has felt like we have found a community that's allowing us to feel more free as designers, by way of positioning ourselves somewhere between art and architecture. We have an interest in thinking about space, thinking about people, and thinking about the world outside of the tools that are typically associated with architecture.

In recent lectures the two of you have given, you've talked about your practice being made of two aspects: building and unbuilding. Can you explain what you mean by this, in terms of the way you work and the different types of work you do?

Jen: That is an inherent contradiction of our practice. We design buildings for private clients and simultaneously we write and produce drawings as a way to understand how so few people are able to accrue wealth to execute such projects. We're not trying to offer a resolution, nor a one-to-one balance between the two. I imagine we will always be working with this contradiction, but a hope is that these parallel streams of our practice will converge at times, in the sense that we can work with stakeholders to instigate our own projects, rather than producing built work only in response to the brief of a private client.

Emanuel: It's been really refreshing to think of the practice almost as a workshop, rather than the type of practice, let's say, that hopes to produce a monograph. A lot of our work is embedded in uncertainty and unlearning a lot of the things that we have been trained to love and respect. We are grappling with our own training and our own education, but also imagining a different type of world. I don't think there should be a distinction between this frustration and commitment to beauty. We're interested in beautiful buildings and beautiful cities, but we want those cities to be equitable. So that creates an inherent friction that is hopefully embedded in everything we produce, whether it's the essays that we're writing or the projects we design.

Do you imagine these two sides coming together at some point, or always remaining separate entities that offer a productive friction and feedback? For example, in your lecture for the Rice Design Alliance Spotlight Award, you mentioned the theory of animist materialism that you adopted for the project Two Markets, and we couldn't help but wonder how that theory might inform a residential project…

Jen: Two concepts of animist materialism that have been very generative for us are the nonlinear representation of time and the atomization of the singular vantage point when thinking about a site. For a building project, that second concept speaks to partnership models, and how to engage the custodians or stakeholders of a site.

Emanuel: We're working on a proposal for a public project right now and we're starting to think a lot about animist materialism again. One moment we might be reading an essay that makes the floor plan we're working on seem completely ridiculous. And somehow, that floor plan might also redefine the essay for us, and vice versa. It's been exciting to find ways to navigate all these spaces and thoughts that are not coherent, but in some way end up reflecting a certain sensibility.

Your work has long been invested in the overlap of geography and identity. How do you think an architect can operate with authenticity when working outside their own geography and/or with people who have different identities from their own? Do you think there are constraints on who can work on particular issues, in particular places, with particular people?

Jen: There are so many degrees of genuine proximity to a project or an issue. We think about it and talk about it all the time: the degrees of outsiderness. Especially when we are doing projects in Ethiopia, where I'm obviously more of an outsider… But having said that, Emanuel left when he was fourteen, so he is now considered diaspora even by family and friends who live there.

Emanuel: When I get in arguments with my mother, she calls me a foreigner. That's her go-to, to end the discussion… By and large, Black neighborhoods in the United States have been designed by white architects and urban designers. The problem historically has been white architects bringing and superimposing their ideas of whiteness, that are about racial hierarchy and dominance, that basically devalue and eventually decimate those neighborhoods. Therefore, we are not interested in discussions that essentialize race or racism. Instead, we are interested in investigating how race continues to be constructed, and how that is the primary thing that we need to actively unbuild—both in practice and academia. Which means if a white architect enters into a Black neighborhood, that white architect needs to deal with their whiteness. There is no neutrality. As architects and urban designers, when we enter unfamiliar environments, we need to make sure that we are collaborating with people who really, really, really know that environment, people who really understand the ways in which that environment has been misrepresented. It's about being genuine and aware of our blind spots when entering into specific territories, and making sure we're not repeating the mistakes made by previous generations of architects.

Jen: Also, designing opportunities for genuine feedback loops is important. With Two Markets, we worked closely with photographers and researchers in Dar es Salaam and Addis Ababa, and then we produced these drawings for an exhibition in Providence. The intention was always to go back and have an exhibition in Ethiopia as well, to discuss how we worked together to produce these artifacts and to invite conversation around them.

Emanuel: But we also have to acknowledge the asymmetry in power when entering into these environments, as much as we might try to acknowledge the people we collaborated with. One of the things we did for the exhibition was print the bibliography on the storefront. Before you enter the exhibition, you actually confront the names of people we learned from in order to produce the work. But even that is not enough of a gesture... because of the circulation of knowledge, when we produce something versus when someone who is based in Dar es Salaam produces something, our work will have much more visibility. So I just think that is an endless project. And we have to find a way to dismantle the trajectory that has been set up by the colonial project, which is what's maintaining this asymmetry.

How does your work consider the relationship between beauty and politics, and also form and politics?

Emanuel: For a long time, the works that we were in conversation with were works produced by other architects. The moment that shifted and we started thinking of ways in which we can produce a spatial intervention that is in conversation with a painting, or that is in conversation with a sculpture, a whole new territory opened up for discussion around aesthetics.

Jen: We were recently on the jury for a public art commission in Providence, and one of the project requirements is an engagement with Providence's history of slavery, redlining, and displacement. As a jury, we agreed that while engaging with this historical weight, the selected artwork needed to convey a certain vitality—to be a project of futuring. When it's a project solely about rendering trauma in a static,

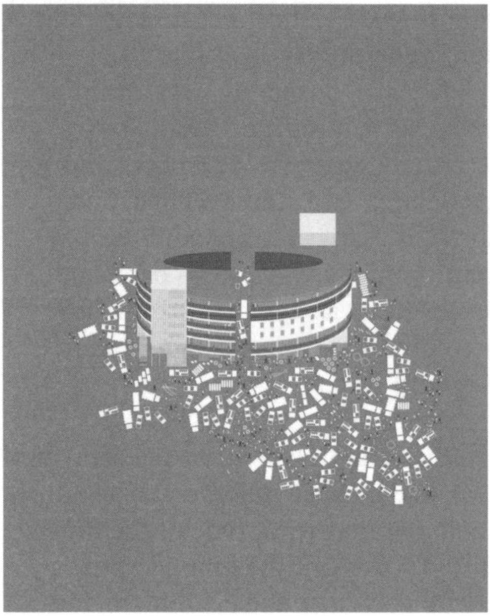

Fig. 13

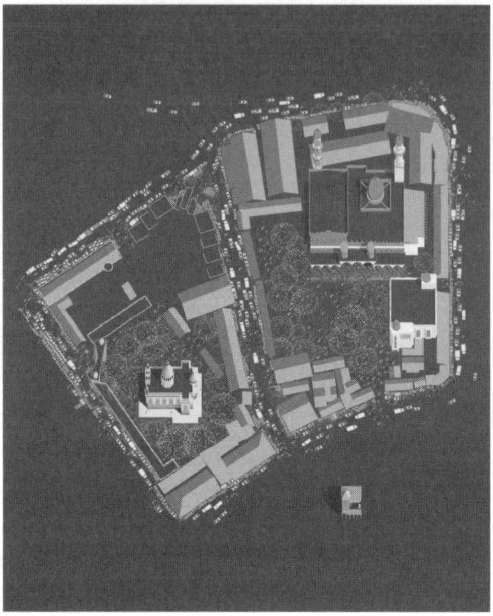

Fig. 14

Fig. 15

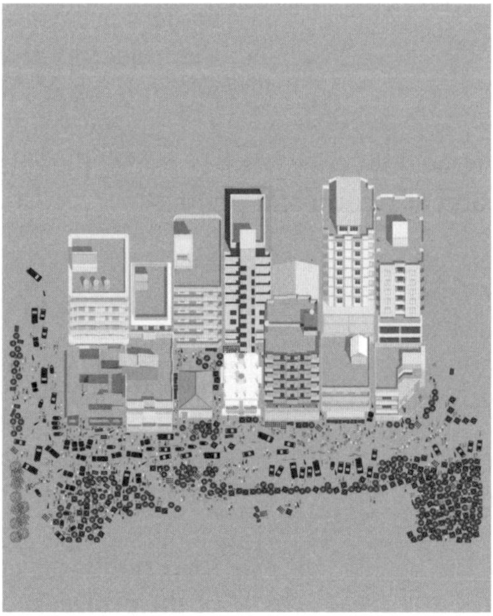

Fig. 16

monumentalizing way, it can foreclose the conversations that need to happen around these issues.

Emanuel: It has to be about transmutation. It can't just be about a representation of ongoing violence or historical violence, but actually has to genuinely imagine a better world. That is where the beauty lies. If you lose either of those elements then it becomes somewhat banal. There are projects that are "futuring" that pretend as if there is no history on that site, that nothing happened before. And those are equally problematic. But there are also projects that are really almost literally representing trauma. And those projects foreclose the potential for multiple forms of engagement.

We'd like to know a bit more about your respective roles within AD–WO, as well as the other things you are involved in. Emanuel, you are also currently an assistant professor at Columbia GSAPP and founding member of the Black Reconstruction Collective. Can you tell us about the relationship between the day-to-day managing of your practice and these various pursuits, and how these other efforts inform your practice?

Jen: There is a delineation of tasks—for example, I manage the nuts and bolts of putting a drawing set together, whereas Emanuel is much more involved with conversations happening in academia and beyond. But, you know, we are married, we live together—we have so much proximity to what the other person is doing, so we aren't producing work in silos. We're constantly critiquing and disagreeing with each other about what we produce. So even though it feels like there's a compulsion to define "Jen is practice" and "Emanuel is project," that's not a true summary of how we operate.

Emanuel: If I'm reading something I'm usually at least giving Jen some sort of synopsis of whatever it is. And similarly, if Jen is working on a CD set, she's usually going to send me at least an iPhone grab or something of every key decision. So, it's really, really porous. The disagreements are really productive. She is able to check me when I get into super academic mode, because she's completely bored with that. And I think simultaneously I'm able to check her when she gets hyper-Architecty with a capital A. That part is really fun. Jen has a certain tendency to veer into territories that are a bit more surreal, from a conceptual standpoint. She usually makes the ideas weirder. Usually when you have

Fig. 17

Fig. 18

this kind of setup, the person who is 100 percent on the practice side becomes the person that makes it a bit more conventional. But in this case, it's an intensification of whatever's unconventional.

Your work inherently intersects with and addresses global challenges such as climate change, the pandemic, and racial injustice. Can you perhaps talk about how the omnipresence of these issues over the last year has amplified certain aspects of your work, redirected your work, or inspired you to work in unexpected ways?

Emanuel: This past year, especially the uprisings and seeing how incredibly conservative architecture has been in its response, has definitely pushed us in a direction of saying, "fuck architects." And that has produced a very different type of sensibility and type of projects. We really want to maintain that. Lately, with things opening up again, there's an assumption that we're all back to where we were before. But we're actually not interested in being back where we were. We want to make sure this becomes a transformative moment, for the discipline and for our practice. We're interested in maintaining both a professional practice and a critical practice moving forward, and continuing to find ways to call each other out. To put it shortly, we want the revolution to happen, and that needs to be made explicit.

What's been the most rewarding moment of your professional careers so far?

Jen: Well, for me, it's being able to contribute to the MoMA show Reconstructions. It was definitely the most difficult project that I've been part of and that sort of struggle was really important for me. I think the project that was led by Emanuel was super strong in the end, and I feel really proud to be part of that.

Emanuel: Yeah, I would obviously have to agree. That project was definitely the most rewarding and, also, kudos to the curators... we've never experienced anything that has been designed that way on the back end. They put together an incredible panel of advisors. It was almost like going back to grad school. We were reading, we were presenting our work. It was an incredible learning process, and I think it's something that we'll continue to reflect on for a while.

Fig. 19

Agency—Agency: Tei Carpenter

What does it mean to practice architecture?

Tei Carpenter: I come from a background in philosophy and visual art. Practicing architecture became a synthesis of those two disciplines, having a broader outlook on things and being able to step back conceptually. What I liked about architecture was the frictions and the tensions that are introduced as a result of the reality that it hits up against. And the possibilities of publicness—the possibilities of experience, not just in a gallery setting, but in a much more public dimension.

Architecture is a commitment, and it takes persistence. Fundamentally, at the end of the day, it is really about practicing. You learn through projects, and it's this layering of information and experience over time. And eventually, you develop what that practice is and how it can become nimble and agile enough to deal with the challenges in the world right now.

Many of your projects seem to be interested in everyday ritual or routine. What are your own everyday rituals that are important to the way you practice architecture?

It's such a funny question because with COVID, and also having a child, there's a lot of disruption, and a lot of destabilization. But I get up really, really early in the morning and have quiet time to think and reflect on what I'm doing, and to set out what I need to get done in a day. I also try to get out of the office, go out to see things. I usually do better thinking when I'm not at my desk, when I'm taking a walk around the block or on the subway or something. There's a level of organization that's required, on a really pragmatic level, but I think it's important to have a looseness around doing the production work to make space for thinking, rather than constantly reacting to every single email.

You have developed a number of projects that engage with urgent and complex ecological issues relating to waste—Pla-Kappa, Testbed, Hamilton Gears Reuse Park. How do you envision your role as an architect relative to these issues? Relatedly, when you work on these kinds of often large and speculative projects, how do you think about the relationship between your disciplinary expertise and interest in interdisciplinary collaboration?

I was just thinking about that question of expertise last night when I was reading an article about Alison Killing, who was trained as an architect, and who won a Pulitzer. She's been doing work in China, revealing prison camps using spatial information. I think she's the first architect who has ever won a Pulitzer, and she actually calls herself an architect rather than a journalist, because she thinks about her work as being able to visualize and spatialize things. In terms of my work, I think it's a question of visualization, and I guess my role is as a translator between much larger, much more urgent issues and something that's part of everyday experience, like the building that's on your block, or a park you visit every day. As a result, these issues get woven into an experience of an architectural project—which has been the case for Hamilton Gears in particular. And I think that's an architectural disciplinary expertise, finding ways to translate or synthesize really big issues into something that's an object or spatial experience that embeds itself in three-dimensional space, where you are confronted with it. I think that's one of the issues with these larger urgent questions, that it's not about a wrist slap, like you can't use plastic bags anymore. Rather, what are alternatives? How do we engage with this? Is it possible to think about this in a charismatic way or in a way that actually brings people in and encourages them to engage with an issue differently, or tries to find alternative routes? I also think storytelling is a part of that—translation and storytelling, and building out the larger context for how we might understand particular issues. The hydrants project is a really tiny project, but it communicates a new narrative about being able to drink water from the city. It's like an unfolding story, and I like thinking about how the experience can be familiar but inevitable, somehow.

Your projects range from built physical things in the real world—buildings and infrastructural installations, for instance—to projective or speculative projects with huge ambitions. Can you tell us a little about how you envision the relationship between these different types of work as it relates to the identity of your practice?

It has to do with this idea of practice, and also what a young architect can do within certain situations. When you get out of school, what kind of work are you doing, versus once you're ten or fifteen years out of school, what are you capable of doing, what do you have under your belt? Some of the speculative work came out of a moment when I didn't think building was the right answer right then—I just wanted to explore and think about how to experiment. I had some time to do research, and I think that came out inevitably from that moment. I'm doing much more built work now, which is great. But I don't think too much about the identity of the practice. There are certain moments in one's practice or in one's trajectory where certain things feel appropriate. And I guess I like to think that there's a speculative dimension to built work. I also feel like you have to have larger conceptual or speculative ideas at the beginning of your career, before you get into nitty-gritty details of a door schedule. I think it's important to lay out what is foundational or influential, as well as the values or ethics of your practice. Architecture is so detailed that you have to really think about what are the big ideas, what's important to you, so you don't lose sight of those things. So, the speculative work and some of the installation-scale work help me to identify those things.

Fig. 20

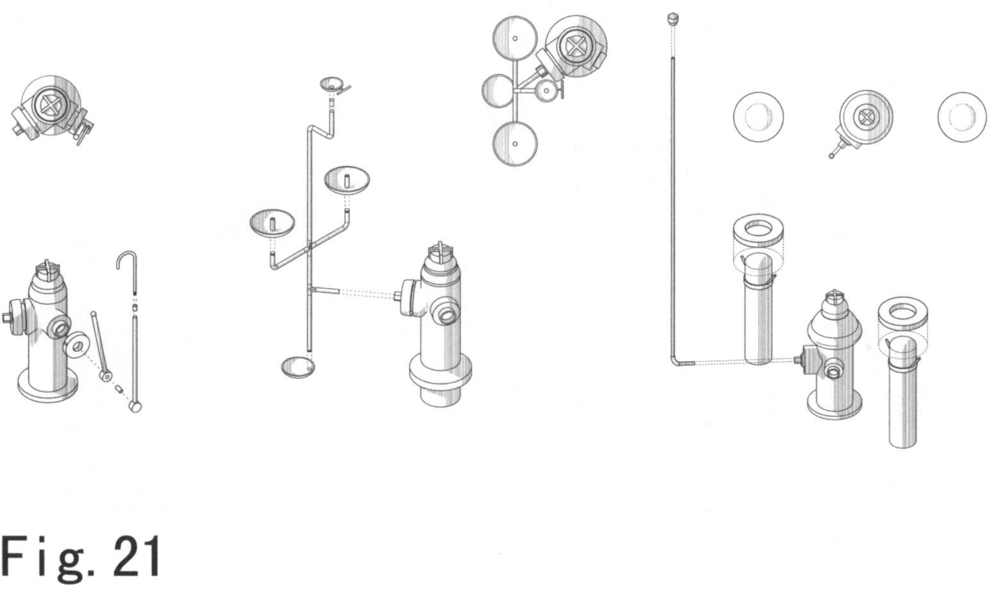

Fig. 21

Fig. 22

Given the range of scales and subject matter, your work speaks to many different audiences—which audiences do you hope your work engages with?

Architects have to wear a lot of hats. I guess I try to think about how projects could get mobilized, or the legibility of a project for someone who's maybe not an architect. It's actually really important to me that the work doesn't necessitate an insider perspective to understand it. I've tried to externalize what I'm doing to bring it into a larger conversation. I'm also interested in how some of the work that I've been doing has formats of representation that come out of the work, like patent drawings, for example, or gifs for thinking about change over time. It's about audience but also about what makes sense for a particular project. And maybe that's because of the different scales that I work at. It's not always orthographic drawings that I find the most useful at communicating a project. I try to think about what might be endemic to the design concept.

What is Agency—Agency's business model as it relates to financial sustainability? How do some of the unsolicited proposals or speculative proposals fit into that business model, or at least into the organizational structure of your practice?

I wish I could say specifically that I have a clear business model, but I don't think I can say that. I'm definitely interested in thinking more about self-initiated work, and how to finance that. I'm interested in how these things can translate across contexts, but also how architects can run their own projects rather than wait for the client to come to them. We don't do bread-and-butter projects. We don't have these secret, back-of-house projects that no one knows about. Teaching has been really important for sustaining a lot of what I do. Maintaining collaborations with artists or certain people has also been part of how we sustained the practice, at least early on. Now it's more straightforward, in terms of how people are getting paid. There's just more client-based work now. I've also learned from artist friends of mine, and have gone after grants and fellowships, and that has been helpful. There's a lot of work that goes into grant writing, but if it's successful, it can be really useful for the practice. So that's something that we've tried for some of the projects that are at more of the installation scale.

Fig. 23

We've talked a bit about how your work interfaces with ecological crises, and by extension, climate change. Have other pressing global issues, like the pandemic and racial injustice, redirected your interests or inspired you to work in unexpected ways? And if so, in what ways? You've done a session with Office Hours—are there other things like that that are newly on the table for you?

Office Hours came out of conversations that were instigated by BLM, among a couple of different groups that I'm part of. It's now been more than a year since George Floyd was killed, and early on I was just trying to find collectives of people to share with and talk through what we do now. Office Hours came out of a bunch of those conversations, and Esther Choi has done an amazing job spearheading and developing the platform. And mentoring has been a clear extension of some of that work with Office Hours. Jonathan Jackson and I both did the high school edition of Office Hours together. Both of us were really interested in not just the grad students from Harvard who can come to Office Hours, but how to instigate these conversations way earlier, with kids who are in high school. It's been important to think about how to make architecture and the practice of architecture more accessible and not so mysterious. It can seem like a completely black box, right? Especially for kids in high school, and especially for people who don't have the means or access or a role model. So I've been trying to just have conversations about it, which has been fun, and enriching for me, too. I think it's incredible, all the organizing across the discipline that's been happening in the past year.

In terms of the pandemic, we did a series of balcony prototypes and fire-escape retrofits—working with existing infrastructure, but thinking about how to recast the New York Tenement Act. The idea of temporality as something that can be transformative, and impermanence as a kind of design technique, is also something I've been trying to think through during the pandemic. I've noticed how we're all reusing the elements of our houses, and how we are trying to reconfigure how we're living. But also, how space and time begin to collapse together, and that absolutely comes out of the pandemic. It's something that I've been trying to pull through the work, thinking about duration and time and really long scales of time.

What has been the most rewarding moment of your professional career thus far?

There are different forms of reward. I feel like there's always this pushing toward the next thing. So, I never really feel satisfied. Teaching is incredibly rewarding. And I think finishing a project after many years is very rewarding. It's great to see people interact with it. But I do sort of feel like it's this endless search, in a way. It's rewarding, but it's like, how do you build on this? How do you learn from it? In many ways, it feels like a feedback loop.

Ajay Manthripragada

What does it mean to practice architecture?

Ajay Manthripragada: When I started on my own, I had a pretty conventional idea of what it means to practice architecture. That definition informed my activities and approach. I was relying on practice as a primary source of income—I was teaching part-time at Berkeley, but I had to focus on practice to make a living. I worked only on things I was being paid for, which is not always something architects do. From the beginning, practicing architecture was about providing a service. Over the years, I've come to a more expansive definition. Alongside commissioned work, it includes being proactive about the conceptual and intellectual aspects of our discipline. In addition to designing, I'm also writing and doing research through drawing. I'm looking more to the history of architecture, as well... not only for inspiration, but to understand how to position my work relative to the past.

In the research aspect of your practice, you often begin with “canonical” references. What is the role of those references as departure points? What does it mean to continue to revisit historical disciplinary narratives today?

Canonical references are always in the back of my mind, but they’re not necessarily departure points. The projects I often refer to don’t inform my design, but they act as corollaries to an approach. For example, I’ve been studying Sebastiano Serlio and how he responded to the irregularities of the sites where he worked. Additionally, his work confronted the division between public and private space in a unique way. I was encountering similar irregularities and confrontations in my work. My projects were being commissioned by private clients, but I had an interest in their public faces, or the way in which they interfaced with the public. That’s why I don’t necessarily think of the references as points of departure. They perform more dialectically—they are in dialogue with what I am doing.

On your website, you have a section dedicated to what you call “Projects” and another to what you call “Buildings.” How meaningful is that difference to you? Do you approach the work within these two categories differently with respect to motivations and goals? Do you think of those two categories as separate or complementary?

That’s something I am perpetually thinking about, and also discussing with colleagues. I’m good friends with Aaron Forrest and Yasmin Vobis, of Ultramoderne, whose website is structured in the same way. Whenever we’re talking about our work, we often talk about the categories of projects we develop. There are buildings, but there are also projects that I have no interest in materializing. When I set up my website, there may have been some naive and optimistic notion that “buildings” would be built and “projects” would be unbuilt. But of course, some of the “projects” on the website are built, and most of the “buildings” remain unbuilt. The categories were more productive for me in the beginning, but now my work is expanding beyond commissioned work and drawing research. For example, I just completed a competition entry, which combines approaches I’ve previously taken in both building designs and speculative projects. The categorization is also tied to the fact that I teach, too. I have a responsibility to understand how work resonates differently with different audiences.

That perfectly sets up our next question: who is the primary audience for your work?

Ideally, there are multiple audiences. A strategy I'm often using is to develop designs that are equally unfamiliar and familiar. In my mind, this strategy opens the work to many viewpoints. There's one audience that would recognize the value in my pursuit of novelty, or uncanny qualities in the work, and there's another audience that would just find that unsettling. I'm open to either response because both suggest the work has garnered attention, even if just for a moment.

Let's unpack that a little more with the Page House and Gallery. There are a lot of games being played in the project—the impenetrable monolith versus the hollow shell, the free aperture against the rigid composition of cladding, the roof as the fifth facade, the recursive organization and plan. How do these disciplinary games confront the material realities of construction and the functionality of the project? Do those two aspects—the conceptual and the material—reinforce one another, or do they operate independently?

The Page House and Gallery is a unique project. I'm very lucky to have received that commission for my first ground-up building. A lot of the conceptual aspects came from the material realities, not from an initial desire for abstraction. First and foremost is the cube. In many ways, the cube was a coincidence. I mean that literally—many things coincided around the form of a cube. When we began to envision the project on the site, the cube made the most sense, not only from an environmental standpoint, in terms of its footprint, but also from an urban standpoint and in the visual relationship the house would have with its neighbors. The cube really emerged from conditions on the ground, as opposed to a desire for me to do a cube as my first project. Of course, working with a cube then bears on materiality. Alongside the design development, we had been searching for the right cladding material. The square tile format was the most straightforward and obvious choice to reinforce the proportion of the cube. Here, the abstract met the material. So, it's strange. Indeed, there are many conceptual games being played, but all of them come from either

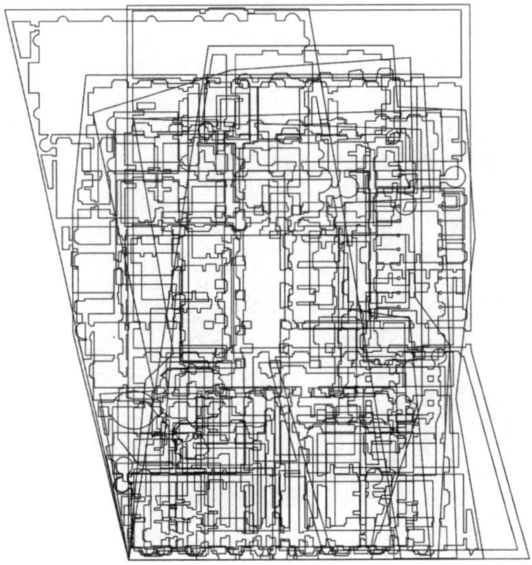

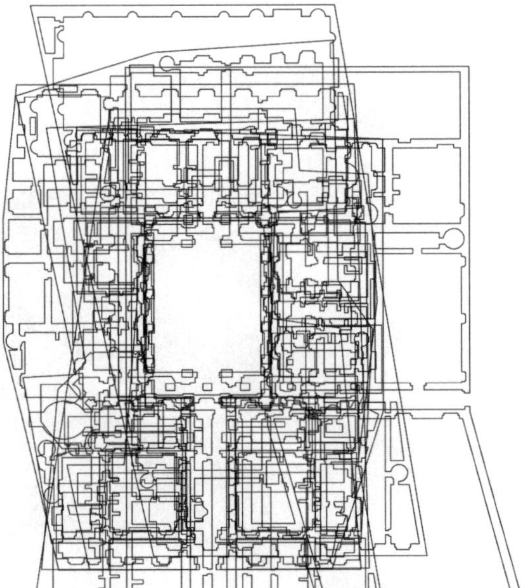

Fig. 24

Fig. 25

Fig. 26

embracing a constraint or acknowledging a condition of assembly or program. For example, the misalignment of the windows to the tile—there was a lot of effort to try to align them with the tile grid in the beginning. In the end, the desire to position each window relative to its optimal interior condition trumped the alignment to the outside tile, but this also produced an interesting result in terms of composition. It's really a curious project because it is very abstract, but each of the individual decisions came out of very pragmatic constraints.

Has the approach that you took designing and realizing the Page House translated to other projects?

That project was unique because of the circumstances of the site and the desires of the client. But what I learned in that project is how much I need to work with preexisting conditions and constraints given to me by the client or that I find myself. In subsequent projects where the client gave me more room with respect to developing form and materiality, I really had to resist the desire to pursue total abstraction. In another project that I've been working on, there are trees in the backyard that the client wants to remove. But I've proposed that we preserve them. In part, that decision was an alibi to create a challenge for myself that would yield a much more interesting form. It created a fortuitous alignment with the motivations I had toward subverting the pitched roof. I look for opportunities in the constraints in many of my projects. I need constraints to limit the level of abstraction—they ideally don't work against abstraction, but rather temper it.

Have the challenges of climate change, the pandemic, and social injustice, redirected your workflow or inspired you to work in unexpected ways?

The work that I've done so far does try to expand the notion of context to something wider than the immediate vicinity of the project, and beyond what's only physical. On the one hand, there's a question of audience. We've already discussed that. There is also an idea in my work of elevating certain constituencies or broadening the range of constituencies that can access and appreciate the work. To do this, I'm moving toward work that is more public in nature. The competition

I completed recently was for a housing project in Los Angeles. The motivation behind entering that competition was to expand the reach of my work, not just in terms of who's looking at the work, but also the reach of the potential constituents of the work itself. I knew it was a speculative, ideas-based competition, but it points toward a new direction. I'm now pursuing a housing project in India. I can't anticipate what the constraints will be, but I'm really interested in taking on new challenges that would increase the capacity of the work to make positive change.

In terms of climate change, that's not something that I have explicitly addressed yet, beyond the basic level of responsibility I hope we all share. A lot of a building's environmental impact is tied to the limitations, or lack thereof, of the client's budget. A budget can equally produce conscientiousness and irresponsibility with respect to material extraction and sourcing. As my practice evolves, I hope the work actively engages with these issues in a more measurable manner, especially as I take on projects in less familiar contexts.

Who have been the most influential figures throughout your career? How has their influence affected the work that you do now, or how has the influence integrated itself into your design process?

I will refer to a couple teachers who have been influential both directly and through their writing. Marc Treib was a professor of mine as an undergraduate at UC Berkeley. Both in his writing and in the way he teaches, he is very selective in claiming new territory. He's a classic historian in that respect. I am being reductive here, but his work is ninety percent description or fact and ten percent introduction of content that is open to interpretation or speculative. I've adopted this sensibility in my work. I'm very particular about where I place emphasis or strive for novelty or innovation. Another influential figure for me is Sarah Whiting, who was my thesis advisor in graduate school. Her theory of an "engaged autonomy" has been a springboard for research and design work that bridges my formal interests in projective geometry with contextual influences or contingencies.

What has been the most rewarding moment of your professional career so far?

A moment during the construction of the Page House comes to mind that was rewarding because of the way it transcends the realm of practice. Initially, I did not design the stair correctly. I was being very optimistic about the structural capacity of the stair at a particular moment. We ran up against the problem of insufficient space for the stair as it was designed. The most immediate solution was to put an awkward angle in the gallery downstairs to support the stair above. Of course, I was not going to accept that solution... and the client was not going to accept that solution. I worked with the engineer to develop a more technically sophisticated way of resolving the issue, transferring gravitational loads in a manner that would not disrupt the space below while retaining the thinness of the stair support. For me, this situation totally challenged a rule of thumb regarding poché and structural depth that I had been taught and believed in for as long as I've studied and practiced. In turn, that experience changed my approach to teaching how construction and material realities confront the abstract and the conceptual.

AUAR: Mollie Claypool and Gilles Retsin

We learned that both of you were recently promoted to associate professor. Congratulations!

Gilles Retsin: Thank you! We get a bit more money and we can finally tell our parents that we are professors!

Mollie Claypool: That's kind of it. Hi, I'm Professor Claypool.

The first question sounds harmless, but it's actually complex. What does it mean to practice architecture?

Mollie: Wow! That is such a loaded question. We don't call ourselves an architecture practice… and that's strategic. We say that we're a design and technology company. When we describe ourselves, we're talking about intersections between disciplines rather than working within a singular discipline. That's really important for the work that we're doing. We're trying to rethink what a practice related to the built environment looks like.

Gilles: We're developing an entirely new model for practice. This ambition grew from the desire to engage differently with the built environment and to transcend the limits of practicing architecture in a traditional manner.

How does this view of practicing architecture inform the way you work together? Within AUAR, there are computer scientists, theorists, architects, product designers, software developers, manufacturing experts… How do all of those backgrounds come together, and how do you sustain the office?

Gilles: The other day I was talking to one of the other directors of AUAR, Claire McAndrew, who is a social scientist. She's not an architect. She also teaches at The Bartlett School of Architecture, and she was telling me how she always feels alienated by architects. It was a reminder that not all of our business partners or business stakeholders are architects. This has to do with the fact that we don't distinguish between our collaborators' backgrounds when determining who does what. We have architects who do programming, we have software developers who participate in architectural design, we have an architect working on robotics.

Mollie: All of our projects are highly multidisciplinary, so we're intentionally an office of people who work across disciplines. This gives us a dynamism within the team that really wouldn't exist in a traditional practice. Regarding how we sustain the practice financially… It happens in a variety of ways. We have a relationship with the UCL, as a spinout, where we find a lot of support. For the first couple of years, we were funded primarily by grants—a mix of private and public grant funding. We've also taken on private consultancy projects, which have provided us with a lot of agility because we haven't had to find investors, like many other tech companies do. This strategy has allowed us the space to play and experiment with what we thought the company needed to be.

Gilles: We are beginning to look for investors, which is the classic start-up route. Now that we've realized what we want with our business, we need to scale up. To do that, we need to find funding. We're talking to venture capitalists and social impact investors, and we're having very interesting conversations with them about architecture and the built environment. Essentially, we're trying to transcend the service-based model of practice and operate from a product-based perspective.

Fig. 27

Fig. 28

Fig. 29

Mollie: We're very thankful to have had the time and space to test different ideas and to design a new market for ourselves. When we talk to potential clients or investors, we can easily demonstrate the value of our efforts because there is a very clear need for what we can do in the intersection between design and technology.

You have expressed a goal to democratize technology and making. How can you operate outside of existing power structures and against the failing systems of profit-driven private corporations, especially as they pertain to housing?

Mollie: We're always operating in tension with existing power structures, and sometimes rubbing up against them or running in parallel to them. Having self-awareness about the way we work and that there is tension gives us an advantage, because we can sit in critique of it, we can weigh in, and we can participate in it. We always ask ourselves: Do we recognize our complicity in the failure of existing power structures? Are we working against existing power structures? In a more traditional architectural practice, there is a lot of complicity because it's so fragile and precarious. We're creating something new. We're trying to build resilience. One of the ways that we've started to work is to develop projects within the demonstrable market that we've developed, but also strategically work with specific partners that share our ethics and values, particularly around community engagement. We often discuss how we can take arts-based approaches to build a strong base for our ideas around democratization and co-creation, or co-design. This creates a resilience in the way that we're working, and allows us to scale up at a pace that isn't as precarious when compared to traditional architecture practices.

Gilles: We're ultimately neoliberal subjects. It's very important to be conscious of that. We wonder if we would operate differently if we would receive a commission to design a large building. We want to keep the values that we have in the company right now, which will be one of our biggest challenges if we keep growing and have opportunities to take on larger projects.

Mollie: One of the ways that we've been thinking about this is through a mission-lock. We're designing a mission-lock not just into our company, but with our collaborations and partnerships and into our contracts. We're looking at how other disciplines and other companies maintain their mission-lock while scaling up. And when we think about scaling up, we know we'll be in conversation with real estate developers, local councils, policymakers, government ministers... These conversations often revolve around the topic of risk. What we're used to seeing, at least in the UK, is that risk as it pertains to social value is not something these organizations are willing to take on. More recently we're seeing a shift in how social value is being built into large pools of funding that are being put out by the UK government. We're at a really opportune moment to be a young company that is starting to have access to this support. And we can provide a framework for these larger organizations to understand social value as a critical component of practice.

In your projects Block West and House Block, your approach is a critique of industrialized modularity and mass customization. What can your discrete kit of parts not do? What are the limits of that system?

Gilles: We are not taking a modernist approach. We're taking an alternative approach. The narrative would radically change if we were to become highly successful. Because we've had opportunities to build lately, we're really beginning to understand the limits of these systems. I've always been interested in things that escape or subvert traditional systems. These discrete blocks are not meant to be totalitarian or universal. We've been having interesting conversations about how these blocks can become a platform onto which other companies can attach their products.

Mollie: When we've shown our work to other companies developing modular building systems, for example, they always ask about HVAC and plumbing services. How we deal with these services is a really important question for us. What we're most excited about is the accessibility of our product to other people, and their ability to imagine it as a template for their creativity.

It's clear that you've been motivated by social and political issues for a long time. Your work is specifically engaged with issues of labor and sustainable manufacturing, for example. Have you been inspired to work in different or unexpected ways as a result of the recent amplification of global issues like climate change or racial injustice?

Fig. 30

Fig. 31

Mollie: We cannot separate our primary focus of housing and the housing crisis from issues of ecological emergency or race. One of the things that we've been pretty strategic about is to build within our projects a real focus on community needs, desires, fears, and dreams. Every one of our projects has a community-asset-based approach. We don't act as if we are the experts coming in and telling you what you need. We work together with communities to discover what they need and how they want to grow. We've been thinking a lot about the tools that we're designing that can support people being able to improve their quality of life and feel a sense of belonging. One key has been to compensate everyone we work with. We don't have volunteers in our projects. We also provide a lot of support with access to technology. One of our main goals is to build trust within and across the communities in which we're working. At the heart of what we're doing is breaking down traditional disciplinary boundaries in design and technology and making architecture and the built environment more accessible.

Gilles: AUAR also exists, in part, because of the pandemic. Previously, we had extremely fragmented lives... Every month we were taking multiple trips to lecture or be on reviews at other schools. We had very little time to focus on creating something meaningful. Confined to our homes during the pandemic, we had time to focus on how we wanted to work together and grow our company. AUAR is our version of a pandemic baby! The flexibility in working hours and locations that was afforded to many of us during the pandemic is something that we've maintained with our employees and collaborators. We are extremely flexible, and because of that extremely agile.

Mollie: This scenario requires that we're really communicative with each other—not in an overbearing way, but in a way that encourages honesty about what we need from each other. We've put a lot of effort into building practices of trust and care with one another and within our team. Giving our team members autonomy and trusting their individual processes creates productive and healthy working environments for them. They don't need to worry whether their time spent daydreaming was valuable. It is valuable!

What kinds of projects do you hope to be working on in the near future, and how do you imagine your practice may evolve relative to those types of projects?

Gilles: We just had a conversation with a business consultant about this. She asked about our dream client. We don't have one. We want our product to be appealing and accessible to everyone. Our dream would be that our products make a positive impact on daily life.

Mollie: We really want to keep communities engaged in the way we approach housing. We want to empower others to participate in the design of their environments. We've been working with a woman named Hannah, who has had a lot of different jobs in recent years and was unable to stay in one place. She worked with us during the construction of Block West. She loved it and really felt like it was something she wanted to continue to be involved in. She's now becoming someone who works on of all of our builds, and has become a community build manager for one of our primary partners, We Can Make. It's been really amazing to see her journey. What she represents to us is the possibilities of empowerment in the community.

What has been the most rewarding moment of your professional careers thus far, individually or as a collaborative?

Mollie: We applied for so many grants over five or six years before we received our first grant, for Block West. That was the first significant grant that we received. Prior to that there was a lot of disappointment. A lot! It's a lot of being beaten down at the very moment you've convinced yourself you have a good idea. When we received the grant, I felt a great sense of validation—that our work wasn't for nothing. This was early 2020. It was really transformative for us to be able to work with our partners on that project and feel kinship. To know that other people outside our small community can relate to and are excited by our work is really rewarding.

Gilles: For me, that moment was my first built project ... Being able to see something materialized at full scale after looking at it in a digital environment for a long time was really amazing. It sounds cliché, but it was an incredible moment, for sure.

Beatrice Galilee

When you were studying architecture, were there any particular moments or influential figures that led you to the alternate path of becoming a curator?

Beatrice Galilee: The most influential person I studied with was Indy Johar, who is now the director of Dark Matter Labs, which is an experimental, multidisciplinary lab that works on strategic design and institutional infrastructure. I also worked with the architect David Turnbull. Both of those individuals were supportive of my unconventional journey through architecture school. I failed studio during my second year, but what I excelled at was organizing class trips and lectures. I was super engaged with everyone else's work, but I was not doing well with my own design projects. In my third and fourth years, I had professors who nurtured these interests and tried to help me find different outlets. At that time, I can't say I even really knew what a curator was. Eventually, I went into writing because that was my main interest. I ended up reviewing exhibitions, talking to curators, and learning how to develop an opinion about the quality of an exhibition. I didn't really have the tools to make these judgments, but it was something I wanted to nourish. So that's the path I took.

Now, working full-time as a curator, do you feel like an architect who's engaging with curating or a curator who happened to study architecture?

When I'm developing major exhibitions or smaller, site-specific interventions, I feel like I have this extra power. My knowledge of the practice of architecture is incredibly helpful. I know how things are made and how to get things done, I know how to talk to the contractors, and through osmosis, being around architects, I have a sense of what the issues are going to be on-site. In other situations, especially when I was at The Met performing day-to-day administrative tasks, it wasn't particularly helpful to have had an architecture education.

How difficult is it for you to challenge conventions and introduce alternative models of curating while simultaneously appeasing your own interests, public interests, and the interests of the institutions?

Every day is a balancing act. For an exhibition to be a success, you need to draw a big audience. It's less about what the critics say. The main thing when you're doing an institutional project is that you need numbers. It's great if you get good reviews, but it's not critical. But you also have to do work that you believe in. When I started at The Met, I had to invent a new way of sharing architecture, because the museum did not have a gallery for architecture—it still doesn't—and there was no budget and no collection. I had to figure out how to create an architecture program without a gallery space. In the end, doing something that is unprecedented or unconventional is a process of negotiation. If you can be direct, persuasive, passionate, and excited, you'll get others on board and make it happen.

What are some of the more pivotal professional experiences you've had?

When I was getting started, I felt a certain power… the power one feels when they are new and young. It's a halo of naivete that provides protection. I felt this when developing my first exhibitions. With my first shows in China, I felt a real sense of opportunity. I'm thinking specifically of the Shenzhen Hong Kong Biennale of Architecture and Urbanism. I was part of a very young team. I was twenty-six and my collaborator was twenty-four. We were both very young and very inexperienced. At the same time, we had a lot of confidence simply because it was a sink-or-swim situation. We were running on enthusiasm—enthusiasm and tons of ideas. From there, it was a matter of envisioning these ideas and then dealing with the politics of the situation. It was in that moment that I learned to read others and communicate effectively. Without these skills, nothing happens. All of these shows are ultimately about developing ideas and working with others to make things happen. That's the real key with curatorial practice... you have to keep yourself motivated and continuously motivate everyone around you. You have to make things happen. When a contributor asks for a translator, or more plywood, or less plywood... you have to make it happen. When you are a curator, you are also a project manager, a contractor, but also a friend. You have to be very versatile.

What is your process for selecting who you work with in a show?

I try to put forward practitioners who haven't had a lot of exposure, or, if they have, I try to put a new project in front of them that pushes their practice in a different direction. To me, architecture exhibitions aren't about a round of applause for someone who has achieved a lot in their career. That is not the type of exhibition I'm interested in developing. It's not the type of exhibition that I would go to, either. As a curator, I'm more interested in creating a partnership between myself and the artist that is mutually beneficial. For example, when working with Wang Shu, who is widely celebrated, I was able to provide a new opportunity for him—I set him up with a curator at The Met who showed him Chinese paintings and scrolls that are not typically on display because they're too fragile. When I include someone in our programming, I'm always thinking of a way that it works for them as well as for the audience. In general, I'm always looking to support interesting young architects, because you just never know what could happen after providing them with an opportunity to share their work.

How do you track everything that's going on in architecture and design today?

In quite a few different ways, honestly. It's not a terribly organized system. I keep a Google

Doc of things I'm interested in, whether they're books or films or exhibitions… I stay very alert. For example, if I come across an article in an architecture magazine listing the one hundred best young architects, I check all one hundred of their websites. If there is an award nomination list, I'll just look at every single one of those buildings and make a very quick pass…yes, yes, no, no, no, no, no, no, yes. I trust my instincts about what I think is good. Then when the time comes to develop a show, I'll review all of these random things I've noted to see what fits. I'm sure there is a much more scientific way of doing this, but that's not for me. At The Met it was more structured. There would be a series of meetings in which an idea for a show would be developed and the roster of participants would evolve. The message had to be clear to everyone, from the education department to marketing to public relations. I would also present the ideas to curators in other departments. In each presentation and subsequent conversation, I would uncover other dimensions of the show. There is also an informal way—conversations with friends, in which I learn about the work of others and develop ideas.

What keeps you motivated?

There are days when I love what I'm doing and feel fortunate to be involved with the people and projects and institutions that I'm involved with. It's easy to stay motivated on those days. On the other days, I remind myself that there are so many other things that I could be doing that would be far less satisfying. Mostly, I'm motivated by thinking through the possibilities of my work, what it can become and how it can change and evolve and get more people involved. I'm motivated by the potential I see in my work.

How do you gauge success in your work? What has been your most rewarding professional experience?

My work is really a reflection of me. In can be stressful to put yourself out there and expose your opinions to the general public. Someone once said to me that one of the hardest things you can do in this field is stand up and say, "I like this!" It takes courage to say that before anyone else does and without knowing what everyone else is going to say. It's especially rewarding when others express gratitude for my willingness to introduce lesser-known individuals to a broader audience. More specifically, I can think of a few highlights throughout my career thus far—I remember the first big projects I did in China and South Korea. I also remember the Lisbon Triennale. So many friends from all over the world came to that show. The most popular show, with the largest attendance, was probably the installation on The Met Roof Garden by Cornelia Parker. That was my first project for The Met, and it was so scary because everything was very unfamiliar to me. We hired set designers to build the installation. I was in the warehouse of the set designer at least three times a week, watching them carve up an old barn and transform it into a replica of the facade of the house from Psycho. At the same time, I was collaborating with Cornelia, who wasn't in New York. I was managing the entire project, which was very stressful. When we were about to open, we had the New York Times come, and Cornelia was there—she was happy with it, and I felt like it was going to be okay. Then the Saturday before the opening, I woke up to see the project on the Times' front page. Only then did I truly feel like it was going to be a successful show. It was a huge relief. The installation went on to get more than 600,000 visitors. I was managing this project on my own and I just had no idea if anyone would like it at all. In the end, it was a tremendously rewarding experience.

What do the next few years look like for you? What kinds of projects do you hope to be working on?

I just finished a book with Phaidon. I really enjoyed the process, and I would like to make more books. I'm not entirely sure how The World Around will evolve, but I hope it will take on other dimensions, beyond the conference. I'm also interested in exploring filmmaking as part of that project, and thinking through how short films can introduce the general public to architecture in a new way.

Fig. 32

Bryony Roberts Studio: Bryony Roberts

What does it mean to practice architecture?

Bryony Roberts: For me, practice means doing work in the world. I participate in research and theory and writing as well, which are really important to me and parts of my practice, but I chose to be a practitioner because it's so meaningful to be embedded in the real world and to work with people to figure out how to get projects done, how to deal with budgets, how to deal with constraints and regulations. Practice for me is bringing ideas into reality through that mess.

How does your work explore the relationship between city and people?

I aim for a dialogical relationship to the city. My projects are always highly site-specific, responding to many layers of a place, from its existing architecture and landscape to its social histories and contemporary politics. But they are also open-ended—because the work is activated only when people use it and transform it. This approach is an intentional challenge to both singular authorship and stable objecthood in architecture.

We need to pivot our understanding of the role of the architect so that we're not thinking that we act as solo agents who come in and look at the situation and solve a problem. There's a much richer way of working that involves seeing people who are already there as experts and understanding the range of creative practices that are already taking place in any given context. Whether it's the domestic lives of people who live somewhere, or the way people use public space, or the community organizers who are already resisting current policy, it's so illuminating to see the world of action that's already taking place, and to learn from that and have that inform design. All of this enables a project to open up to future transformation.

How can you succeed as an architect while staying true to your own values and ethics?

It's a constant tension. It's about being very particular about partnerships, whether with a client or a collaborator or an institution. There's a moment before you enter into a relationship where you can ask critically, "Is this really in alignment with my values?" There are also challenges once you enter into a relationship. You find out that what you want from the project is not necessarily what they want from the project. I'm thinking particularly about clients who don't incorporate extensive community engagement processes, or have unequal fee structures, or are more interested in the "Instagrammable moment" than in the rigor or depth of a project. For me, it's always about making all that very overt from the beginning—being clear to them that my process involves community engagement. I have to make sure that there's funding for that and that the timeline is going to work. It's not easy! Sometimes it involves a lot of pushback and compromise. But I've been lucky to work with many clients who believe in that. To get to that point, I took a lot of risks. I pursued a conceptual practice from the beginning. I started teaching right after graduate school so I could do my own thing, and do research and teach at the same time. I knew I didn't want to do residential practice or commercial practice. I wanted to be able to do work that felt true to what I cared about. So, I had teaching as my lifeline, my support system, my community. Teaching allowed me to be very selective about the projects that I did professionally. It's tough in the beginning, but the work eventually snowballs and accumulates. Over time, it turns into a business model. But it's a really difficult thing to navigate in a market economy. If work that has a social purpose is really important to you, it's important to secure financial stability through something else so that you can keep the integrity of the projects.

How do you communicate your ideas to users, clients, or collaborators from other fields?

The question of translation is really important. I keep coming up against my own assumptions that other people are going to be thinking architecturally. When you ask someone what they need in a space, you assume that they're going to name something spatial. But, of course, that's not at all how it goes. WIP Collaborative, a feminist design collective that I'm part of, completed a research project that ended up feeding into an installation, called Restorative Ground, where we started learning about design for neurodiverse populations—people on the autism spectrum or with other intellectual or developmental disabilities. We found that there's really very little work on that in architectural discourse. It's important to think beyond conventions of universal design. We conducted many interviews and had conversations with experts and advocates. We had a Miro board with clusters of images of materials and scenes that would evoke a mood or an atmosphere. Then we would ask people to look at the board as they would talk about the need for a calm space, a space of retreat to get away from overstimulation and bring down energy levels. We'd say, "Okay, well, is it like a soft, feathery environment? Or is it more like a green garden environment? Or is it more like a dark cave, a low-sensation space?" Then they would say, "Oh, well, you know, that's good because of this, but that's not good because of this." And it was really helpful to bridge the gaps between different ways of understanding space.

Where does your visual language come from?

I've been obsessed with patterns for a long time. I'm not entirely sure where it comes from. In general, pattern is an exciting way of creating complexity and variety using almost mathematical logic with very simple shapes. I like the accessibility—patterns are easy to fabricate, and it's easy for people to jump in and understand them and imagine different versions. I've always been a little allergic to a parametric design process. It seems to put the machine in the driver's seat, rather than the designer. Instead, I'm interested in how simple systems of choice can produce variety and complexity, and then how the material can be an important element in subverting or transforming that system. I tend to use versions of Platonic shapes but then design many different permutations. This is also connected to my interest in craft traditions and textiles. Patterns are amazing vessels for cultural exchange. Familiar patterns through history have often traveled around the world and appeared in different forms and materials in different places. I looked at that a lot in Italy when I was there for the Rome Prize. In Sicily, in particular, there are buildings where you see patterns from Muslim, Christian, and Jewish cultures, but they've started to merge and influence and transform each other. It's fascinating, because it's a slow process that craftspeople are producing over time, and yet it has all this historical and geographic meaning to it.

How did you find yourself interested in combining architecture and performing arts?

I actually used to do really bad performance art in college. Hopefully no one will ever see that work! I also did set design for experimental theater. I was really interested in the history of performance art and public space and politics. I'm only now understanding why it matters to me. I can explain it retroactively. For me, it's a way to get at the lived experience that people have in space that's specific and embodied. It's about their own life stories and how they come to an architectural space and understand it. It's very difficult for architecture to capture the specificity of lived experience and corporeal bodily reality, the kind of day-to-day, fine grain of that. Performance is about individual lives and individual bodies and the way that people interact with each other and space. We Know How to Order, Marching On, and Corpo Estraneo were all about the particular individuals in those performances, that their lived experiences had not been celebrated enough in those spaces.

Fig. 33

Fig. 34

In terms of the process, when I first met with the choreographers and the performers, I brought these architectural drawings of the spaces and different diagrams of grids and points, but they were totally useless. I learned from the choreographers that it's all about the physical experience. For the medium of choreography and organizing performance, you have to figure it out one-to-one, walking through the space, moving through the space. I was bringing an initial idea about structure and sequence and the relationship to the street, and moving in and out of the street or the public space. But the choreographers really understood how the specific movements of the body could make that complex and interesting over the trajectory of the performance. My thinking about sequence and entry and visibility was informed by architectural analysis, but it had to be communicated through physically walking the space and standing somewhere and thinking, "Well, what if we start here? And then what if we go here?" Dancers and choreographers know so much about space. There's an inventiveness about three-dimensional movements and how to occupy a space that we can learn from.

What was your design approach for Soft Civic, which feels like it's referencing performance in a different way?

I'm interested in working with existing structures and figuring out how to respond to existing buildings and social systems as a form of care and maintenance. It's not just about responding to the built structures, but also about the intangible heritage, the social histories. Understanding and supporting the social lives of a place is part of a process of responding to that place. That's part of recent discourse in preservation. Both We Know How to Order and Soft Civic were about responding to the concrete material and formal conditions of the architecture. They were also about responding to the social histories of each place. With We Know How to Order, it was about expanding the frame on purpose. Federal Plaza is in downtown Chicago. It's a place that's been heavily invested in by the city government. We were intentionally expanding the frame to think about the history of the South Side of Chicago, which has been the site of disinvestment and divided from the Loop through racial segregation. The cultural traditions

Fig. 35

Fig. 36

Fig. 37

Fig. 38

of the South Side are incredible—like the drill teams that were a part of the performance. We were thinking about how the social histories and architectural histories of a city could start to meet, not without friction. With Soft Civic, which took place at City Hall in Columbus, Indiana, it was about that building and its geometry and how it defines the experiences of governance in that city. We did many studies of the circles and the diagonals and the way that they intersect, and how we could kind of break that apart. We also looked at the ways that building has been used in its lifespan. We were really interested in the patterns of movement and how protesters and performers and ceremonies occupy that space, the way they follow particular geometric patterns created by the architecture. The project aimed to expand the possibilities for occupation and gathering on that site, adding new structures to support a greater range of scales and types of interaction with the civic institution.

What has been the most rewarding moment of your professional career?

That's a tough one! Can I have a top five? Before Soft Civic opened, we were tightening the last of the zip ties that were holding down one part of it, and this family with young kids came running up the steps of the building. The kids threw themselves on the project. They started climbing up it and jumping on it and swinging on it. The parents were like, "Is this okay? Is it finished?" That was so cool to see. Before that kind of moment, you just don't know how people will respond. You don't know if anyone is going to want to be there. To see people engage with the installation and want to climb on it was super gratifying.

Dream the Combine: Tom Carruthers and Jennifer Newsom

What does it mean to practice architecture?

Jennifer Newsom: Recently, I was talking with Mira Henry and Jerome Haferd about practice as a continual state of becoming. It's continually evolving, it's not a static enterprise. We've tried to think consciously about the type of work we take on—how we have to design both the work that we do, and also our lives.

Tom Carruthers: Hopefully we're not defining ourselves only in terms of our work. Practice is about opening up sustained engagement with one's self. It's reflective. There have been really challenging moments when I can't face myself. There are moments when things feel so overwhelming that I need the help of someone else to settle down. That is also where the work gets good, or maybe unpredictable... where vulnerability is important. If we're in an uncomfortable place, if it feels sort of weird, if it actually *feels*, then it's actually worth the investment of building a practice around that feeling.

Dream the Combine designs things, but you also make things. Yet you don't identify as a design-build practice. Why not?

Jennifer: It does feel like in the world of architecture there's a division between designing and building, but these two terms are equivalent for us! We care about how things are made. We care about who is making them. The integration between designing and building comes from a deep consideration of process and how things come into being.

Tom: The how doesn't fully circumscribe the work, or the practice. The rationality of our thinking is not solely what shows up in a set of documents or some text. There's intelligence and muscle memory. We want to be able to be present at multiple levels of our process … "How can material be formed?" is an open question that includes both craft and experience. What is the eye doing? What are people doing? Where are the invitations and are they legible? Whether you're talking about design-build, or something else, I just don't care what it's called … Is it called architecture? Is it called art? Simply stated … I want to do more of this. You can call it what you want.

Given your design and fabrication interests, affiliations, and experience, who is the primary audience for your work?

Jennifer: The term audience implies directionality and passivity of reception. We are more interested in the work being a platform for an energetic exchange between us and other people. We're setting up a platform for things to happen. I don't think of it in a singular direction of experience or knowledge passing from one place or one person to another. Once we make the work … that's actually the beginning of the project. I get to observe how others engage with our work. That's when I feel like I'm then the audience. I get to learn about what we've made.

Tom: When a work is "done," we start to see this call and response with people as they're coming through, and how they're beginning to author the work in their mind. In a sense, the things that we build physically are not actually the piece. The material and intellectual experience of our work is the piece that people carry away with them.

Jennifer: I'm on the board of the DIA Art Foundation. There's a new group called the BTA, the Black Trustee Alliance. At our first gathering, Courtney Martin was talking about art institutions and the use of the word "community." The terms community and audience both have a kind of distancing effect. Courtney has said that she refuses to let people at the Yale Center for British Art use the word community. She prefers "neighbors." That parsing between community versus neighbors and audience versus publics or just people... We don't need so much distance. We're all here in the world experiencing these things together.

Can you tell us a little more about your idea of distributed authorship? How does that model play out in your work currently, and how do you imagine it as your practice moves forward?

Tom: When my dad was in medical school, he went into an exam somewhat panicked. And he had a friend who just said, "Alastair, relax—things will become apparent as we go along." And that little phrase became a sort of permission, to sometimes work more intuitively, and just trust that you're onto a good thing. Coming from a sculpture background, I understand that sometimes projects begin to have a life of their own. When they start getting good, they start to speak and ask questions. This prompts a question of the bounds of authorship, and the territories and terrains of authorship. When you're working in the built environment, you're also working textually within a number of narratives, some of which are expressed, and some of which are oppressed. When you're navigating that terrain, do you start to participate in certain fictions or lies, or do you begin to pursue a naked approach to things? We've been saying, "What if we're not the complete authors of our own work? What does that mean?"

Jennifer: We may set some sort of intention, but then it passes through so many other bodies on its way to being a real thing that others can experience. We are authoring the work with the people who make it, with the weather, with other nonhuman species who encounter it. Plus, most of our work has been temporary... it exists in memories, photographs, and videos. Somebody goes to it, they have an experience, they carry that with them, they have the remembrance of it, which is also changed each time they remember it. That's another form of coauthoring the work. Conceptually, we're really interested in looping, recursion, and this simultaneity of experiences.

In addition to your work with Dream the Combine, you are each cofounder or co-owner of other organizations. Jennifer, you are cofounder of Dark Matter University and an educator. Tom, you are currently co-owner of the metal fabrication practice Jacobsson Carruthers.[1] Can you tell us about these respective efforts and how they interface with Dream the Combine? We're interested in how all the puzzle pieces fit together to construct your larger efforts of practice.

[1] Since this interview was conducted, Jennifer has become Assistant Professor at Cornell AAP and Tom has shuttered his fabrication business and become Assistant Professor of the Practice at Cornell AAP.

Tom: We're not defined only by the work we do, or by any one of our many roles. Even more fascinating to me, we can feel a number of emotions simultaneously. Jennifer had a student, Sam Schaefer, who talked about the social geometry of material. In architectural terms, we're talking about materials in terms of matter, but we don't talk about how anything actually gets done. This person knows that person ... there are little networks of trust, and those are the pathways and tunnels through which these projects flow. At a conceptual level, my work as a fabricator has been a way to gain fluency in the language of material. There are real ways that it is helpful. There are also distractions associated with it ... Do I really need to make another railing or a hood for somebody? There is a changing terrain. Five years ago, the current setup made sense. Going forward, I think there will be some adjustments.

Jennifer: When we moved to Minnesota five years ago, we discussed pursuing different forms of capital. Tom went after capital capital, literally starting a new business with a fabricator we had worked with on previous projects, and I developed social capital by teaching. We found certain things that drive us, but it does feel like we're at a kind of pivot point. There's some renegotiation happening now. Getting us both on an academic schedule will be great for us and our two kids. Finding more time to work together in the same room, doing the work that we really want to be doing and feeling like we are resourced enough ... we need to make that happen. We are entering a new phase, and I'm excited for the continuation or deepening of the themes that we're interested in.

Fig. 39

Fig. 40

There has certainly been a lot going on in the world lately, especially in Minneapolis. How do you acknowledge and integrate ongoing global challenges such as racial injustice and climate change into your work and into your design process?

Jennifer: As architects or artists, we're making the environment, we're sculpting the environment, we're changing the environment. We can't be people who live in 2021 and not think about everything happening in the world. Quite honestly, these global challenges are ongoing—there is nothing novel about them. We have been concerned with these issues from the beginning of our practice. We're also trying to figure out how to operate with the tools that we have, and with the skill sets that we have. I don't think that I'll ever go into a situation feeling totally at ease. I'm always trying to pick away the little paint flecks on the underside of the surface, to see what can be unearthed. That's something that we share…it's probably part of why we're together. We both approach the world through continual questioning.

Tom: In a recent interview, we were asked if we see our work as political. The answer is yes. How can it not be? If we don't see it as political, it's definitely politicized. Even the privilege of being able to be here and talk with you…even this moment is political.

Jennifer: The question is very direct, but the answer is complicated. For instance, for the Miller Prize project that we're working on in Columbus, Indiana, what we're trying to do is understand the specificity of that place while understanding that it's not specific at all. It is part of a global, colonial, and imperial narrative, regarding Columbus as a historical figure, and the project started by European colonial powers. Our project has been about thinking through multiple narratives that are framed by this really pernicious and pervasive network of cities called Columbus that exist around the world. The piece is titled *Columbus Colombia Colombo Colón*. Each one of the elements in the installation refers to a specific geographic point on the map that is named for Columbus, and each element has a different narrative from these places written on its surface. It is literally a text that unfolds cinematically as you move through it. The installation reconstructs a narrative—it develops a palimpsestic text of the larger system. With the tools that we have and that we feel like we're adept at using, it's one way to address things like racial injustice, to address land theft, to address resource extraction, to address settling and unsettling. Part of the haptic movement through the installation is meant to be unsettling. It's meant to induce a kind of dizziness, to throw you off course. It's a metaphoric construct or way of modeling these issues in a way that feels true to us.

Who have been the most influential figures in your careers, and how has their influence affected the work you do now?

Tom: Someone that I'm really fortunate to have had as a mentor is the sculptor, Ursula von Rydingsvard. There's real depth in her commitment to practice. As a mentor, she fosters a sense of possibility and permission in the world to be certain ways. She's invested in the ways that she can realize ideas in any material and is open to metaphors asserting themselves and claiming authorship in her work. I'm inspired by her acknowledgement of the impossibility of fully knowing things.

Jennifer: I had a meeting with Billie Tsien when our son Ogden was six months old. I said to her, "How do I do this? Am I just a milk machine now? What happened to *me*?" She encouraged me to keep my intellectual life going. She reiterated that I'm not going to become a totally changed person and that it's okay to recognize that being a mother is a really important job. Deborah Berke has also been wonderful to the two of us. But my friends and my family have probably been the most influential because they're the people I talk to every day. I really cherish my family.

What has been the most rewarding moment of your professional careers so far?

Tom: When preparing for my undergraduate thesis show, and before curators and artists from New York arrived, I hung a casting I made on the wall. There was a feeling in that in-between time, before anybody saw the work. I had done the work of conceiving, trying, iterating, and getting it up there. I was sitting in an old beat-up office chair at a little desk in the gallery. My feet were up on the desk. Someone was playing Neil Young's "Harvest Moon." There was gratitude. I thought to myself, "I've said a thing, and I'm pretty good with it.

I'm at peace with it. Come what may, I'm going to just celebrate this moment of peace right here." I was flush with the downslope of an effort.

Jennifer: My moment was in a similar state of in-betweenness... It was when Hide & Seek was complete and before Warm Up had started, before our work really had been inhabited more deeply. I just remember walking down the stairs into the courtyard from the entrance to the museum at PS1. I thought, "This was in my mind and now I'm walking through it." That felt so amazing. It was so incredible. It sounds really straightforward, truly at the root of what we do as architects, but it was really powerful.

Fig. 41

Fig. 42

FreelandBuck: David Freeland and Brennan Buck

What does it mean to practice architecture?

David Freeland: Practice allows us to translate our values and ideas about architecture that we develop through teaching, reading, and writing into built form and test their validity in three dimensions in a cultural, economic, and ecological context. It also is where our architectural ideas can have an impact on the world. Building is the fullest realization or our ideas and values as a practice.

The two of you are split between Los Angeles and New York. How do the locations of your practice affect your work?

David: My first impulse is to say it doesn't really affect anything, meaning that within the abstract geometric space of the digital model, there isn't an imbued context. Work in a virtual environment is not situated. But at the same time, it would be very short-sighted for any architect to say that place or context is not a component of a project. There is a balance between the development of a project in abstract space and the way that context becomes inscribed into a model. We are always working on how to embed a physical context into a design developed in virtual space. With Stack House, for example, the complex topography of the site was incorporated into the digital model early on. We modeled critical contextual parameters that would constrain the project.

Brennan Buck: "Place" or "context" as ideas have a long history within our discipline. Think of critical regionalism, an idea that Ken Frampton developed about the need for architecture to be specific to its geographic context. That is not an idea that we subscribe to. But cultural context is definitely important in our work. New York and Los Angeles have very different administrative and regulatory contexts, for instance. You have to build differently in New York than in Los Angeles. We are also a part of very different academic cultures at Yale and SCI-Arc. In that sense, we benefit from the distance between us.

You've designed and built temporary installations, retail environments, restaurant interiors, and single-family residences. What do you think gives your work coherence? Is your approach to each project unique, or is there something that you bring to a project regardless of program or type?

David: We constantly work between mediums. There are gaps that exist between two-dimensional mediums, like drawings and images, and three-dimensional mediums, like models, objects, and buildings. We're really interested in interrogating the gaps and developing unique representational techniques that unpack two-dimensional and three-dimensional modes of communication. Artifacts we've made that we call "image-objects" are an example of this. Our critical approach to representation lends itself to multiple layers of engagement. We strive to produce work that can sustain the attention of a group of architects, as well as makes an appeal to a more diverse audience. There's accessibility at different levels and for different groups of people. The ambition to create visual and conceptual openness is something that guides our design strategies regardless of project type.

Do you view models as simply representations of buildings during the development of your projects, or do the models operate independently?

Fig. 43

David: In our recent projects, we're really asking models to do many things for us. Models are sometimes representational and oftentimes built at a particular scale. A model, by definition, points to something other than itself. But more recently, we've been creating models or objects that point only to themselves. They have unique qualities and conceptual ambitions beyond scaled representation. We are intentionally undermining conventional categories of architectural representation to liberate drawings and models from mere reference. Many of our recent projects are conceptualized as built drawings, or three-dimensional drawings. These drawings fall into the category of conventional drawing with regard to the practice of architectural representation, but they are also full-scale constructions. Our ceiling installation in the Renwick Gallery at the Smithsonian American Art Museum, Parallax Gap, is an example of this. Our work intentionally confounds categories of representation, and, in doing so, hopefully opens up other possibilities for architectural representation.

Can you tell us more about how your two-dimensional drawing work relates to or informs your three-dimensional work?

David: In our earlier conceptual projects, we were interested in creating drawings that used abstraction to produce effects rather than simply serve as representations of other things. I'm thinking of our drawing-series Slipstream. But where these drawing projects operated more autonomously—independent of cultural reference and engagement—our newer drawing projects try to do much more. This is related to my previous answer, where I described our interest in building drawings. In general, we are interested in moving away from complex digital techniques and transformations as a primary focus toward engaging a larger cultural audience. We are invested in geometry and form-making as well as creating images, objects, and buildings that have broad appeal.

Brennan: Almost all of our recent projects are attempts to do both: to operate through abstraction and elicit engagement through visual association and illusion. This duality is something that we struggle with. People engage architecture in states of distraction—architecture is rarely something the general public stops to think about, and it largely informs their activity through

Fig. 44

affect, and subtle things like color, temperature, and spatial relationships, rather than through direct attention. That said, there are a couple of reasons that we've looked beyond abstraction to association and reference. First, distraction has become our default state of mind in everyday life. Focused attention now feels rare. We have also realized that narrative and association is a way of appealing to a broad audience. In the Renwick Gallery project, all of the elements in the installation reference relatively well-known Victorian-era ceilings. The installation both produces an abstract array of lines and colors and reproduces familiar architectural elements, such as the ceilings in Cincinnati Union Terminal and the Palace of Fine Arts in San Francisco. We now realize that we can produce work that is abstract and open to interpretation and also engaging for people who stumble into the gallery and are more interested in a narrative about the history of different buildings across the country. This is a powerful thing that some of our earlier work didn't tap into.

You both pointed to an ambition to make your work accessible and engaging. Does a desire to be popular factor into this ambition?

Brennan: It doesn't. Popularity may be good for business, but being popular is not our primary motivation. Our goal to realize projects that are accessible and engaging is related to an ambition to have a positive effect on the world and to make spaces that are useful and stimulating. The Renwick project was about very old architectural traditions—drawing and illusion. But it was also about capturing the visual effects of beloved buildings scattered across the country. There was a direct connection between the content of the installation and familiar architectural references. It wasn't just a narrative that people could read in the wall text. It was more of an optical puzzle. That's one way we talked about it—a visual riddle for people to solve. They might read the wall text and try to find all of the different projection points for all the three-dimensional drawings. We tried to produce a narrative that would pull people into the space and allow them to experience the effects of the installation rather than just read about them.

David: The desire to create work that is accessible and engaging is also another way to be inclusive. The disciplinary issues that fuel us are not necessarily accessible to most people. So, we believe we have a responsibility to explore the potential of these disciplinary issues to affect a broader audience and produce broader cultural effects.

In relation to the idea of having positive impact, do you think that the clients of Second House experience the house as you intended them to? Do you think that they acknowledge and appreciate the complex formal, spatial, and visual effects that you were pursuing in that project?

Brennan: We are suspicious of anything universal or assumptions that anyone will experience something the same way we do. In Second House, we were exploring ideas about alternation and contrast. We had alternating spatial zones—a checkerboard pattern of interior spaces and exterior spaces, and corresponding floor materials. The ceiling heights move up and down to reinforce the idea of contrast or difference. As you move through the house—and it's a very small house—there's a constant alternation of very different conditions. Light, temperature, volume, and so on… there is continuous difference. In that sense, our interest in effect is probably more about variety and registering difference rather than prescribing something universal.

David: Because this project is for private clients, it's more focused. The conversation about broader cultural engagement is curtailed in favor of creating spaces tuned to the desire of the two people who will live in the house. Unlike other projects where we pursue particular legible effects, this project seeks to work on bodies in spaces in a much more subtle manner.

What has been your experience with getting your work built?

David: The frustrations are myriad. I cannot recall who, but someone once said to me, "The happiness that you have as an architect is measured by the degree of grace that you can bring to the work every day." There's an art to the balancing act, to managing different priorities and issues that come up in a project on a daily basis. Balancing of all these different pressures is the art of practice. One thing that people often think demands the most attention in practice is getting clients, and getting them to believe in whatever your vision is for a project. But that is merely the beginning of a much

Fig. 45

Fig. 46

more delicate balancing act that moves from concept through completion over a great deal of time.

How have recent global events related to social justice and public health affected your approach to practice?

David: For us, these recent events call attention to who we are responsive to in the development of design work. While a commission may be for a specific client, there are larger concerns that have to be addressed, balanced, and at times advocated for. We've adjusted our design process to listen to more voices, recalibrating which are most important and focusing on what we can do to make a change in the built environment. We are rethinking typical responses to design problems, such as working with commercial and institutional clients to support gender-neutral instead of gender-segregated restrooms.

What has been the most rewarding aspect of practicing architecture thus far?

David: I'm interested to hear what you say, Brennan! You go first.

Brennan: A few years ago, we were in Nashville to present a project proposal to a panel of jurors. I was speaking with one of the competition jurors after they awarded the project to someone else and she said, as consolation, "You guys live interesting lives." That hadn't really occurred to me—there are a lot of frustrations, as David described. But to interact and collaborate with so many different people and work on very different problems, to think through different ideas through teaching… the variety in terms of daily life that we've been able to develop through the practice has been great.

David: Architecture is a marathon, not a sprint. There are very high highs balanced by very low lows. Our model of practice puts us in the position of the endurance athlete. We have to pace ourselves. We're cautious about getting too excited about things, and also cautious about getting dragged down by things that don't fall in our favor. We're told "no" a lot, and we've worked on so many projects that we never completed, for reasons beyond our control. But we have to put these moments behind us and keep pushing forward. The fact that we always have things to keep us moving forward is very rewarding.

French 2D: Anda French and Jenny French

What does it mean to practice architecture?

Jenny French: To practice architecture with a focus on collectivity, we advocate ceding certain agency in favor of greater input or finding new agency depending on our shifting roles. We find it important to state that collectivity is not everyone doing everything together, nor is it everyone doing the same thing. Finding ways to support a project with collective effort means that, at any given moment, our roles are different but dependent on one another and our collaborators. If we've learned anything from project to project, it is that success comes not from having fixed roles, but from filling in where needed.

Anda French: For us, practicing architecture—and we believe in a broad definition of that task—requires transparency and trust. By nature, we have always built trust through transparency and breaking the fourth wall—not by being cool. We find that to talk about the thing, we have to talk about how we are doing it and, most importantly, why we might be doing it. We would argue that the urgency of the moment calls for breaking down the fourth wall.

Your professional partnership is unique because you're siblings. What are the advantages of having such a close personal relationship with your partner?

Anda: We call what we do "close practice." Part of the collaboration is familial, but a lot of it comes from the kind of shorthand of our close relationship that then grows into a collective artistic vision. In partnerships, each person is very vulnerable. You have to trust the other person. As siblings, that trust exists naturally, and we already know each other's pressure points and weaknesses. We take the individual egos out of our conversations and operate as two people thinking together.

Jenny: We don't curtail the ways that we think or talk about things. We let our entire lives filter back into architecture. There are no boundaries for where our references can come from and there's no judgment about the origins of our ideas. Probably ninety percent of the time the references are not architectural.

How do you balance the goals and demands of clients and contractors with your own goals in any given project? How do you make sure that everyone is satisfied with the process and result?

Jenny: That is a typical struggle for small practices. Throughout the course of a day, we might be working on eight different things. The different audiences that we're trying to communicate with or produce things for have very different desires or requirements. Ensuring that we're balancing these requirements is an ongoing struggle. We're always recalibrating, because we know we need to make time for the intellectual project.

Anda: A good portion of practicing architecture is maintaining interpersonal relationships. Learning how and what and when to share with clients and contractors is so important. Each contributor sees the project from their own perspective and has their own values and ambitions within a given project.

Jenny: The firm Kwong Von Glinow uses the phrase "smuggling in the architecture." When you're a young practice, you're always trying to smuggle in small details or conceptual issues that you're really, really interested in and focused on. Maybe those interests and issues account for only five percent or ten percent of the overall scope, but, for many architects, it's the heart of the project. We're always fighting for aspects of projects that most align with our values to be included in the budget. And we hope that, in the end, everyone understands and appreciates the work in their own way.

You're currently working on a few housing projects. Will you continue to focus on housing? What types of projects would you like to work on in the future?

Anda: We often say that our interest in housing is related to our interest in civic work, which is not an association one would typically make. We are interested in types of housing that address different social structures. So, in some ways, in the next project that comes to us or that we seek out, we will make an attempt at tying our design approach to an existing or nascent social structure. There are only about 130 cohousing communities in the US right now. It's an emerging and evolving typology. We're interested in participating in larger ideological conversations related to this project type.

Jenny: It's not about housing as such, but it's about how housing intersects with nested privacies and economies, and questions about relevance that we all face.

How do you relate your representational style and interests to the overall identity of your firm?

Jenny: It took us a long time to take the way we literally see and the way we want to project ideas onto the world to create a legible attitude or disposition in the work. Through our representation, we hope to convey seriousness, but also levity through experimentation. There is work going on behind the scenes in our office to arrive at moments of clarity and playfulness through our particular approach to representation.

Anda: Building something and then having to re-present it back to ourselves and our peers creates unique opportunities. There is a curious relationship between representation that appeals to our colleagues and representation that appeals to clients or potential clients. We've been surprised at how much those two audiences have come into alignment with respect to our style of representation. At first, we thought clients would want to see only straightforward drawings. It turns out that the drawings and images that our clients are most drawn to—like, cartoonish elevation obliques—are our favorite drawings and images as well.

Jenny: To engage individuals outside of the architecture community is so important if you want to realize your projects. The way we've approached representation and communication has enabled us to participate in disciplinary or academic conversations, and, at the same time, communicate with and make our work legible to a broader audience.

Outlier Lofts is an interesting project as it relates to operating on an existing building. How much of the existing building was maintained, and how did the history of the existing building relate to your design?

Anda: There are two answers to that question. As far as the City of Boston is concerned, it's the same building, just with a third floor added. The reality is that when working on a building that is 150 years old, much of it is removed and rebuilt. There is an entirely new structure for the building, new walls and floors—though we had to maintain the same floor-to-ceiling heights, as well as the building foundation.

Jenny: The building's history definitely influenced the design. We reoriented the building in relation to the corner.

Anda: Right. We actually reintroduced openings that existed in the original building that were removed in previous renovations. What's interesting is that the building is actually a non-conforming building. Under current zoning, we could not add an additional floor. Because we uncovered that the original structure had a third floor, we were able to add it on. Intellectually that building has always existed, but physically it is rebuilt.

Many of your projects use bold colors, patterns, and graphics, but that is not the case in Outlier Lofts. How did you arrive at the material palette for the project?

Anda: From the interior looking out, you see across twelve lanes of traffic and the city skyline. We muted the interior to set up a reverse gallery, in a sense. The windows frame the context and all of the textures and colors it contains.

Jenny: Frank Lloyd Wright's Guggenheim drawings were originally in pink. This question of how the character of the built form may emerge

Fig. 47

Fig. 48

without the literal color and all that it implies in the original drawings is important. The colors we used in Outlier Lofts acknowledge the context and play with a particular kind of preservation in the neighborhood—one that is formal rather than representational. It's not historical reenactment. It's about remaining neutral and flying under the radar. The white allows for a kind of scalelessness to happen and also a kind of neutral position about the future occupants.

Anda: Also, we were aware that we needed to convince the neighbors that our design belongs... that the building is part of the context. Maybe we'll take more risks with the next one. The roof alone is almost scandalous!

Beyond any singular project or recurrent aesthetic sensibility, how have recent global events related to social justice and public health affected your approach to practice?

Anda: Prior to the pandemic, our practice was engaged in the reevaluation of home through the lens of social justice and resource sharing, and the challenges of childcare, isolation, and accessibility. As the pandemic creates urgency to address many aspects of living, we are considering short-term and long-term ways in which we approach spaces of work and play in the home, and the effects of space on our general health and well-being. For us, the reimagining of housing in a post-Covid world is as much about the renewed social contracts that come with living together as the spaces themselves. Echoing the call of many, we believe that we cannot pursue a return to "normal," but instead must begin to address conditions of inequity, division, and isolation that the pandemic has laid bare.

Jenny: As architects we've been engaged in designing and researching collective housing, particularly the Danish-influenced model of cohousing, and its potential to strengthen community resilience, combat loneliness, and reduce environmental impact. For cohousing to expand as a viable popular option, we have to reconsider the idiosyncrasies of the model, both the positive—rethinking the nuclear family, shared resources of care and support—and the negative, including its struggle to be more inclusive and economic barriers to entry. At a moment when fundamental challenges to the social,

Fig. 49

economic, and political fabric are imperative, we think collective housing can be pushed, pulled, and remolded as a fertile ground for critique, experimentation, and action at broader, more inclusive scales.

What has been the most rewarding or fulfilling moment of your careers thus far?

Anda: We've been very fortunate to work on projects that align with our interests. And we've had a lot of freedom in most of our projects. Partly because of this situation, validation, for us, is internal. We don't often seek or rely on external validation. When we were included as winners of Architectural Record's Design Vanguards, it was unexpected. We were very happy that others were acknowledging our effort, because we have sort of existed in our own feedback bubble.

Jenny: But it is particularly rewarding to receive external validation for things on which we had to take a risk. For example, in the photographs for Kendall Square Garage and for Outlier Lofts, we decided to turn the task of photographing the project into a project in and of itself. We sewed our own dresses for the Kendall Square project and used virtual staging for Outlier Lofts. We hope that these extra efforts help to communicate the design agendas more clearly. But the extra efforts were not necessarily encouraged... We had to trust ourselves. Sometimes you have to say, "Well, if this fails miserably, that's okay."

Anda: At the end of the day, the most rewarding aspect of practicing is having the confidence to do those things because I get to work all day with my sister.

Fig. 50

Iben Falconer

You are now the global marketing and business development leader at Skidmore, Owings & Merrill! How do you foresee this role evolving in relation to today's political and social climate?

Iben Falconer: It's an important question! There are business development and strategy fundamentals that if you can get right will serve you well all the time, not just during a time of intense instability. I've often thought about what those fundamentals are and how we make sure we're not making plans now that are simply a response to the pandemic. We're working on how to stay disciplined and strategic at all times—when everything is going our way as well as when things are really uncertain, which is how they feel right now. This was the catalyst for the first column that I wrote for the online magazine *Madame Architect*, which was a response to the high levels of anxiety I saw in colleagues. This anxiety led to bad business development. I was wondering how I could help others I was interested in helping to find a path forward for everyone that transcended the frantic response to quickly recover from the downturn that resulted from the pandemic. There are some obvious differences during a recession or during a time of instability that you pay attention to with respect to which markets are most affected, but new opportunities emerged at this time that were not present before. I used my column to help others find these new opportunities.

What exactly does a business development leader of an architecture firm do on a daily or weekly basis? How would you describe the role of the strategist in developing a practice?

At SOM, I have the pleasure of working with a global team of thirty-five colleagues, who include marketing coordinators, marketing managers, business development managers, graphic designers, and researchers. I participate in many of our weekly marketing meetings which are organized by office, functional market, or region. I made a point to get to know our leadership across all our offices, to understand how they think about marketing and business development—what's working, what's not. A lot of what I have been doing is getting to know not just the people and the work, but also how we approach business development. I'm in the process of overhauling our business-plan creation and implementation process, which I find tremendously exciting. While it might sound dry to some, business plans are like a road map that tells us where we want to go and how to get there. They're essential for a firm of any size, but particularly important for us at SOM, where we work across so many sectors and geographic markets.

How have recent global events related to social justice and public health affected your approach to business strategy?

Sharing goals and values related to social justice and public health are no longer a "nice-to-have," but a must-have. Our clients are asking more of the team; they want to know about a firm's approach to sustainability and equity, and they ask up front. It's exciting and long overdue.

On a personal note, I'm thinking more about who contributes to our business-strategy creation and implementation. Being in business development or marketing for the world of architecture and architectural engineering is already so specific. It's a profession that is getting closer to gender parity, but we have a long way to go when it comes to having diverse racial and ethnic representation.

For many people who want to be involved with architecture, they think the only way to do so is by being an architect. There are many exciting alternate careers, and it's important that we talk about that from early on.

Does your current skill set differ from the one you left school with? What were the circumstances that led to you acquiring your current skills?

This is a good question, because I'm always asked where to find good candidates for strategy positions in other firms. It's such a niche field. There is no degree program that caters specifically to business development and strategy in architecture. My education in architecture equipped me with research and writing skills. It turns out that writing is a skill that not a lot of architects have. There's always a place for good writers in larger architecture offices, often in marketing departments. When I began working in architecture offices as an intern alongside other architects, I quickly discovered that I didn't want to be a practicing architect. But I liked to write and I was good with clients. More and more, I had opportunities to work on business development, to work with clients, and to write. I had a wonderful mentor when I was working at BIG—Kai Bergmann, who's the partner in charge of business development. I've been very lucky to work with really, really smart people who took time to invest in me. With their help I was able to cultivate the skill set that I have now.

What drew you to SOM? What is the most exciting project you're working on right now?

One of the things that drew me to this role was the chance to work at a firm with such an incredible legacy, one that's so deeply known across the world. This is the biggest firm I've ever worked for. That comes with really interesting challenges. I'm coming from a role that was very client-facing. I loved gaining an understanding of what clients care about. In my new role, I'm not on the front line with clients anymore, but I work with a wonderful marketing team, and together we must build up a system for marketing and business development. I really enjoy this aspect of my job. But to your question about the most exciting project… A lot of people don't really understand what the business aspects of architecture are. I remember a panel discussion years ago that included Gregg Pasquarelli, of SHoP. Someone asked the panelists about their favorite project. Greg answered that his favorite project was his firm. He was thinking of his firm as a project in and of itself. This answer has stayed with me, and it's something I'll never forget. I got really excited thinking about how a practice is a design opportunity. Business development is something that intimidates many architects. I love the challenge of helping them approach strategy and development with creativity.

You mentioned earlier that you wrote a column for *Madame Architect*. How does this writing intersect with your role as a strategist?

Madame Architect was a wonderful outlet for me. It came about because I called Julia Gamolina in early April 2020 to discuss how we could collaborate. I saw many colleagues and friends struggling as a result of the pandemic and I wanted to offer professional support. With *Madame Architect*, Julia had a place where I could share advice with others. So, in my columns I wrote conversationally, to share the types of conversations with Julia's audience that I was having with my consulting clients.

There is this vacuum of knowledge about things that I care deeply about in our industry. I have no interest in pretending that business development and strategy are some sort of secret thing that only I can do. Some of my peers want to treat it that way, but it's not true. That approach holds our industry back. I'm really interested in being very open and having honest conversations about what it means to think strategically about practice and business development. If there's a lesson I've learned through writing the column, it's to make business strategy more accessible.

What have been some of the more rewarding or enjoyable aspects of your professional career?

If I have a professional calling, it is to demystify business development and strategy for designers. It isn't well taught or even often well modeled in firms, so unfortunately it becomes something magical that only certain people can do. I urge my colleagues to think about business development as a creative endeavor. What is truly rewarding for me is watching the light bulb turn on when someone realizes that business development isn't as scary as they thought it would be.

Independent Architecture: Paul Andersen

What does it mean to practice architecture?

Paul Andersen: To practice architecture is to contribute something to the discourse—in the form of models, essays, drawings, gossip, or buildings. The goal is to open up new ways of thinking and designing, which is different than, say, practicing piano, which is geared toward refinement.

What do you think makes your office unique compared to other emerging offices?

The most obvious difference is that we're in Denver, which is on the fringe, at best. When it comes to buildings, Denver has a lot of corporate schlock. But it also has some pretty good suburban architecture, which influences the office's culture and work. The pop sensibility in the suburbs is fantastic. It tends to be accessible and unique. Pop practices accept that their work isn't essential. It acquires value when people like it—and those people might be friends, experts in the field, the general public, or any number of groups. This seems like a good approach for architecture, too. If people don't absolutely need great design, we can feel free to do strange, irrational projects…and even to fail. We also borrow material from the suburbs. Sometimes we incorporate everyday objects, like giant party balloons, statues, and letterforms. In other cases, we use a familiar material in an unorthodox way, like in the project that Paul Preissner and I are doing with wood framing at the US pavilion at the Venice Biennale. Occasionally we look for new design principles in idiosyncratic examples of ordinary suburban buildings.

Who commissions your work? Do you have to spend a lot of time finding work, or do clients come to you?

Some of both. There is a lot of chance involved in finding the type of projects that we enjoy. Some offices have a structured approach to finding work, but sometimes it's just a matter of being in the right place at the right time. A related issue is the low percentage of projects that we actually finish. Of all the projects that we've started, only ten to twenty percent are built. In the end, I'd say that finding clients who want to do the same kinds of things that you do is what matters most.

What types of projects do you hope to work on in the future?

More houses and arts projects would be great. Mainly, I hope to keep designing, curating, and writing.

Motherhouse recently completed construction in Denver. The description of the project on your website references plan diagrams of houses by Palladio, Le Corbusier, and O. M. Ungers. What was the role of these projects, and of precedent, in the design of Motherhouse?

I was looking at the Ungers House in Cologne before we started the Motherhouse project. I often hear other architects describe it as a minimalist project. Even Ungers said that it was an experiment in making a totally abstract house, where you can't recognize materials or scale or use. Oddly enough, the minimalist tilt is completely contradicted when you look at the plan, which has an outrageous number of doors. The house has 178 doors, including six in the hedges. So, the minimalist exterior is a mismatch with an interior that's beyond

Fig. 51

excessive. I like the bizarre combination of rational and irrational design in that house. It turned us on to some aspects of Motherhouse. At the same time that I was looking at Ungers, I was also looking at houses in Englewood, Colorado, that are quirky, very odd 1960s houses. The point of Motherhouse was to merge these two references—to do a suburban American version of the Ungers House. The walls have the same thickness as the Ungers House, but instead of using that thickness as a set of foyers, we use it for closets, which we needed because we couldn't build a basement on that lot. The water table is too high. So, the first floor of the house ends up being a single room lined with doors—no walls. The second floor is a more or less rotationally symmetrical arrangement of rooms that all have different ceilings. Throughout the house are examples of excessive repetition... in the gables, doors, stairs, and colors, for example.

We understand the project was commissioned by your mother. Was the open ground floor plan a requirement set by her?

My mother will not actually live in the house. As you might know, there is a tradition of architects building houses for their mothers early in their careers, because it's a moment when your mother is the only one who thinks you can actually do whatever offbeat thing it is that you want to do. Corb designed and built a house for his mother. So did Richard Rodgers, Robert Venturi, Charles Moore, Harry Seidler, Charles Gwathmey... the list goes on. In my case, my mother didn't want a house for herself, but she wanted to support me by commissioning the design and construction. We're going to sell the house, and as soon as we sell it, we'll do another one. It'll be an ongoing project.

Earlier you mentioned that you're drawing inspiration from the suburbs. What has been the response to Motherhouse from people living in Denver?

Most people are either enthusiastic or confused. The work that we do in schools gets further out of the mainstream than we realize sometimes. It could be that there is something unnerving when an architect messes with the familiarity and comfort that people expect in a house—especially in a suburban house. For example, the extra-flat facade is a problem for a lot

Fig. 52

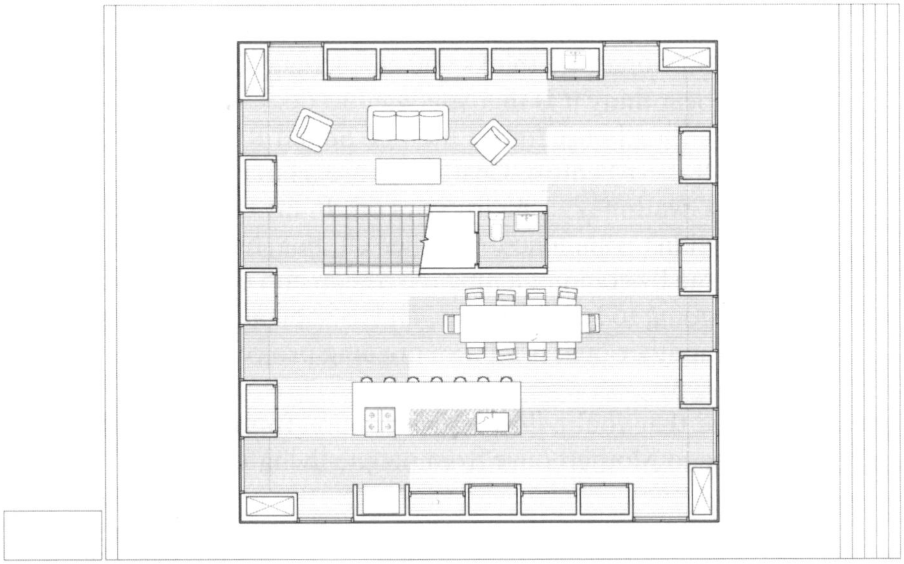

Fig. 53

Fig. 54

Fig. 55

Fig. 56

of people. They don't know what to make of it. However, when I get a chance to talk to people about the house, to explain the design strategy, they usually come around. They understand that the stripes on the facade and the gabled roof are already in the neighborhood, in Victorian bungalows that have been there for a century. They can see that this house is just a different version of the typical houses in the neighborhood.

Across many of your projects, there's a recurring use of strong geometric figures in plan and three-dimensional figuration, as opposed to complex three-dimensional form. Can you talk a bit about your interest in figuration?

It's a deliberate reaction to things that I learned back in graduate school at UCLA. In my second year, I worked with Greg Lynn on his Embryological Houses. He had a brilliant argument regarding variation and difference, how the project inverted the modernist kit-of-parts logic... but I always wondered if the argument could be stronger with figurative geometry. Working with geometry, and curvature in particular, is an interest that continues to play out in many of our projects. Teaching at the University of Illinois Chicago, where a focus on figure and shape has been an important part of the discourse during the past decade, has definitely helped. For years, we intentionally limited figuration to the plan in our projects. Motherhouse is the first project where we are aggressively pursuing figuration in elevation and section.

You mentioned that only ten to twenty percent of your projects get built. What happens when a project stops prior to completion? Do ideas find their way into other projects? And what about the temporary installation projects—do those concepts evolve into building projects?

A few years ago, Paul Preissner and I designed a structure made of two barns for a contemporary arts festival in Denver. The barns were up only for a day—actually, more like eight hours. They were made out of an off-the-shelf steel barn panel kit. For years I've been trying to build houses made of the same system, just assembled differently. It hasn't happened yet. In other projects, we've gotten all the way through construction documents before cancellation. There are many ideas from those projects that we hope to incorporate into future work. Even with projects that don't get built, there is material or structural-systems research that will become valuable again someday. There are also some bubble-gum projects…I have yet to build a cruciform column out of bubblegum, but that would be great.

In another interview you stated that you're not as interested in creating *good* architecture as you are in creating *interesting* architecture. What did you mean by that?

What I meant by good was *moralizing*. There's a lot of talk these days about what architects should be doing. I got into architecture for the complete opposite reason. I like the idea that if you're a good architect, then you're figuring out what you shouldn't do. You go against the grain and attempt to open up new ways for others to see the world. Sometimes, the only way that can happen is by pursuing something uncomfortable, even for yourself.

Perhaps a question that's not entirely unrelated…How have recent global events related to social justice and public health affected your approach to practice?

We can have an impact as architects in a few ways. In our office, we do our best to take care of the people and places around us, both professionally and outside of work. We've always done projects for underserved communities and people who improve environmental and social conditions for others. Moving forward, we can make a bigger difference through carefully choosing who we work with.

What has been the most rewarding moment in your professional career?

I really enjoy the surprises when I see a project get built. You know, there's stuff that you drew and modeled and imagined, and then all of a sudden, there it is. But sometimes it isn't what you expected. It turns out to be weaker or stronger in some way. In Motherhouse and a few other recent projects, we've been trying to see if we can produce qualities through excessive, consistent repetition, rather than variation, or repetition and difference. We don't really know what kind of sensibility will come out of it until it's built. So, we do it and we get to find out. I really love that. And also, that in any given day, we might deal with bubble gum, framing plans, and Catholic theology, all with equal seriousness and irreverence.

Jack Self

What does it mean to practice architecture?

Jack Self: The easiest way to answer that question is to say, I know what architecture is, and I know what architects do. Different schools take different approaches to how closely or not they want to follow a classical definition. For example, at the Architectural Association, where I studied, a poem could be architecture. In Switzerland, at the ETH, where I have taught, buildings are architecture. I would argue that you can't really have architecture without the architect. The pyramids, the Parthenon... sure, there was an architect involved, but architecture as a concept and the figure of the architect is a Western invention. We have to be really careful when we use the term "architecture" outside a Western context. In that sense, there are maybe two possible definitions of a modern architect. There's the social function of the architect, which was invented in the fifteenth century, in which you call yourself an architect and you take control of the building process. You're an assembler of other artisans and craftspeople, as well as engineers. When we say architect these days, we mostly mean the figure created in the nineteenth century, which is a professional figure. So, I know what architecture practice is—it means getting a degree and earning professional recognition by an institute or professional body, and then practicing a very specific and limited form of building-making.

But the more important question is, what can you do with an architecture degree? What can you do with architecture training? That's a much more open question. There are two really amazing things that studying architecture has done for me. The first is the concept of the project as it applies to design. The modern world was made possible by the scientific method. We think we know something, but it's always open to interrogation and doubt. The world participates in a process of constant correction. So, the concept of the project, the notion that you start with an idea and you always end up with more knowledge about the world around you—that is really valuable. The other is the way in which architecture makes you look at the world and gives you so many different potential ways to understand material interactions.

In a recent lecture, you said, "I don't think you can have a career like mine if you're not prepared to break the rules." Can you talk about your decision making with respect to how you wanted to contribute to architectural culture?

My family was very wealthy when I was a child. Then my father went bankrupt. My parents divorced and my mother was on food stamps. From when I was about seven until I was sixteen, we were very poor. One of the great things about having been poor for a considerable period of my life is that I have absolutely no fear of poverty. Middle-class people generally have anxiety about falling through the cracks and worry that they're going to run out of cash and end up in a dire situation. I know that I can live on very little money. I don't fear that, and therefore I have a disproportionate sense of the risks that I can take. Everyone is always assessing their futures in relation to the level of risk that they're comfortable taking on. After internships in Paris and London, and after working as a typesetter, I had very little money… It was a dire situation. To get into the Architectural Association, to receive a loan to pay for school, I had to forge my financial situation with the government. When I finished at the Architectural

Association, I took inventory of my resources. I asked, what are the abilities that I have? What are the skills that I have? I spent a lot of time trying to develop writing and web development skills. Early on, most of my income came from working as a web developer. This led me into graphic design and writing, which I thought was one of those jobs I could do in my spare time and on the weekends. I learned that simply writing more words didn't amount to more income, and ultimately, that became an increasingly unsustainable model for me. What I did—and what I've done for the last five years, since founding Real Foundation—was raise my labor costs by at least twenty to twenty-five percent. I changed the amount that I charge, while at the same time overestimating the amount of time it takes me to do something by twenty-five percent. So, over the five years, I've worked the same amount but doubled my income. I haven't taken a pay raise. I've used that surplus income to finance projects that otherwise could not exist. You tend to think that as you go on in life, you have a bit more money each year—you get a nicer car, you get a nicer apartment. If you don't do those things, you can use the money for making books and doing other types of cultural projects. This is how *Real Review* was started. My path was not a conventional one. It wasn't easy, and it came with a very high level of risk. Thankfully, it has worked out.

What roles do lecturing and writing play in your practice?

When I graduated, I didn't want to work for someone else. I prepared lectures on a variety of topics, and I wrote to more than 100 universities in Europe inviting them to invite me to lecture to their students. I didn't get invited to top-tier universities, but I was invited to small, regional universities in places like the rural Czech Republic or the countryside of Poland. I would make €250 per lecture, and they would pay for my flights and accommodations. I would go to Krakow or Vilnius for one night and I would give my lecture. As long as I could do five or six of those a month, I could make enough money and I could pursue my own projects. Also, I would write articles for journals and magazines, and I would get £200 for each article. I was recently asked if I wanted to publish a book of my writing. I looked in my writing folder—I've written 750,000 words in the last six

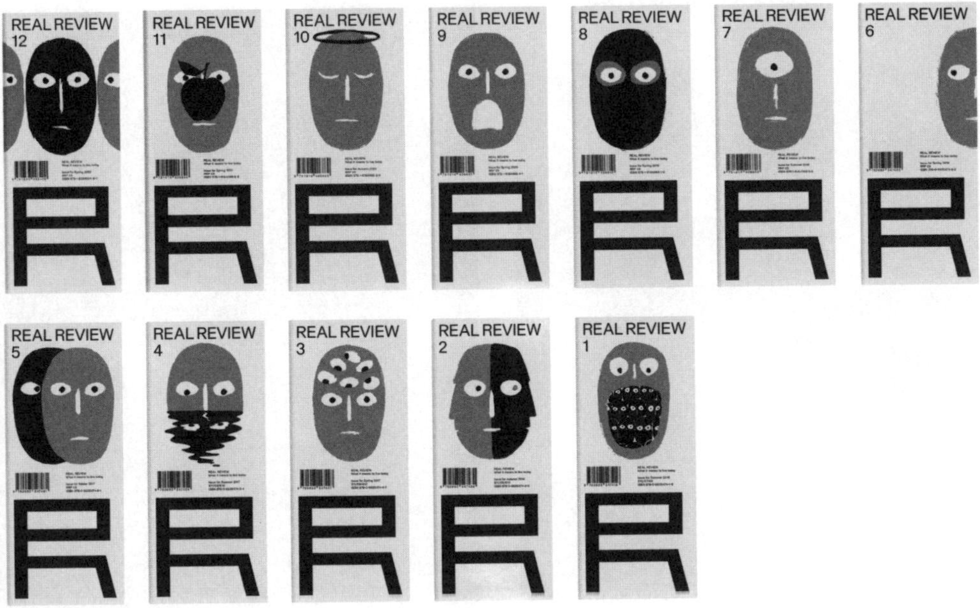
REAL REVIEW
12
REAL REVIEW
11
REAL REVIEW
10
REAL REVIEW
9
REAL REVIEW
8
REAL REVIEW
7
REAL REVIEW
6
REAL REVIEW
5
REAL REVIEW
4
REAL REVIEW
3
REAL REVIEW
2
REAL REVIEW
1

Fig. 57

Fig. 58

Fig. 59

or seven years, of which 400,000 have been published. It's a colossal volume. It was purely in order to be able to survive financially and keep doing the other work that I thought was interesting, but for which I wasn't necessarily being paid. At a certain point, universities stopped asking me to give lectures about the history of the double bed or the history of the apartment and started asking me to present my own work. This was a big shift for me. Since then, I've been scrambling to continuously produce work that will in some way be useful to others. While teaching and lecturing over the years, and presenting myself publicly, I learned that I've accumulated cultural capital. With it comes a strange phenomenon… through exposure to my words and design work, people constructed their own idea of who I was, which, since they've never met me, was completely divorced from my own idea. It became difficult to manage the gap between my public persona and my private persona. I've tried to make sure that those two things stay as close to each other as possible. One can use public platforms to either promote themself or to share their values. Through conversations like this one, I hope I give enough emphasis to my ideas and values. That's my focus.

How do you see your career evolving?

If we look at someone like Rem Koolhaas, we can see an architect who is always slightly ahead of the rest of the profession. From about 1991 onward, each year he moved further away from being recognized only as an architect and attempted to be seen as a cultural figure. In order to do that, he needed to talk about more than just architecture. This PR strategy is a time-honored strategy. First, you have to have a method that you can teach other people, and you develop that method by becoming a teacher. Second, because you need to be able to influence the next generation, you have to have a manifesto. For Rem, it was Delirious New York. And you need to have designed a house. Rem said to me once, "The problem with you is that you don't have a house." He said that no one would believe that I'm a real architect until I design and build a house. He strongly recommended that I design and build a house. He thought that I was trying to follow the template for how to become a great architect. I'm not interested in that model. Like Rem, I am trying to distinguish myself as a cultural figure, but I'm not trying to become a famous architect.

We appreciate your ambition to break with tradition and pursue alternative paths for yourself as an architect. How does this apply to your practice, and how do you see models of architecture practice changing?

I can share an example of how we are trying to change the way we practice. At REAL Foundation, we work on models rather than instances. For example, we were asked by clients to design an apartment renovation in London. The problem was that they had a very small budget. So, I said, "We'll do it for free." We agreed that when they sell the apartment, we'll take one or two percent of the final sale value. The longer that they hold onto the apartment, the more it will be worth, given its location in central London. I tried to turn the risk into an advantage. During that negotiation process, we hired a lawyer to draw up an amendment to the Royal Institute of British Architects' standard contract, which we then published as an open-source document that any architect could use as a model. I'm not obsessed with developing a personal style or a personal aesthetic—rather, I'm much more interested in developing a methodology that can be repeated. We're not focused on the outcomes of practice. We're focused on changing the process through which projects are developed and through which architects are compensated.

Can you talk more about how new forms of practice intersect with current financial models for development?

Once I realized that you can put whatever the fuck you want in a contract, I realized that there are so many other ways to develop and build buildings. I looked for loopholes within the system that I'm examining and for ways to insert other products into that system. If you can create a product that is more attractive than what already exists, then you can eventually wash out the existing condition. As it pertains to housing, I want to start with high-density urban environments, because in the metrics that I'm dealing with, considering the way that capitalism works, you need to build faster and cheaper and more dense. I started by designing a system that is thirty-percent denser, forty-percent cheaper to build, and about forty-percent faster to construct than existing high-rise models. Additionally, through REAL foundation, I want to offer a new ownership model to people who might normally be excluded from the housing market. There is an idea about incremental ownership that I'm developing that will enable residents to build up shares in their building. I found that if you have a building of 100 apartments where everyone owns one apartment, if there's a leak on the roof, the people on the ground floor don't give a shit because it doesn't affect their property. Whereas if those 100 people each own one percent of the building, a leak is everyone's problem. It also means that you have a different sense of investment in common spaces and in the building as a whole. Even really minor things, like shifting to a share option—which is built up slowly over time through savings, rather than a mortgage—can be a positive change in our current system.

Overall, what I'm trying to suggest is that, of course, the ultimate ambition is to transition to an entirely new model of society that is more just and more equitable, but I'm looking for opportunities within the existing system where you might be able to create modest and incremental change. We should not be discouraged by the amount of time that it will take to make substantive change. If you can find very small and incremental ways to improve the lives of the people around you, that in itself is already a step in the right direction.

What has been the most fulfilling moment of your career so far?

You're asking the wrong person. I'm always unhappy. I'm always disappointed. I'm an atheist Jew who was raised in an evangelical high school. So, I ended up Judeo-Christian with a healthy dose of atheism. This means that I feel great guilt to feel pride. I need to learn to take pride in my accomplishments. I can't look at any particular moment and think that I did an amazing job. I always see room for improvement. That's my own psychological failing. Mental health and well-being have really risen to the fore in the last couple of years. We need to take moments to congratulate ourselves and to be grateful to ourselves for the work that we do. Unfortunately, I haven't quite arrived there yet. I am very hard on myself. I wish I could say that there was a moment where I was like, "Fuck, I did it."

Fig. 60

Fig. 61

Jess Myers

What does it mean to practice architecture, and do you consider what you do to be a form of practicing architecture?

Jess Myers: The profession has been extremely insecure in defining itself. There's this idea that we'd be taken more seriously if architecture were more aligned with engineering and technology, so a lot of schools have moved toward STEM-focused education. But the profession really started out of the humanities. What this produced is a combination and integration of mathematics and human life. That's where I find the most purchase with my practice. I always talk to my students about how architecture is essentially about creating a stage for life. The built environment is a stage on which human life unfolds. I consider my work to be a part of reframing the practice in those terms. If we are concerned with creating a staging ground for life to unfold, then we have to understand what lives are out there. That's where my podcast is coming from. It's definitely where my writing comes from.

You've moved through a variety of institutions and offices: Princeton, MIT, Superfront, the Centre Pompidou, and Bernard Tschumi's office, to name a few. How did each of those experiences bring you to where you are now, with respect to carving out a particular approach to contributing to architectural culture?

I wanted to be an architect from a relatively young age. I structured my middle school and high school education around this desire, but I panicked about a lot of things because I was aware of how difficult it is to become an architect. I wasn't top of my class in math or drawing. Also, I did not and still do not see a lot of Black women in this profession. In order to be taken seriously, I thought I needed to have a very serious, brand-name degree. So I went to Princeton for my undergraduate degree in architecture, but I did not know that the program was very focused on the humanities. I found that frustrating because I didn't think I would acquire a skill set that would help me get a job. In other ways, it was ideal for me, because it encouraged me to find different ways to be a part of the profession. I ended up at Bernard Tschumi's office, working in administration and publications and preparing a show at the Centre Pompidou. After a while, I realized I was unfulfilled engaging with architecture only through theoretical and aesthetic issues. I wanted to participate more in the political and social aspects of architecture. So I decided to go back to school and study urban planning. I became very interested in neighborhood resource allocation and management, and narratives and frameworks surrounding identity and insecurity in the space of the city. I wondered, How do you frame insecurity? How do you frame safety? I wanted to ask people questions about their sense of security and insecurity in their cities. All of this eventually led me to begin my podcast.

A question about that podcast, Here There Be Dragons—you've indicated that your goals are to understand how people negotiate their identities through the space of the city, particularly in relation to issues of safety. What have these conversations revealed to you about how architecture and urban design can alleviate some of the problematic aspects of identity and safety in the city?

What the podcast reveals is the entanglement of architecture and politics. To be more specific, the conversations I've had really reveal who gets provided for and who gets protected versus who gets policed in the space of the city. I've become very interested in understanding how people negotiate their position on the spectrum of protected versus policed. I spoke to a Swedish-Somali woman in Stockholm who was pregnant at the time of our conversation. She told me about how people of color in Sweden who were visibly pregnant were being attacked because white Swedish people were afraid of what an increase of families of color could indicate for the country. She would wear certain types of jackets on subways, for example, to obscure her pregnancy—that was her strategy to stay safe. In my conversations, no one said that they would go to a city planning office or the police to change the outcome of their circumstances.

Now, where I see architecture and city planning coming into this situation is understanding that architecture is set up to create a certain amount of ease for certain people. Look at a well-resourced downtown compared to a neighborhood on the outskirts of a city that's considered a servicing neighborhood, where people commute from that neighborhood to service the city. How do the lights look in those two areas? How do the streets look in those two areas? Who gets an aboveground train or subway station? Who gets warm lighting? Who gets surveillance lighting? All of these design elements make it clear who is being resourced and who is being surveilled. Returning to the idea that the built environment creates a staging ground for life, the financialization of the built environment creates certain assumptions about how people are leading their lives, and, in turn, a certain amount or a certain lack of resources.

What triggers a societal need for architects? What is architecture's superpower, and how can it be used for good rather than evil?

We already have a social place. Right now, architects are seen as a luxury expense rather than something that the middle and working classes need. I'd like to say that it's our fault that the general public understands the profession in that way. This condition has been created by privileging aesthetics over effect. We need to do a better job understanding the social impact of architecture. We need to rearticulate why the built environment and stewardship of the built environment is inherent to life. Architecture school needs to become a bit more mundane... We need to cut a little bit of the grandiose factor of every student having their own projects, spending thirteen weeks in isolation to solve a design problem. We also need to expand the content of our design studios and design problems. We should talk more about how buildings are financed, where materials come from, and who we build for. Because we educate students in the manner that we do, they exit with their own brand identity that gets formed into a portfolio that an employer will barely look at before shuffling them into an entry-level job. We need to restructure our educational model to help students understand current realities of the built environment and seed their vision for how these realities can be transformed. Giving up some aesthetic agency in order to make things happen in the built environment is part of being an architect. Embracing the administrative, bureaucratic, and political processes of building is part of being an architect. This is the first step in creating a class of architects that is much more flexible, much more grounded in where they can move and operate.

Beyond advocating for a more inclusive and equitable built environment for everyone through your work with The Architecture Lobby, you're also an advocate for more inclusive and equitable professional environments for architectural workers. How might what you've called "worker power" change professional practice in the future?

Over the course of 2020, we saw how workers are putting in unpaid overtime, how women and femme-identified people who are caretakers are treated in the workplace, and how people who are disabled are treated in the workplace. Before the pandemic, it was said that there's no flexibility in the way that we work. And then as soon as the pandemic happened, as soon as lockdown happened, all of a sudden there was flexibility and work still got done. So there is this framework where we tell ourselves what is and what is not possible because of ways of working and thinking that we've become addicted to, instead of trying to think of new ways of working and engaging with different types of client groups and different types of financialization models in the built environment. Worker power is crucial for architecture to become more inclusive and equitable, and to retaining any level of relevance. What is important about tools like unionization is the structure of transferring power in the firm from the hands of one into the hands of the actual workers of the firm. How can we restructure the types of contracts that rely on unpaid overtime in our workplaces? We need to find ways to create jobs that provide a livable wage and a humane set of work hours, as opposed to passing the burden of extra work onto the workers. A lot of people can't afford to take on this burden. It's not right that you need to have come from money or have a second job to be an architect. A union for architects can push for policy that provides political power to the workers. A union can change wages and work hours and parental leave. It would be incredible if architects could join together and have power in a progressive way. I'm not here to say that unions are a cure-all for the profession, but they can be a tool that could give us a lot of power to make positive change.

We know you previously worked as a strategist, which also seems like a meaningful way to direct efforts of other professionals toward positive change. Do you have any desire to move back into consulting and strategy? If not, what other avenues may you seek out, and what kind of projects do you hope to be working on in the near future?

Doing strategic work was not the the best fit for me because it exposed the difficulty that really great institutions have getting over the hurdle of the structures that they themselves are so invested in. It was incredible to see how entrenched and how deeply immovable people in institutions felt those structures to be. It was very frustrating to me. The difference between the outward optics of those places versus their actions was significant. This experience reiterated to me that to move the needle, we need to alter our professional frameworks. You don't necessarily need to start with the CEO, you don't necessarily need to start with the board—you can start with students. You can start with workers to create forms of solidarity that they didn't know to be possible. Something I like about the podcast is that I can sit in rooms with people from very different walks of life who you could not see coming together on their own. But in the space of audio, I can use their voices as beads on a string, where the hip hop producer in the suburbs of Paris and the economic development director in Versailles can have a similar concern and share space together in the podcast. There exists a sense of solidarity through the podcast. The threading together of perspectives and concerns creates opportunities for overlaps that would have previously gone unregistered.

What has been the most rewarding moment of your career thus far?

Definitely watching the podcast evolve as we have access to more resources and funding. Something that was always an ambition was this space of sound—using sound that is orienting and evocative. We were building toward that from season one, when I was working alone, to this season, in Stockholm, where we are working with a sound designer, capturing different types of sound and building moments in the podcast that do things like orient people who are not familiar with the city, as well as those who know the sounds of the city. Being able to orient people without visual prompts has been really, really exciting. We're hoping to push that even further for our next season, in eastern Europe.

Julia Gamolina

The figure of the architect has historically been and is reiterated as a white man. Do you believe that by giving a platform to successful women in design with your online magazine, *Madame Architect*, you will help change this narrative?

Julia Gamolina: When I was in school, I had a lot of concerns about joining the profession, because as much as I loved studying architecture, I didn't really feel that there were a lot of options that aligned with the career that I wanted. Between who was presented to us as role models and the unhealthy lifestyle that was being depicted and even celebrated, I didn't know if it was going to work for me. So, I sought advice from my female professors about how to navigate the profession as a woman. I was and remain inspired by their trajectories and how they've chosen to live their lives. Ultimately, those encounters are what fueled *Madame Architect*. I do hope that my efforts will help to continue to rewrite the narrative of women in architecture.

In what ways does your current skill set differ from the one you left school with? What were the circumstances that led to you acquiring these skills?

Surprisingly, it's not very different. I'm still the same person I was when I graduated—I'm of course more experienced now, but I had all of the skills I use now when I was coming out of school. After school it was simply about finding the right place and the right outlet to direct my skills and energy toward. I always liked to write, which is not always everyone's favorite activity. While I was in school, I was also much more interested in talking to my classmates about their projects and organizing educational and social events where I had opportunities to curate lists of participants. I'm doing a lot of those same things now.

How do you think about the balance between emphasizing interviewees' identities as women and normalizing women in the industry by not highlighting gender identity?

We make sure to focus on what makes up the identities of the people we've spoken to beyond their gender. We've profiled people who are leaders in sustainability, high-rise construction, development, product design, criticism, and so on. They're not just women—they are experts and leaders in their respective fields. That being said, we don't ignore the fact that they're women. We're not going to say gender identity doesn't matter, or that gender identity has not affected people's experiences. It definitely does. I think we have been able to strike a good balance. In interviews, I don't ask "What is it like to be a woman in the field?" because the challenges are very well-known. We know what these challenges are and we're working through what do we do next and how to celebrate accomplishments of women in architecture and design. We want to highlight and share the female perspective, one that is not the status quo or the establishment perspective, while highlighting excellence in the field outside of gender identity.

What responsibility do you feel as a writer to engage with political, social, and environmental issues?

I have a responsibility to cover people who are truly doing the right work, and not just talking about it. There is a lot of talk at the surface, but my responsibility is to dig deeper, to highlight those who are truly working toward change and delivering results. I'm also looking for lesser-known or undercelebrated people who are doing really meaningful work in the world, with regard to design, but more importantly in relation to climate change, politics, social issues, sustainability, and so on. That's one responsibility I embrace. The other responsibility is to make sure we're covering women from all kinds of backgrounds—design and professional excellence comes from everywhere.

You were previously the director of strategy at Trahan Architects. What activities were you involved in on a weekly basis in this role?

As director of strategy, my focus was on the intentional growth and evolution of the firm, and essentially paving the way for the firm's future—which projects do we want to work on and bring in, which personnel, which issues should we be talking about? I was involved in business development, branding, marketing, and client relations, and developing a strategic plan. All of this to say that in professional practice, we tend to associate creativity with visual output, but creating architecture is so much more. Architecture school can construct a limited way of understanding how your skills can be applied after graduation. Classes like design, building technology, structures, construction, history, theory, and representation come in multiples, and every other aspect of practice is compressed into one professional practice class. It's not a reflection of all of the realities of practice. There are so many alternative modes of practice. Despite not being directly involved in design, I still feel like I am practicing architecture.

Can you expand on that? What does it mean to you to practice architecture?

To practice architecture means to create our future world. That's a huge responsibility. Practicing architecture doesn't stop at creating a building. Architecture's inception is from other players in the ecosystem, and the maintenance of the organism is by others…so in practicing architecture, you are interfacing with everyone else in the process. No one does anything alone.

How would you describe the role of a business strategist in developing a practice?

A role in strategy is all about ensuring and encouraging the holistic synthesis of design, operations, business development, and marketing in order to healthfully sustain and develop the firm. These topics and departments may be siloed in terms of personnel and teams in firms, but they are certainly not siloed as it relates to a practice's evolution. I see my role as really deeply understanding the ecosystem of people that it takes to shape our world—those in design, those in construction, those in financing, in development, in government. If you think of the "production chain" of getting a ground-up building built, it starts with the financing and ends with the PR, but then the life cycle goes on through occupancy, maintenance, and aging. Our built environment is a living and breathing organism that takes a lot of people and a lot of professionals to make it perform in a way that's good for us all—ideally—and making sure that an architectural practice is playing its part responsibly and with excellence within that is a big part of strategy.

You are now a Director of Business Development at Ennead Architects. What does this role involve?

My role with Ennead is very focused on bringing in new work to the practice (whereas in strategy, that was one aspect of it). Business development has three facets—research, outreach, and tracking. Then, there is a lot of match-making of people and initiatives internally to opportunities that we find externally. For example, we look at recent projects a partner or principal has led, in addition to their research and geographic interests and "pulls," and point them in the direction of opportunities in those veins. Just like in strategy, you need to have a very wide view of both your company, and of the industry, for this matching to be most effective.

I travel very often for this role as well, and it has been fascinating to see how design professionals and the general public approach design and architecture in different regions. Chicago is very different from Los Angeles, Austin is very different from Miami, and so forth. Also understanding what is being built in each city and why, based on the very specific history of that place, is fascinating. We gain that understanding by looking at everything through a socioeconomic lens, and then we look at what could be through the same lens, but also through a filter of sustainability and social responsibility. There is a lot of keeping with the times—we talk a lot about the effects of the pandemic on various cities, and what we see coming up, so a lot of forecasting that is based on the past.

How have recent global events related to social justice and public health affected your approach to business development at Ennead Architects or your work at *Madame Architect*?

Architects often tend to operate and think of themselves as existing within a design bubble. There is no bubble. Everything is connected—design, social justice, public health, creativity, editorial, all of it. These events were global and were movements for a reason. In terms of approach, it's been critical for me to lean into everything that's happening. You can't deny these things and not participate! What I've learned in terms of approach is that you have to stay informed, engage with it, and do your part—and your part will depend on what your strengths, focuses, and outlets are. With Ennead Architects, we ask ourselves what we could do given the resources that we have, and which partnerships and conversations we can pursue more. With *Madame Architect*, I made sure to focus our editorial approach very prominently on these topics.

How do you define success in your work?

Success for me exists in really deep fulfillment. I was pretty unfulfilled working as a junior designer early on in my career. I remember hearing statements like "Do what you love and you'll never work a day in your life" and just wanting to roll my eyes. I didn't think that that was real and that anyone could feel that way about work. But now I truly do feel that way with *Madame Architect* and with my work with Ennead Architects. That's what success means to me right now—doing what I really like doing, having opportunities to meaningfully connect with others, and being able to meaningfully connect people with each other.

What keeps you motivated?

With *Madame Architect,* I really like everything about the process. It's a huge creative outlet for me. People often ask me if I miss design. My answer is that I have my creative outlet with *Madame Architect.* It's very visual, and the writing aspects require a lot of creativity. It's very stimulating in that way. To be honest, I like it so much that I don't struggle with staying motivated. There is another side to it… I'm an immigrant, and I've immigrated twice. I was born in Russia, and I moved to Toronto when I was eight and moved again to Colorado when I was thirteen or fourteen. Our entire family foundation was shaken up two times. I had to say goodbye to my grandparents and my best friends. When my family moved, any community of support I had was suddenly gone. I've always had to be proactive when it comes to building relationships. Because of my experiences, I want to make sure it's easier for other people to find systems of guidance and support. That definitely keeps me motivated to keep going with *Madame Architect*. I want to make sure people appreciate and celebrate their own uniqueness and the different combination of qualities that they bring to the world.

What has been the most rewarding moment of your professional career?

There have been so many rewarding moments in my career. One that stands out—Paul Goldberger tweeted about *Madame Architect* and stated that it offers the best combination of insight and information on the internet, and that it's beautifully packaged and one of the best architecture websites today. I basically cried tears of joy. When I read statements like that and see how people connect with and appreciate *Madame Architect,* it's really rewarding.

Knowhow Shop: Justin Rice and Kagan Taylor

How does Knowhow Shop practice architecture?

Kagan Taylor: The way that we generally describe what we do as being different from the work of a traditional architect is that we have a material- and craft-oriented practice, which means we design with feedback through construction. Part of our design process is the building of things, and that influences what we design. It becomes the field that we find a direction in, through specific details or practices or ideas within construction and craft.

Justin Rice: Part of our process is a back-and-forth between physical and digital. We still build physical models, and we'll send clients renderings occasionally, but we've found that building something physically allows the client to engage more with the project. They get way more excited about a project when they have something physical that they can pick up, whether it's a small model or a large model that they can stick their head in.

How did the co-op structure that you established when you started your practice allow you to continue to experiment and innovate?

Kagan: When we started, we were just trying to make it work. There were a lot of potential sources of revenue that we explored. We allowed people to come in and use the shop. We taught classes for a while. They all had advantages and disadvantages. A disadvantage of allowing people to come in and use the shop was that we were constantly playing the role of shop manager. An advantage of teaching classes in the shop was that we met a lot of really cool people. The downside was that we had to come in on the weekends and work. Over time, we've tried to focus on doing things a little bit more architecturally, a little bit more like a traditional design-build firm. We have been interested in retaining the community engagement that we had when we first started off, so we always try and participate in competitions or community projects, or anything that will allow us to show and discuss our work.

Justin: Education has always been important to us, and what we felt like we could give back, rather than going into full-time teaching, was doing workshops. Workshops allow someone to come in for a couple of days and learn something interesting, something that they previously didn't know, or hone their skills in a certain way. We haven't done as many workshops in the past few years, because we've just been so busy, but the community aspect of it is a huge draw for us. Ultimately, I think our workshop model actually ended up evolving more into a party model. We stopped doing workshops and just started having parties.

Your firm's logo establishes a strong visual identity. How did you start curating your image as people and as a studio?

Justin: Well, we can't shave our beards because of the logo.

Kagan: Justin and I are both so frustrated with architecture practices and architects that take themselves too seriously. There's nothing worse than getting on an architect's website and it just being the most obtuse thing in the world and impossible to navigate. We wanted humor and fun to be part of our practice. Especially because we were developing something that we were going to do for a long time, we wanted it to be enjoyable. We wanted to have a community within the shop and not take ourselves too seriously. So having a logo that doesn't take itself seriously is part of that, as are the videos we have on our website. The impression that we put out there is that we're skilled people who want to have fun doing the things we love to do.

Yes, we have seen a lot of the videos that you have posted on your website.

Kagan: Oh god! Yeah, maybe we should take some of those down.

We especially liked the safety one.

Kagan: Yes, that's the one! That's the one we should take down.

You have described your beginnings as a firm as taking on small projects and unusual requests. What was beginning your practice like given the socioeconomic circumstances of the time?

Kagan: In the beginning, there was no threshold for someone to call us. People may think, "I want to build a house, so I better call an architect." But they don't see us that way. With us, people think, "I need a board cut—I can call Knowhow Shop." When we started, we would take anything, for better or for worse. Once you take anything for a while, it's a hard reputation to shed. So, for the last few years, we've tried to be a little bit more selective about the projects we take on—projects along the trajectory we want to follow. Ultimately, if someone contacts us with something interesting, we'll do it. The most interesting projects are where there's room to inject our own agenda and what we're interested in at the moment. It may be a really conventional design project, but it becomes interesting when there's room for us to do something unusual with it.

Where does your interest in traditional craft and digital fabrication originate?

Kagan: I have a woodworking background, so I had broad knowledge of what was possible within craft. And Justin got really interested in running the CNC and pushing the boundaries of what we could do with that machine while we were in school. There was a good marriage of his interest in pushing the CNC and me having a sort of a broad understanding of directions in which to push and what had traditionally not been done with digital fabrication. We started seeing architectural opportunities within this combination of interests.

Justin: So much of our work deals with material feedback, in that not only do we push a tool to do something that maybe it isn't exactly designed to do, like the CNC maxing out what it's capable of doing, but then we also get material feedback. We're maximizing what a material can do, too. For example, a specific technique we used a lot early on is called kerf bending, which is a very old technique for bending wood. And we used it architecturally in a project called The Oinkster. Usually, all the kerf bends are covered up, but in that project, we left them open. So, you can see the way we did it. It showed our hand.

When we look at projects like Lighthouse Office and Lunar Cat Lander, we see a consistent aesthetic and specific formal choices that you've made. How do you think your aesthetic translates across these various scales and objects?

Kagan: It's more about ideas or themes, and we'll often do three or four projects within a given theme. The Lunar Cat Lander and the office… those are both the same idea. Another example is the peeling of a wall. If that's the starting idea, we'll try peeling in a bunch of different ways. We'll say, "Okay, this is how you traditionally build a wall. What if we wanted to peel the drywall away from the wall?" We tried that idea on a gallery project called Slow Culture, and again on a residential project called the Listening Studio. It's the same idea, but with different geometry. Slow Culture has a curved geometry, where we peel a wall into a curve. And the Listening Studio has a faceted or folded geometry, where we imagine the surface of the wall being something that we can fold.

Justin: Another idea I think you can see play out through a series is darting. One of our very first projects that we worked on together in school was a skateboard that was tailored using techniques that Charles and Ray Eames developed for bending plywood. It's how they made a lot of their chairs, but specifically their leg splint for wounded soldiers in World War II.

Fig. 62

We've continued to use those techniques throughout the history of Knowhow Shop. We designed a mini-golf course that we tailored in order to give geometry to an otherwise flat material. We've also scaled that idea up to a coffee shop where we tailored wood to bend around the cash register and the countertops. That's one technique that I'd like to scale up further to see what it means architecturally for, say, a roof or a wall.

Can you describe your process of construction and how it differs from more traditional practices?

Kagan: When we started, we were doing fairly small projects where we could do everything, and we did. That's not a sustainable model if you want to scale up the work, and that is something we're interested in. We recently designed an accessory dwelling unit, and most of it will be built by a traditional contractor. We'll use the normal framework of an architectural relationship with a client and contractor to communicate exactly what we want done, but we'll identify some element of the project that makes sense for us to build ourselves.

Justin: We may build a complex part of the project, or a part for which we have a very specific idea of how we want it done. It would be a difficult thing to explain to a contractor to get it done the way we want—it wouldn't be impossible, but it would be difficult, and probably also very expensive. So, our model has really shifted to one where we focus our fabrication energy on just one or two specific moments within a project.

Kagan: This model is also interesting in terms of our relationship with the client and the contractor, because we'll be hired by the client to design a project, and then we will be hired by the contractor as a subcontractor to build some element within that project. So, our relationship to the contractor is both as the architect, who has the responsibility to the client to ensure that the contractor is doing the project per our instructions, and as an employee who builds some scope of that. That's interesting and pulls us in a few different directions.

Does your current skill set differ from what you learned in school, and if so, what circumstances led to you acquiring the different skills that you use now?

Kagan: By necessity, when you start your own practice, you develop new skills. Business skills, specifically, weren't things that we learned in school. Dealing with clients and vendors and other people and getting the best work you can from them is a skill set we had to learn. But just running the business has been the biggest challenge.

Justin: A lot of what we've learned isn't necessarily about architecture or fabrication. It's really about human relations in a lot of ways. So much of running your own practice is how you communicate with other people. It's something we've just learned over time. We've been pretty successful at it. We've generated a lot of goodwill in the community.

Kagan: The other thing that's really important is the working relationship that the two of us have. The relationship I have with Justin is not without conflict, but we have found in each other someone who we can work with over a long period of time. That involves having different skills and recognizing each other's skills and weaknesses, and being open and honest with each other about that.

What has been the most rewarding moment of your career thus far?

Kagan: For me, it's the fact that we've designed in the flexibility to have lives outside of work. Justin just got married last week. I got married a few years ago and had a child last year. The fact that we are able to do things that we love outside of work is something we care about deeply.

Justin: One of the most rewarding things for me is when a project is finished. When we're in the midst of several projects, it feels like we're in the middle of a tornado. Then, finally, a project is finished and you get photos of it and it looks amazing and the client is happy. Since we're so involved in the fabrication, it's so much sweeter because so much of our own sweat has gone into the project…To see it finished is always amazing.

Fig. 63

Fig. 64

LA Más and Office of: Office: Helen Leung and Elizabeth Timme

You started LA Más as a nonprofit. What has the combination of your respective expertise—design, and public policy and community engagement—made possible?

Elizabeth Timme: I started LA Más the year before I met Helen.[2] At the time, in 2012, there were no other design nonprofits in Los Angeles, nor did I have peers working in Los Angeles to support lower-income communities or communities of color. However, there were planners and people with policy expertise, like Helen, who were having a deeper conversation about the city, and I just intensely wanted to be in that conversation with them. I found the issues being unpacked in those conversations and the ways they were talking about systemic change to be really valuable and substantial, and that they really reflected my lived experience in Los Angeles, and the needs I was seeing and the kind of challenges the city was facing at that time.

Helen Leung: A lot of what we've been known for in our work has been a reflection of our tools and our discipline. But how we connected was through our values. When I decided to join LA Más, Elizabeth hired me as director of social impact. I had no idea that it was a design organization. I first understood LA Más as a nonprofit working in community development. In the years that followed, I began asking, "What does it mean to do work that's meaningful in communities where I grew up?" I'm a child of working-class immigrants. I was born and raised in Los Angeles and grew up in working-class neighborhoods. They are my backyard, my lived experience, and to see them rapidly change because of new investment that wasn't for the average person, but only for a specific group, was frustrating. I felt that there had to be a way that development and investment could be done differently. This is what the journey of LA Más has been—to develop strategies that represent community values.

How do you make a community nonprofit sustainable as a business?

Helen: Running a nonprofit is just like running a business. As a way to think about how to start a nonprofit, I have three broad buckets of advice. One is that doing it alone is hard. You actually have to have a board when you register for your 501(c)(3). It's hard to do real, meaningful, systemic change or committee work all alone. The opportunity to have your founding board be part of that effort can be really helpful. Second, you have to understand what impact you want to make. If you were successful, what would that outcome be? It's very easy in our space to think about inputs and outputs, but then you forget to think about the broader impact you're trying to create. Are you trying to resolve poverty, hunger, homelessness? What is it that you want to see changed in the world because of the existence of your nonprofit? The third is about financing—every organization has its own revenue model. For us, we had some seed funding, and after building our reputation, we slowly received larger foundation grants. It's important to think about having a diverse funding stream. Our foundation grant strategy was one strategy. Another strategy was individual donations. The third way was through fee-for-service, which is a pretty common approach in the design field. We took on a lot of projects because they were something we could do, despite the fact that they may not have been aligned with our mission.

[2] In January 2022, Elizabeth Timme and Helen Leung uprooted their organizational structure and formed two distinct organizations. Elizabeth now leads a new design organization called Office of: Office. Comprised of a team of planners, architects, and builders, Office of: Office translates community vision into neighborhood projects and uses policy and design to help people see themselves in the places they live. Helen remains at LA Más, which continues its evolution into a place-based organization that fosters community ownership and builds power among working-class communities of color in northeast LA. LA Más partners with community members to identify solutions related to affordable housing and economic resilience.

Elizabeth: That's not to say we had any of that out of the gate. That is seven years of experience refining our approach. When I started, I did not have a chart of accounts. Helen came into a mess. And we've actually had three missions so far. We had a public health– and urban planning–focused mission, and then a place-keeping– and urban design–focused mission, and now we're moving into a community-based mission, which we hope to keep, but these things change. There was a lot of flux and change in the beginning. We did work that wasn't necessarily in line with our mission. The entire team that existed in the first three years left, except for Helen and me. That was traumatizing. In those first three to four years, every day was like a week of learning.

Helen: With COVID, this will be the third year in a row we're going say to our board that we're not asking for a raise. Our board is not happy about that, because they want to make sure the nonprofit is sustainable. We could probably be making twice as much if we were to work elsewhere, but we thought it was important for us to have our team be compensated fairly and to have long-term sustainability on both personal and professional levels. We hope we can get to a place where we're not in this mindset of scarcity. It continues to shock me every single time that there are people who, if you make your vision compelling and clear, will say, "I want to support that." I just got an email from someone who wants to donate $2,500 . . . and I thought, "Wow! Really?"

Elizabeth: I recently participated in a panel discussion at the University of Southern California. It was about architects doing social-impact projects. The two architects who spoke both talked about their social-impact work as pro bono—for free—which is totally unacceptable. We try to never do anything for free. This is because in order for LA Más to be sustainable, our work needs to be valued and compensated. Never work for free! There's always room and a discretionary budget for hiring consultants to do work. You become their arm investing in their community. If you know the value of your role, make it clear and ask to be compensated. If you don't know what your value is as a partner, don't do that work. Never do anything for free.

When the COVID-19 pandemic began, you halted your backyard-homes initiative and began providing aid to the area around your office, in northeast LA. What prompted you to begin this initiative and how did your status as a nonprofit affect your response to the pandemic?

Helen: We put a halt to not just our backyard-homes work, but most of our projects, because how we were doing our work wasn't possible. As people were thinking about what to do with their finances, investing in an accessory dwelling unit was probably not the first thing they were thinking about. We also had to figure out, as a small team, how do we work remotely and adjust to this new situation? We have people on our team who are parents or take care of parents. We provided space for that. While we were doing that, we checked in with neighbors and community members. We learned that there was something that was already happening. There was an invitation by our neighbors to help them. That was the beginning of seeing what's already happening…this informal, beautiful, rich, network of people helping each other out, calling each other, checking in, buying groceries. We brought our skill set of being great project managers and being able to find resources, being able to organize and put an infrastructure in place to provide direct aid. What has come out of it is a greater sense of trust and a greater understanding of who we are as an organization—even though we've been in northeast LA for five or six years already. Not a lot of people saw us necessarily as a community-based nonprofit. It was a way to build partnerships and trust that wasn't about us coming up with an idea and putting forth a solution, but instead honoring what was already happening and sharing the privilege of our resources.

Elizabeth: We had been coming to terms with the fact that the model under which we were working didn't reflect what we wanted to be accomplishing. We'd been having that conversation together for at least six months before COVID hit. We had been chatting with community-development leaders and community-based organizations. In addition, we were having a series of similar listening conversations around emerging needs in the community. We already had an idea of where we wanted to start and whom to reach out to in our response. Inspired by an existing system of support within the community, we developed a phone

Fig. 65

Fig. 66

tree with trained volunteers to reach out to and check in on residents. We were able to reach out to around 2,000 residents in a month or so. We spent maybe six weeks making calls and recording that and then talking about what we were hearing, and then over three or four weeks, we started the Community Response program. We knew we had to move quickly.

Can you tell us more about the importance of putting residents in the driver's seat in the type of work you do?

Helen: I've always envisioned myself as a community-development advocate, rather than a planner, even though that's my training. I'm for the people. Part of our work is reckoning with what we've done and what kind of work aligns with our values. If we proclaim to be of service and to be in partnership with whomever we're working with—whether that is middle-class people, veterans, seniors, those who are homeless—it's common sense that if you don't honor and listen to those lived experiences, whatever you're creating is not going to be aligned and it's not going to work. Because of my upbringing, with immigrant parents, as someone who grew up poor, I have had so many experiences of never being listened to, or being the other, of feeling like I didn't belong. I would love for my work and how I contribute my time to not contribute to that, and to honor and listen to voices that mainstream society doesn't often listen to.

How do you work within and serve a particular sociocultural community that you're not part of without the community feeling that you're an outsider coming in?

Helen: That's something that we have struggled with. In our previous work, when we've worked in different neighborhoods, we often spent a lot of time listening first. So however we approached the work, there were community partners who were our advisors, who were grounding us, kind of checking us. We've done that in the past, and we have always tried to hire in a way that is racially, socially, economically, and culturally diverse. In some ways, our office represents Los Angeles. What's wonderful is we recently hired someone in the neighborhood to be a part of our community response. That comes out of the desire to invest in people who are part of the communities that we serve. This is so important to us. I grew up in northeast LA. I share my story with the community. There's space to be personal, and to share parts of yourself. There are other elements of your life that allow people to connect and understand why you're doing the work. That's important as a way of building trust. Why are you here? What are your intentions? Vulnerability builds trust, and it's something that we're going to have to continue to be open to in terms of how we build trust in the communities we work in down the road.

How do you measure or evaluate your impact in a community?

Elizabeth: It's a challenge to measure the impact of imparting identity. It's one of the main issues surrounding Black Lives Matter—it's about having a right to the city, having a right to protest, a right to speak. How do you measure a community's right to have an identity and a voice in the way their community moves forward? How is design culture going to support that? With our Storefronts LA project, we looked at increased foot traffic, increased sales, but the challenge with these public-realm projects is that the issues were more systemic than we could address. Also, funding is not available for us to conduct a post-occupancy study. In retrospect, I'm embarrassed that we had a design-based nonprofit, because—and this is indicative of an issue that I've been talking about in lectures—positioning the designer and the architect at the center of the conversation is problematic. That being said, it takes a lot of effort to truly be a part of the conversation from the beginning, as a problem-solving team member working in community development. Otherwise, design culture has taught an architect to solve things superficially that are quite systematic and intense from a very pragmatic point of view. It takes a lot of resilience on your part as a designer to be engaged and let others lead while also being explicit about what you're going to contribute as a team member. For all the talking we do, architects are not in the habit of being explicit enough about the value of our contributions that are translating or being translated into design purchase. We need to do better to communicate our value to others.

Fig. 67

Fig. 68

LAMAS: Wei-Han Vivian Lee and James Macgillivray

What does it mean to practice architecture?

Wei-Han Vivian Lee: It is important to us that to practice architecture is to navigate between our experimental interests, be considerate of our clients' desires, be empathetic to the trades that have to build our designs, and be conscious of materials and detailing choices so that we are responsible stewards of the environment.

We see a strong relationship between your practice, research, and teaching. How do you work across these three areas, and how do they benefit each other?

James Macgillivray: There is an economic relationship between practicing and teaching. I think people who teach and practice are more willing to take risks with competitions and even with private clients. You can present things that are more conceptual because you always know that it's not the only job. It's important to point out that this is a condition from which many of the practices you are interviewing benefit. It also creates opportunities to apply our academic research in our professional work from time to time, effectively allowing us to transcend simply providing a service. We can test design concepts in a client-based situation, and if they don't land, they can be offloaded to our academic research. For example, at the beginning of Townships Farmhouse, the client was very interested in agricultural buildings—farmhouses and barns. So initially we had an academic response. We looked at the history of those building types and researched how they worked. Whether we apply that research is separate from the value the research has for us in an academic context.

Vivian: It's also important to note that these three areas don't always overlap. We're always doing research, and we try to inject that research into our professional projects as much as possible. But practice is more often the outlier. There's a clearer alliance between our design research and the work our students produce in classes we teach.

James: Beyond practice, research, and teaching are our hobbies. Sometimes our hobbies inform these other three areas.

Along those lines, both of you have different interests and backgrounds. Vivian, you have a background in painting, and James, you're interested in film. How are these hobbies and your unique backgrounds folded into your practice?

Vivian: I studied painting as an undergrad. My undergraduate thesis used painting as a medium to explore methods of perspective construction in architectural representation. As projects come to us, there's a constellation of maybe four or five things we are interested in and looking to incorporate, whether it's film, representation, or any number of other interests. To be honest, I'm not sure we even have a game plan when we start working on a project. Sometimes it's liberating to know that we don't have to force certain interests or aesthetic ambitions into each project. We let the defining features of each project emerge naturally and over time.

James: Regarding my background, I did two theses on film. One was at the undergraduate level, at Princeton, where I studied under P. Adams Sitney and Alessandra Ponte. Then I did another film thesis at Harvard, with Preston Scott Cohen. Since then, I've been writing academic research papers on film—not "operative criticism," but film history, film criticism, writing on film technique. I also completed a research and teaching fellowship at the University of Michigan that featured film as a primary topic of interest. At that point, after I got it out of my system, we did a bunch of studios that dealt with optical or "op" art and architecture. Op art was a way to address film as a method of engaging optical aspects of architecture… We were interested in exploring how architecture produces different effects as you walk around it, rather than simply look at it. This particular interest has found its way into more than a few of our projects, but mostly it's something that occupies my time in the background, something that we do in our spare time. We recently traveled to Greece to go to a film festival in the middle of the Peloponnese…

Vivian: James also makes films… weird, experimental films that are actually now mostly family films.

James: Yes, I do make films, but they don't screen anywhere.

Vivian: He's being modest because he just showed in the Telluride Experimental Film Festival… I just wanted to voice one kind of practice where not everything ties up neatly in our orbit of interest.

James: That reminds me of a show we've been watching recently. In *Terrace House,* this Japanese reality TV show, there's a character, Shohei, who insists that he's going to be equally good at every single thing he does. He's a carpenter, an actor, a chef… and it drives the other members of the house crazy. They can't deal with the fact that he wants to do several different things at the same time. Sometimes we're like that character on *Terrace House,* which is not necessarily a good model to follow. To Vivian's point about an intentional lack of overwhelming coherence across our work, either by circumstance or because of our personalities, the capital-P "Project" is not something that we were interested in pursuing. We tried, but every time we did a new rendering, we were interested in testing a different rendering style. We're comfortable with a consistently evolving aesthetic and set of interests.

Why did you decide to start your own firm? Was it an ambition, or was it born out of necessity, or something else?

Vivian: After graduate school, we both thought we would work our way up in an office and maybe become partner at whichever firms we were at. We started working together in 2008, and the recession did affect us. I actually quit my job at SHoP because I started another firm with two female colleagues of mine. We had a lot of work in Williamsburg. This firm lasted for six or eight months, and then the recession hit—and that was the end of most of our commissioned projects. Around this time, Monica Ponce de Leon became dean at the University of Michigan, and she was looking to hire new lecturers. Fortunately, I received an eight-month teaching contract at the University of Michigan, thinking that I would move back to New York immediately afterward. James continued working at Peter Gluck and Partners, in New York, through all of this. But long story short, the eight-month teaching contract gradually evolved into a tenure-track position. What I realized was that when you begin teaching, you can essentially be a graduate student again. You can initiate your own projects and start thinking about architecture from other vantage points that are not solely practice-based. The practice was, in part, born out of this realization.

You are very experimental with tools of production. For example, the food cart for the Stop Night Market experiments with a marble texture, where you mixed liquids to achieve a marbling effect. In other projects, you've experimented with hydrographics and thatching. What is the inspiration or idea behind these handcrafted production techniques? How do they help you during the design process?

Vivian: We've always been interested in things that are indeterminate or messy, where one can't quite figure out the exact processes executed to accomplish the overall assembly. Having come from SHoP, I felt pretty versed in digital fabrication and thinking about the assembly of parts. When I started teaching, I was interested in revisiting vernacular oral traditions through the new lens of contemporary technology. I was very interested in materials reacting to control imposed from an external source.

James: When we started working with hydrographics, it was the first indication to us that the digital could be something that was not smooth and could have something in common with things like marbling and other processes that were indeterminate. Some of this was a reaction against the version of "digital" that

Fig. 69

we came up with. We were in school during the first wave of digital technology being applied and mastered in practice. But there was no way into that digital work, because it was so smooth. It evaded engagement by being completely worked out and completely seamless. We wanted something that was a little bit broken and appeared to have cracks in it.

Vivian: While working at LTL and SHoP, I contributed to installation designs that were the assembly of many parts. The infinitely unique components in the digital environment simply made for an increasingly complex process of physical assembly. So, expediency is another thing that was interesting about traditional crafts. As much as they're indeterminate, they're messy and fast. There's a relationship to labor that seems more interactive, rather than demanding the human laborer act like a super-precise, fast robot.

Do you think that having a child influences your design approach?

James: Our son was born in 2012 when we were doing Townships Farmhouse, so in the first two weeks of his life, it was a very good sleeping schedule to pull all-nighters and make models while we were up with him anyway.

Vivian: You think your kid is so brilliant, usually. So I think my kid is super brilliant. He has good ideas about competitions. But I think all kids do, they're not labored with preconceived ideas yet. But I don't know that we've specifically designed in such a way for children. Since having a kid, I am actually more interested in doing a children's book. I think when you're an architect you're such a generalist, you think you can do something better.

We have learned that the client for Townships Farmhouse is an artist who paints the landscape around the site. Did her interests affect the concept and design of the house?

Vivian: The client is an artist, and her husband studied agriculture and is a farmer. She's also been collecting work produced by emerging Canadian artists. That commission was in part related to their interest in fostering young talent.

Fig. 70

Fig. 71

Fig. 72

James: The working relationship with the client was very, very good. It was an unorthodox sequence of design in relation to how a project would typically develop. We went all-in on 100-percent schematic design for two schemes, which we developed to a significant degree of specification. It's much more than what we would do in schematic design now. Each scheme was represented through many drawings and a quarter-scale model. Through conversation around these two schemes we arrived at the configuration that was eventually built.

Vivian: The reason there are two schemes is that she was very interested in a design that related to the context. The brief called for design of either a farmhouse or a barn, two types of buildings that are very common in that area. Each scheme is our take on the barn or the farmhouse, both of which we conceptually reinvented. The barn scheme was built. We uncovered an old courtyard barn type and repurposed its form as a view-framing device.

Did you face any significant difficulties during the design or construction process of the project?

James: In Quebec, there's an interesting situation where in the middle of summer, at the peak of any kind of ability to build, they have a two-week construction holiday and all work seizes. Even most engineering and architectural firms take those two weeks off. So, they found a way to be more productive in winter and remain unburdened by weather.

Vivian: The project had a unique schedule. We were doing design work in Revit over the course of almost two and a half years. When it came time to build, we really understood every aspect of construction in great detail. The house had to be wheelchair accessible, and even the foundation was cast to make sure that all the different depths of finishes were completely flush. Everything was fully resolved prior to construction. The contractors were very helpful throughout the process, and we had a very good working relationship with them, in part because we had such a complete drawing set and a long time to discuss everything. Nowadays, we're involved in a lot of projects that people want fast-tracked, and they don't want to decide on a contractor until after the bid process. In Townships Farmhouse, collaborating with the contractor early in the process made it easier for us to draw the project exactly as it would be built.

How have recent global events related to social justice and public health affected your approach to practice?

Vivian: On the topic of public health, Canada has been quite strict about quarantine, and Toronto has been on lockdown on and off. While there are a lot of difficulties to working remotely, we also realize that quite a lot can be accomplished with a flexible schedule. We hope to apply this knowledge to have more flexible hours for our employees and focus a bit more on the importance on the other aspects of life, such as family and health. Since we both teach, the concern for social justice has been extremely formative, in the past year but also before. Diversity, equity, and inclusion are so essential to how we address the subject of architecture and how it is relevant to our students. We're constantly trying to reevaluate how we reflect and address those issues.

James: On the practice side, most of our projects are based on the goals of the client, *and* we mostly do single-family residential, so there is less opportunity to address those issues. But this has prompted us to reevaluate how we acquire projects and, in the future, to take a more critical approach to serving a larger, more diverse group of end users. Whether this takes the shape of pursuing more RFPs or looking at nonprofit business models we haven't settled on yet, but the direction is there.

What has been the most rewarding aspect of practicing architecture?

Vivian: There is satisfaction in the relationships we have with our employees. They bring a lot of ideas to every design decision, which really enhances the overall project. It is very rewarding to have the privilege of having employees.

MAIO: Anna Puigjaner

MAIO has four partners. How and when did the four of you come together to begin the practice?

Anna Puigjaner: We started practicing together in 2012, following the social crisis in Spain in 2011. At that moment, we felt the need to involve ourselves in that situation as designers. The four of us shared interests and ambitions and wanted to create a space for discussion and designing together. The crisis encouraged us to open a space not only for us to practice together, but also to collaborate with other colleagues and friends in fields related to architecture—graphic design, landscape architecture, and engineering, to name a few. We thought that situation was going to be temporary, but it ended up being quite productive and defined a lot of what we do today. We're a family in that space…we all learn a lot from each other.

How do your previous academic, personal, and professional experiences influence your approach to practice today?

I believe that every generation responds to the previous one. Through our work, we are responding to the previous generation of architects in Spain. Where we studied, in Barcelona, there were many limitations. For instance, color was forbidden! So for us, it was necessary to break through some of the limitations imposed on us when we were students. Also, the relation between theory and practice was lost after the Olympic Games in Barcelona in 1992, because of all the practices were so busy with commissioned work… suddenly, the theoretical side was lost. Since the beginning, we have aimed to combine writing, theory, and practice, partially as a response to the time that came before us, which was mostly service-based practice and didn't involve much criticality and speculation, but also as a response to the social crisis we were living in.

Do issues outside of traditional boundaries of the discipline of architecture influence your work?

When the economic crisis hit Spain in 2008, most of the architects we knew left to work abroad. We stayed, and we started gathering with artists and designers. We were deeply influenced by the underground practices that were able to survive during those years. For instance, we began designing many things other than buildings—art objects, temporary installations, pavilions. It was an exercise that was super necessary for us to push the discipline beyond its boundaries. This moment also influenced my approach to teaching. I was encouraging my students to read philosophy rather than architecture. I wanted them to engage with contemporary issues rather than historical ones. In a moment of social change, if you don't understand how and why you are living, you cannot meaningfully respond through design.

What about your personal interests—how do they influence the work?

Well, from the beginning of my time in school, I was interested in housing, partly because I was really uncomfortable with how housing—collective housing, and not only public, but also private housing—was approached in Spain. I built up a critical awareness of the production of too many gender-biased and speculative housing projects in Spain. I started to look at cooperative housing from the 1970s that was really popular in Spain and was very successful. At that time, cooperative housing was developed by banks to promote collective living and positive social reform. Meanwhile, in the 2000s, banks lost interest in promoting well-being and engaging social and political action through housing. Housing became a mere financial issue. The notion that housing could be tied to social issues was totally lost. So, that's why I started to look at—and continue to look at—housing from a critical perspective.

Your office is one of the few we're connecting with that is not based in North America. How does being based in Barcelona influence the development and execution of your projects?

Now that I spend a lot of time in the US, I understand that problems in the US are really different from problems in Spain and throughout Europe. So we are still a local practice, but we have to be aware of the global market in order to know how to navigate and grow. Compared to the US, in Europe there are mostly small practices, which provide quite a richness in the landscape. The economic weight of running a small practice in the US seems like quite a lot to carry. So, in the US, there are far more large firms, and developers have much more power. Despite the challenges, I'm always encouraging students and young architects in the US to find cracks in the system, to be proactive in finding ways to practice that don't rely on partnering with corporate offices or waiting for developers to call and ask for your services.

Do you intentionally pursue a particular aesthetic sensibility across projects, or do the aesthetics of your projects emerge naturally relative to context and parameters?

That's a tough question! The aesthetics of our projects evolve as we evolve as an office. The members of MAIO are quite diverse. We have different interests and different backgrounds. So our aesthetic predilections are different as well. That's positive. The outcomes that we achieve in our projects are the result of long conversations and debates among us. For us, it's important to take time to evaluate the status and evolution of cultural constructions and aesthetics, which are always changing. If we do not also evolve, our identity will become fixed and we will be left behind.

We have a question about 110 Rooms. We know that the plan organization is inspired by an apartment type that is common in the the Eixample neighborhood, in Barcelona. How does historical precedent factor into your projects? What is the role of context in 110 Rooms?

This question is a bit related to the previous one, because architecture is stuck in between competing demands. Architecture has to be timeless because buildings last for decades or even centuries. At the same time, architecture has to be rooted in contemporary context. Because of this, we always look at the context of our projects and the history of the context as a starting point. In 110 Rooms, the floor plan is a reenactment of the original nineteenth-century housing type that defined the neighborhood, in which rooms were similar in size and allowed programmatic change through time. Regarding the plan organization… We also acknowledged that the conditions that we have today mirror those in the 1970s. Concepts of flexibility were on the table and really important at the time. But the way we understand flexibility today is very different from then. Our daily life changes slowly—our needs might change from one year to another, or every five years, but they don't change from one day to another. We pursued flexibility not by means of moving elements, as designers did in the 1970s, but rather in the relationship between fixed space and assigned activity. In 110 Rooms, we are making a claim that housing should be much more generic and should lack preset hierarchy in order to avoid social biases and welcome all kind of social structures. Nowadays, most of our market is defined for the prototypical heteropatriarchal family of two parents and one or two children. Meanwhile, our society is much more diverse. So, the concept of flexibility that we're dealing with is related as much to use and activity as it is to space.

What types of projects would you like to work on in the future?

It's always good to have a five-year plan! Once a year, all of us meet to discuss the next five years. We know that every decision that we make will influence the future. So, if you decide to do one project or another, it's likely going to influence what comes next. We hope to keep on working on social justice, on gender justice. Also, one thing we always agree on is to maintain

Fig. 73

Fig. 74

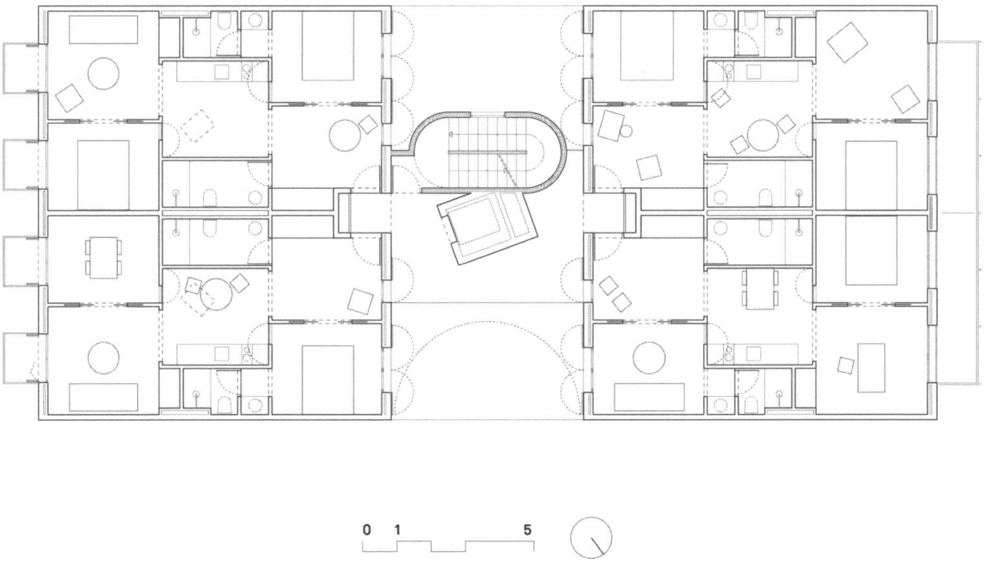

Fig. 75

a balance of big projects and small projects, super-practical projects and super-conceptual projects. This is our ideal situation because the most conceptual and smallest projects usually influence the large ones. I'm saying this because they have different temporalities. An installation might take three or four months, but a building takes a minimum of three years to complete. So, the smaller, short-term projects provide us with opportunities to experiment with ideas that might influence the large, long-term projects.

What has been the most rewarding moment of your professional career?

The most rewarding moments are when you witness the positive impact architecture can have on society and on individuals. From their perspective, it's not something that comes immediately, so you have to be patient. But when you meet a former client and they share how much their life has changed for the better as a result of living in a space you designed, it's very rewarding. It seems obvious, but good architecture is really important in order to make everyone happier. Most of our society is not aware of that. We've been fortunate to have opportunities to create spaces for people to live in. And some have shared with us how they've been deeply transformed by space we designed. That's such an extremely nice compliment to receive.

Fig. 76

MALL: Jennifer Bonner

What does it mean to practice architecture?

Jennifer Bonner: Architecture is a total thrill and lifestyle. I am someone who nerds out on ideas all of the time. In this sense, I feel very fortunate that I have discovered a way of practicing within the discipline that is flexible and malleable—meaning I am able to think about nonarchitectural things found in pop culture, like sandwiches or food photography, as conceptual material, while at the same time obsessing over real materials, like stucco or cross-laminated timber. In my worldview, anything goes. Developing both technical and aesthetic positions that are constantly being refreshed is the way I practice architecture at MALL. As another way of thinking about your question, I love to think about the word "practice" as a verb because it explains very succinctly what we do: we practice, practice, and practice—rehearsing architecture repeatedly over several spans of time and in a range of circumstances. Friends and mentors of mine, Mack Scogin and Merrill Elam, always say something like, "The moment you approach architecture without a kind of naivete, you have lost it." I interpret their provocation to mean there is an art to "practicing" architecture, which includes equal doses persistent, relentless inquiry and curiosity.

Can you tell us how MALL began, and more generally about your path from graduate school at Harvard to today?

I finished at the Harvard Graduate School of Design in 2009, during an untimely moment, just at the start of the financial crisis. I had already worked in London for Foster + Partners and David Chipperfield Architects, but wanted to work for another architect before starting my own practice. Unfortunately, there were no job openings anywhere, so I applied to teach at various schools. Georgia Tech offered me an adjunct position for a semester. The question then became, "How do you start teaching and build a practice at the same time?" This marked the beginning of what MALL looks like today, with one foot in practice and one foot in academia. During the recession, my work was directly linked to design and research questions and the majority of the projects were speculative ideas installed in galleries or within the institutions where I was teaching.

Initially, I founded Studio Bonner with full intentions of getting licensed and using the word "architect" in the name of my firm, but that never happened. After practicing for five years in Atlanta and Los Angeles, I moved to Cambridge to teach at the GSD with an ambition to rethink the identity of my practice. I was interested in the history of using an acronym as the practice name but leaned heavily toward the OMA model—Office for Metropolitan Architecture, which has nothing to do with Rem Koolhaas's name—over names such as SOM. MALL is acronym that is flexible and changes from project to project. There have been a few different variations—Mass Architectural Loopty Loops; Maximum Angles, Little Lines. Beyond the name, the practice has been running for about ten years now. The first five years were hard work, figuring out my architectural interests by setting up a series of conceptual projects, while the last five have been really enjoyable and productive, and have included building those ideas.

What is it like to run an office by yourself?

During my first three years in practice, I partnered with Christian Stayner, an architect in Los Angeles. It was very useful to gain momentum together, especially in the beginning of our careers. Now we are working independently and developing very different types of projects. That partnership and pursuing public art projects was one way of coping with the recession. Today, MALL is what I call a "one-woman band," and I hire employees on a project-by-project basis. It is liberating to run an office on my own and to define what that looks like with fluid collaborators.

You are a mother, a sole-practitioner, a curator, a writer, and associate professor and director of the MArch II program at Harvard. How do you manage to stay afloat, and how do you bring together all of these different identities? In particular, do you reflect often on your identity as a female architect?

I won a Progressive Architecture honorable mention award in 2019. Apart from one other firm, eight other winners were male, and it got me thinking about the importance of being a female solo practitioner. I also asked myself, "Why aren't there more women winning these awards?" and whether I should be teaching less and practicing more. At the same time, I wondered how I could devote hours to teaching and administrative roles while also making highly creative work. Part of the magic at MALL is the ability to remain small and to be highly selective about the projects I take on. Most projects begin with a research question, not an inquiry from a client. In the case of the P/A Award, the project began years ago as a body of conceptual work titled Best Sandwiches. Later, we pitched it to several developers as a mid-rise tower, Office Stack. To answer your question about how I balance all of these roles, after a decade of being in the thick of it all... I couldn't imagine it any other way.

We know that you're really interested in pop culture and encourage your students to look outside of the discipline for ideas about representation. Can you talk a bit about your sources of inspiration and how you incorporate them into practice and teaching?

Yes, I am very inspired by popular culture and tendencies found in art. I often wonder, "Can we push architecture in new directions today?" I believe

Fig. 77

Fig. 78

it's possible. For example, when selecting materials for Haus Gables, I was looking at contemporary artists like Mary Corse and Barbara Kasten and traditions found in the American South, not references from the discipline of architecture.

From a geographic standpoint, I'm constantly moving—seemingly every three years over the past two decades. I'm always in a different city, which creates a persistent curiosity that encourages me to carefully observe the world around me. I also believe that Instagram is very useful for this, because now I have access to what others are observing in the world even if I'm sitting in a basement studio space in Cambridge.

Regarding teaching, I just started a new course at Harvard called "Representation First (!!!), Then Architecture." We're not looking at architectural representation. We're looking at art practice, popular culture, and material found in the everyday as a way to encourage inspiration from places other than within our own discipline. We're looking at cake-decorating techniques from the eighteenth century that include intricate piping from French masters, but also methods found in America, with the use of marzipan in the 1950s. Other things we obsess over in that course: food photography, 1980s bubble letters, or the origins of clip art. Perhaps these cultural eccentricities can offer architectural design and representation something new, or at least unexpected.

When you share your work, have you found that these non-architectural influences and modes of representation resonate with a broader audience? Do you alter your presentations relative to your audience?

It's important to know your audience, but I don't think we have to make such a strong distinction between academic audiences and the general public. I'm interested in using devices that already have a broad appeal—like the image of a gable or the medium of a guidebook—to draw people in, to educate them by making them feel included in a discussion about architecture. For example, in the interior of Haus Gables, I wanted to select a material palette that linked the house to local cultures in Atlanta. The soft white wood used in the primary structure of the house draws associations with Scandinavian architecture. But I was building a house in Atlanta, in Goodie Mob's "Dirty South." It couldn't have been a Scandinavian house. I put pressure on myself to create environments on the interior that resonate with Atlanta's aesthetic culture. This is where the faux finishing comes in. There is a tradition of faux finishing, where southerners could not afford precious materials, like Italian marble, and instead painted them onto domestic surfaces. To answer your question about audience…is it locals who rent the house out for amateur photoshoots with big ambitions to "fake it until you make it," or the fan base of the Atlanta rapper Mulatto, who shot her video for the song "Longway" there, or is it architectural academia all along? Perhaps it's all of them.

Beyond the faux finishes, Haus Gables has a very playful array of colors, patterns, shapes, and textures on the interior. How did you select these interior finishes? Is it simply a matter of taste, or is there some science behind it?

It may be a bit of playing out taste… You have to start somewhere. But the design of the interior environments was also very intentional and conceptually oriented. There is an idea about combining expensive materials with inexpensive materials, like rubber vinyl you might see in hospitals or fake wood vinyl from Home Depot. The expensive materials elevate the inexpensive ones. So, there is an economic argument to make here, too. Overall, each room took on a unique identity relative to the material selections. To reinforce difference, transitioning between rooms and around corners became important moments. When I received the final architectural photographs of the house, I saw something that I did not anticipate. All of the colors tend to flatten space. It reminds me of a trend in contemporary fashion, color blocking, where bright yellow, pink, and mint green become a color block. In one fifty-five-foot-long view through the house, you can see similarities to color blocking in fashion. The bedroom, dining room, and kitchen start to look like a Marni sweater.

Given that you've thought so much about the color and the overall visual experience of the interior of Haus Gables, why is the exterior white?

The cross-laminated timber that is exposed on the interior is monochromatic. As I mentioned earlier, it's a soft white wood. And I knew that the finishes should be kind of daring or bold, to create an

Fig. 79

Fig. 80

Fig. 81

environment that the soft white wood could not create alone. The idea for the exterior in white was really because of Domestic Hats, a project that served as the conceptual precursor to Haus Gables. I was drawn to the idea that Haus Gables is a full-scale model, almost a replica of one of the massing models I created for Domestic Hats. So white, as a color, links the built house to the white-foam architectural massing model. The exterior of the house also has a unique texture. I was inspired by John Chase's Glitter Stucco & Dumpster Diving. In that book, Chase writes about how ordinary houses in Los Angeles finished with stucco are often additionally finished by the owner with glitter, to make the house sparkle—a kind of upgrade. The glitter in Haus Gables is a reference to this phenomenon in Los Angeles. I was also inspired by Mary Corse, who painted with glass beads, the same glass beads that are used by the Department of Transportation in road striping. Chase's Glitter Stucco and Corse's reflective beads become a "dash finish" in the facade of Haus Gables. Maybe it's a house with way too many ideas, but it was my first building at MALL—I couldn't help myself!

We recently learned that Haus Gables had no client. How did this affect the design, and what was it like to design a house without a client?

I have a bunch of family members—aunts, uncles, sister, mom, dad—but none of them have asked me to design a house, and it's fair to say that they don't see the value in architecture. And then there's me… I've invested twenty years of my life in architecture. As you may know, many architects receive their first commissions from a family member. This was not going to happen for me. We, meaning me and my husband, decided we had to do it ourselves. We bought a piece of land in Atlanta when we were teaching at Georgia Tech and applied for a construction loan. On one hand, there was a lot of freedom. Nobody was presenting demands like where to put the bathroom or how many closets to have. But there was still a budget, and there was tremendous stress associated with taking on the financial risk of such an experimental construction project. For example, the CLT panels were from Austria, and the company required payment in full before they started manufacturing the product. That doesn't totally align with bank financing.

Overall, there were many difficulties as a result of moving forward without a client. Still... it was totally worth it! I believe I was able to achieve several of MALL's architectural ideas faster than if there had been a traditional client involved.

How have recent global events related to social justice and public health affected your approach to practice?

Like most of my colleagues, I was deeply rattled by the most recent racial injustices toward various BIPOC communities within the United States. Germane Barnes and Shawhin Roudbari, the guest editors of Vigilantism, a forthcoming issue of the journal MAS Context, invited me to write an essay about these events. In this text, I connect my observations as a witness to Samuel Mockbee's pedagogy at the Rural Studio while living in rural west Alabama with what might constitute vigilante architecture today. I certainly do not have all of the answers as to how architecture can respond to the vicious murders of Black people in the US, but I do know that we must end racism within our institutions, practices, and individual selves. I am committed to changing the way we have valued architectural practice as a white, male-dominated profession for centuries.

What has been the most rewarding moment in your practice thus far?

That's an easy question for me to answer—completing Haus Gables. To build something after talking about it for years and years... was very liberating and very rewarding. Despite the struggle to get it built, I wouldn't change a thing.

New Affiliates: Ivi Diamantopoulou and Jaffer Kolb

You met in graduate school at Princeton. How did you come together to start an office? Was it something that you planned for some time, or did it happen rather quickly?

Ivi Diamantopoulou: It was quite organic for us. We started very informally. There was a project we started looking at together while working for other offices. And it made sense: working together was fun and interesting and exciting, and we wanted to keep doing it. We convinced ourselves that if the infrastructure was there, everything would work out. We had no clients, but we had insurance! It's been about three years now, and it's somehow worked out.

Jaffer Kolb: Part of it was working through an inquiry into the formula of how practice works. For us, it was really about coming together as two people who are very different. Ivi had a much stronger background in practice, and I came more from curating, writing, and working on installations. We wanted to use these differences to test architecture as a variable condition that we could play around with using the small office model to combine teaching, practicing, writing, and research. But instead of trying to do it all at once, we use every opportunity to trial various combinations of our skills.

What does it mean to practice architecture?

Jaffer: We're drawn to architecture's expansiveness—that is, the openness of architecture's possibilities. For us, practice can mean designing a building, developing a program, or collaborating with an artist. It can also mean advocacy, invention, curation, and writing. In other words, it can take many forms. But ultimately, it involves some form of engagement: a way of relating, or of communicating. We never shy away from architecture's implications as a service industry, but at the same time, we never accept practice as totally determined or fixed.

Ivi: We started our office with a desire to practice, to build, to be in the real world and participate in larger networks of design and construction in New York City and beyond. We were eager to spend time at dusty construction sites, take on bureaucracy of many kinds, and think through real clients' needs and desires. Not every day is glamorous, but we find it all fun and full of potential. And as Jaffer said, during this all we have found ourselves inclined to take the profession on as a similar kind of project itself.

From residential work to installations to warehouse conversions, your portfolio is full of very diverse projects. Do you have a unique approach to each project type?

Jaffer: We really like working on different kinds of projects. Within each project, we are less concerned with type than we are with a general approach to design. We've designed a lot of exhibitions and residential spaces. The projects are unique, but it's not necessarily because they have different programs or are different types. It's more because we bring different interests at the beginning of each project. We like those strange hybrids, which we seek out regardless of the project.

Ivi: But there are differences between the exhibition projects and the residential projects. They each have very different timelines and budgets, and different degrees of openness to experimentation. For example, if we want to test a particular material application, we can do that in an institutional context more easily, because those projects are often fast and temporary. And then we can use that material again in a project that is commercial or residential, where we generally have less room to take risks and experiment. The two different speeds at which projects get developed generate slightly different approaches and opportunities.

You both teach, as well. How do you balance your time between teaching and practice? Do you view one role as primary? Who do you consider your primary audience?

Jaffer: These are good questions. We're really interested in academia and are grateful for opportunities to teach and be included in academic events like this interview series. We both teach, but teaching is secondary to our practice. For now, neither of us is looking for a full-time job at a university. Practice comes before teaching, at least while we're figuring out how to run the office. Hopefully, over time we can refocus our attention back and forth between the two, because we find the dialogue productive.

Ivi: We come after a generation of architects who somehow managed to juggle everything at once—not only teaching and practice, but also academic administration, curation, experimental work, writing… It seemed admirable, but also overwhelming to us. We'd like to start with practice. We are invested in making it work while maintaining a loose relationship to academia. We see it as a space where we can observe, grow, develop expertise.

Jaffer: And to answer your question about what audience we're catering to or speaking to—on the one hand, we want to be recognized within our peer group and in academia, but most of our work tends to have an element of public engagement. Right now, we're putting a lot of our energy into communicating with the city and working through formats that have broader audiences. It's very difficult to make something interesting to the discipline of architecture and architects specifically while also communicating broader principles to a larger audience. When we do our best, we're doing both.

Given your interest in construction- and demolition-material waste and reuse, do you think about the second life or the material life cycle of projects while you're designing them?

Ivi: Absolutely. This is something that we have been looking at very closely, especially with exhibition design. It's only through our ongoing involvement with these types of projects that we're able to look closely and internalize such issues before we begin to address them through design. We recently did a show on Leonard Cohen for the Jewish Museum in New York, and at the same time we were collaborating with the Department of Sanitation to understand museum waste. From the outset, we looked for materials that could be taken apart and reused after the show was over. This changed both the kinds of finishes we were using and how we detailed their installation. We made sure that everything resisted wear and was easily removable. Following the exhibition, most of those materials were donated for new uses all around New York City. I'm super excited about that!

Jaffer: Our reuse projects are in this really weird niche, where we're mostly looking at what architects make and how we produce waste—looking at what we produce that's superfluous or excessive—and treating that as inherited material. But this work is less about responsibility and more about methodology—investigations into local economies and material flows. I don't want to pretend that we're experts in reuse. We use these projects to think about detailing and assembly, but also to think about how architecture operates as a narrative within the city. In this sense, the second life might intersect with things like form or program as a means of perpetual reinvention.

We'd like to ask a few questions about the Tunbridge Winter Cabin, in Vermont. Did your experience in exhibition design influence the design of this house?

Jaffer: To start, we really wanted to avoid the typical modern cabin design and be strategic about how we used framing and aperture. Those motivations come from exhibition design, where we are thinking through perspective as an immediate visual issue. We were interested in how different events would unfold in a contained space, as a time-based medium. We coupled

Fig. 82

Fig. 83

Fig. 84

an idea about how one moves in a domestic environment with an idea about how to organize an exhibition relative to framed views and orientation. We were thinking a lot about landscape painting—not just about the content of the image, but about arranging landscape paintings, which become interior elevations.

We read that the project was designed and constructed very quickly. Did the pace of the project limit your ability to explore different ideas? What was your relationship with the client throughout the process?

Jaffer: It was very fast. It was also very collaborative. Sitting together with our client, we would literally project a Rhino model on a wall and rotate it around to ensure that there was no room for misinterpretation. Issues could be addressed and problems could be solved together in real time. We did not follow the typical model of preparing polished presentations, receiving feedback, and spending a week making revisions just to present again. How we work is honestly a bit messy and impromptu. We're more interested in what we can learn through collaboration with contractors, clients, and even with living artists in our exhibition projects. We understand working with others as a chance to express something about a collective, even if just for a moment. We're not here to push an agenda.

Ivi: Working on the house was very fast, informal, and conversational. We didn't have the luxury to study every design detail or to iterate through thousands of options. We were lucky to work with a contractor who was a great communicator. We often joked that he was like a 3D printer—we would sketch something on-site, and then a day later it would be built. The process was easygoing and laid-back: let's do it this way, let's try this other thing, let's improvise. It's a big part of how our practice was formed, in terms of our early experiences.

Can you give an example of the way the collaboration played out?

Jaffer: We didn't go in with a seventy-page construction document set and ask the contractor to execute our drawings. We knew the form of the cabin and we had an idea about what the interior and exterior elevations would look like. It's not that we came with nothing, but we were trying to draw from his expertise as someone who's been working in Vermont his entire life. We had some ideas of how we wanted the project to look and how interior spaces would relate to one another, but we needed guidance from a local expert, especially when it came to details and environmental issues. One example was with the baseboards. We kept resisting certain tolerances that he insisted on given Vermont's extreme temperatures, but in the end, we followed his recommendation. He did it as a custom inset baseboard, though. While we listened, we also never wanted to go with an easy default.

Ivi: Working with him, we were able to strike a balance between an exquisitely designed house where every detail and material transition and connection is considered and precious and a house that is durable and casual and provides a sense of comfort. It's kind of funny for us to realize that with the Vermont project, we established a standard for our practice where we leave certain things deliberately incomplete. We have a client right now—a graphic designer—we leaned on to help lay out a pattern on a large custom millwork element of his home. We had a conversation where we told him, "You know, you do this for a living—you should just do this. We should do this together." This is not a matter of us knowing better than anyone else.

Did your interest in material life-cycles, waste, and reuse inform the design of the cabin?

Ivi: Yes, definitely. There's a material sensibility in the cabin. For example, the baseboard material is all recycled plastic. That plastic comes in large sheets, so we were compelled to make room in the design to retrofit all off-cuts—you'll see it pop up between windowsills and panel frames to avoid excess waste. Also, we worked to incorporate passive strategies that will enable the house to climate-control itself through the winter, even going back to the windows being smaller framing devices instead of giant picture planes. It's a bit introverted, a bit closed.

Jaffer: I would say… unfortunately, not as much as it should have. For example, there was nothing on the land when we got there. In order to make a half-mile driveway, we had to cut down a lot of trees—which is not a huge deal, because there are a billion trees in Vermont. We also had to blow up a lot of ledge, but that ledge became the front porch and paving. The trees have all been milled and that wood is going to be used on the main house structure. There is a sense that everything that gets destroyed on the land to clear space for the house gets reused in the house. It's almost a semi-enclosed material economy. But I wouldn't take credit for that. That came from the contractors and landscapers.

Beyond considering the environmental impact of your work at a broader scale, how have recent global events related to social justice and public health affected your approach to practice?

Jaffer: We think often about expertise—what we know, but more importantly and more often, what we don't. Recent events have made us particularly aware of, and sensitive to, the need to make space for others to share their knowledge and their expertise—whatever that may be, and whether formed through lived experience or professional practice. As architects we orchestrate and coordinate—material flows, client desires, possible programs—and we do our best work when we're open enough to accommodate the perspectives and views of others around us. This has always been really important to how we work, and has only become more so in light of the events of 2020—a year that taught us how much we don't know and how to adjust our practice to accommodate new forms of knowledge in real time.

Ivi: On the public-health front, much of what has been going on is counter to the work we've been doing. A lot of our community-geared work in the city's gardens, for example, is really possible only through real-time collaboration in groups. At the same time, outdoor public space that is equitable and accessible does feel more important than ever right now. So…let's see. We hope to figure it out!

Where do you see yourselves in ten years? Do you hope to continue to work on smaller projects, or would you like to evolve into a practice that can take on bigger projects?

Ivi: I don't even know if the two of us are on the same page about this, but I can tell you what I hope for. I imagine that these two worlds—institutional and private, temporary and permanent—might begin to move closer to one another. I'd love to think that our ongoing affiliation with the art world and our increasing expertise in design and construction could enable us to work on projects that are larger and maybe more permanent.

Jaffer: Ten years is a long time from now! The easier answer is for the next few years. Originally, I had always imagined that we would keep growing. More recently, I'm resisting the desire to grow. We are still exploring how to create an interesting form of practice. If you'd asked us this question two years ago, I would have said that in ten years, we're going to be forty-five people and we're going to have large commissions. After being in this for a couple of years, I actually want to slow down and invest more time and energy into figuring out how we can do better work before we start getting more work.

What has been the most rewarding moment as a practice thus far?

Ivi: Not quitting on ourselves! Every single day we decide to not apply to work for a corporate office is very rewarding.

Jaffer: I'm going to give an earnest answer: I think this moment is one of the most rewarding. I'm being very sincere. When I woke up this morning, I was thinking about how meaningful it is that our work can sustain the interest of a class, that it can sustain a close read or prolonged attention. It's incredibly gratifying!

Fig. 85

Oana Stănescu

What does it mean to practice architecture?

Oana Stănescu: When you're young and you get projects, you just start doing things organically. If you're lucky, this continues, and you eventually have an office with other people involved. There comes a point when you have to pause and ask yourself, "What am I actually doing?" After five or ten years of practice, you also start wanting different things and you're less excited to maintain a status quo. Recently I've been asking myself that question over and over and over again. I try not to define the practice of architecture for myself, and I rarely use the word architecture, for that matter. I am an architect and I have the skill set of an architect. However, for me, joy or reward comes from doing many other things that don't necessarily materialize as buildings. I've been thinking more about how the skill set that I have can be applied to many different disciplines, and I've removed myself from the specificity of architecture—at least mentally. That being said, I know for a fact that making architecture is also the thing I excel at.

We watched the video you sent to us of Benedict Cumberbatch reading the letter from Sol LeWitt to Eva Hesse, and felt that his message was very powerful and relevant to young architects with regard to the notion of "just doing." How do you engage in "just doing?"

As architects, we have a lot to learn from artists and their approach of just doing things, of inventing a practice. Their job is to just do things—not to be asked to do things and respond to something, but to just do things and to really dig in deep to see what they care about. We, however, are trained to wait for someone to ask us to do something, and to respond to requests. That's not that satisfying or a great position to be in, and also not very tenable in 2021. Growing up in Eastern Europe when I did meant that the only secure career options were doctor, economist, or lawyer. When you come from a place like Romania, you're not thinking of becoming a writer or an artist. That's not an option. So, I felt I had to learn the value of writing, of making art, of doing things for oneself, of creative fulfillment, of experimentation and play—of fun, for that matter. There's value in a lot of the things that we do as architects that don't necessarily materialize as buildings. There's value in the creative process; there's value in conversations; there's value in many things that won't be measurable on an x-y graph. We need to value the process of "just doing," which really just means establishing our own set of values, or a measure for how we choose to spend our time.

With respect to building your practice and allowing room for it to evolve, what do your work day and work week typically look like?

After graduating, I began what I call my second education, which was working at a bunch of offices across the world. I did this for a decade—working my ass off, doing the whole twenty-four-seven thing, living far from family, and always moving. I took a lot of joy in it as I went through the machine of just absorbing architecture and was so excited about it and so incredibly dedicated. But one cannot do this forever. Things changed when I started my own office, as well as when I was dealing with my cancer diagnosis. It became crystal clear to me that my work needed to become secondary to my life. It might seem banal. I always learn the obvious the hard way. I've been trying to get better at this. I don't always succeed, but every now and then I find some distance from my work and can appreciate other things. After surgery, I took three months in the woods in Romania, doing next to nothing. What I realized is we never get to do that as adults. Maybe you take a two-week vacation from time to time. By the end of a two-week vacation, you're actually ready for a proper vacation. But this was the first time since high school when I felt like I had space to think, where I could just look at the world. I asked myself, "Why don't we do this more often?" It was incredibly liberating. The notion of being in an office for eight hours a day or the idea of having to be somewhere for a specific number of hours is killing me to this day. It's a very infantile reaction to the world. It's a very terrible way of moving through a capitalist society. I don't function well under those terms. All of this is to say that my every day now incorporates my dog, or being in the forest for hours, going for a run, or taking in museums, or doing all sorts of other things in addition to working.

In your piece, "On Breathing," in which you reflected on your cancer diagnosis, you reference Marcel Duchamp, "Oh, I'm a breather. I'm a respirator. Isn't that enough?" Can you share with us a little more about how your experience with cancer has been informative of what you do now?

I'm glad you read that piece, and I'm glad you're asking about it, too, because I've been very open and upfront about the subject, partially because I felt I learned so much in it and it was so momentous. I think it makes many people uncomfortable talking about it, not quite knowing how to breach the topic. First of all, I was very lucky in a way, because it was a brief period of, let's say, three months that I had to be confronted with the issues, have surgery, and then recover. So I didn't undergo years of chemo or anything like that. There were physical issues that came with it, but after surgery I healed rather quickly.

I wouldn't wish it onto anyone, an experience like that. But I also don't remember what I was like before, and I can't imagine my life without that experience at this point. It became part of my DNA, probably in the most literal terms for that matter. You learn so many things and it puts things into a really dramatic perspective. The things that mattered became crystal clear.

Fig. 86

Fig. 87

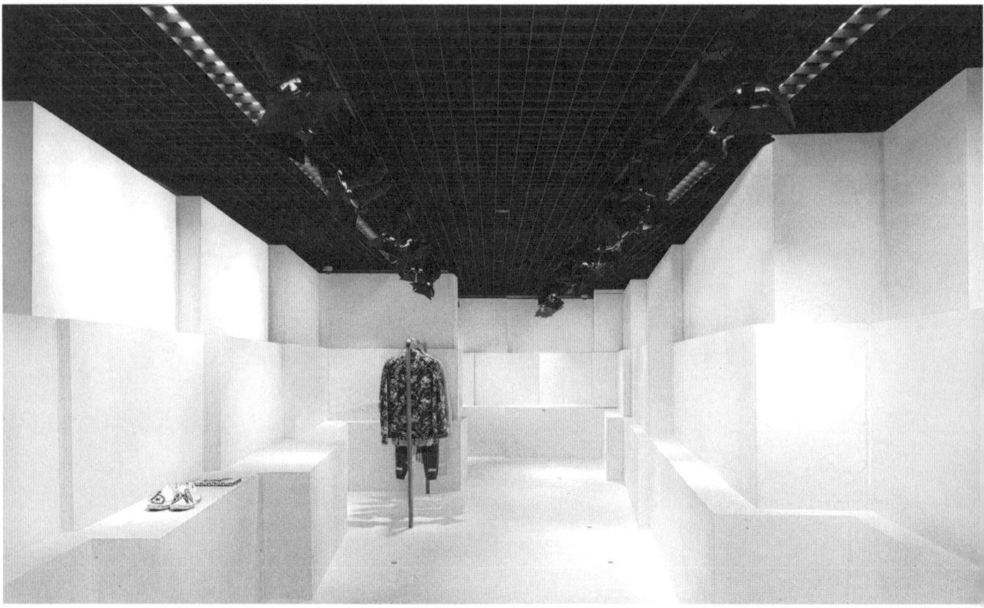

Fig. 88

After my diagnosis, I chose not to go back to work and I chose to take time off. I owed it to myself to move forward, to make something of this experience and to make sure I live the way I want to live. There are layers and layers of input from society, from ourselves, from anxiety, from all these things that keep us from acting on what matters to us, and it is a very unsustainable way of going through life. Really appreciating and honoring one's own work and finding one's own strength outside of the moving pieces around it, provides a certain sense of freedom. That sense of freedom also meant allowing myself to fall on my face. It's so easy to be cynical, to say no and step away, but the possible rewards of allowing yourself to fail, to fall on your face, to embarrass yourself, are so much higher than the potential bruises of an ego.

You've previously talked about how you aim to create work that is generous—in what ways do you feel that your work has given back and engages a more diverse audience who might be typically marginalized by architectural practice?

It's always something that I hope to achieve with my work. I believe that design, at its best, can make people's life easier or better. To me, the whole joy or beauty of a project lies in how people are able to overcome things. I'm interested in the invisible side of architecture, in the invisible things that it creates and enables. The tangible, the physical, is really just in service of the invisible. From an architectural perspective or design perspective, I'm not interested in a very specific language or trying to impose my likes on everyone else. On the contrary, I'm more interested in the different perspectives and the friction between different people. I think the disagreement and the nuance is where the whole beauty of this thing lies. So in that sense, that's why I think, in designing, you have the ability to allow people to use space or engage with space in ways they haven't before.

In the case of the Long House there was a very powerful moment when I met with the clients. They initially had another architect on the project, and they had a really good idea of what they wanted because the constraints were very specific. In their mind, the house was pretty much designed. They didn't see much room to play with because the constraints were so specific, but we were able to put something new on the table that still fulfilled all the requirements, while adding other possibilities. Having that conversation with a client and to see them understand and absorb the power of design, that's always the goal. It's such a powerful moment that brings me so much joy, because then someone starts to understand the potential of architecture, the potential of design, and how it can do more than it needs to.

You've worked with a series of high-profile individuals—Kanye West and Virgil Abloh, for example, and there are many others. How does collaborating with professionals outside the field of architecture influence your work?

I get bored very easily. Working with different professions provides me with opportunities to continuously learn new things. It's such a privilege and such a privileged position to be in. Through these collaborations, I've learned so much about myself, and also the world at large. For example, working with Kanye when he was recording *Yeezus* in Paris . . . I would meet with him at 8 a.m. for architecture, and he would subsequently meet with others throughout the day to discuss other projects. Slowly, throughout the day, the whole thing would merge into music. Seeing his process with the album shed new light on what I do as a designer with my projects. The process of *Yeezus* was quite beautiful. Witnessing that album come together made me understand so much better how I design. I'm reminded of a book by John McPhee called *Draft No. 4: On the Writing Process*. The book is about writing. How he describes writing is really no different than what the design process is for me. He talks about the first sentence always being terrible. But to make a better sentence you must have a sentence. It's all about continuous editing. It's the same way I look at architecture. So, I enjoy collaborations because I'm always learning a lot, finding new ways of making sense of the world. Through reflection, you can learn so much about yourself by seeing yourself reflected in other fields or other peoples' worlds. Ultimately, these collaborations enable me to go in different directions with my own work.

In working in so many different fields, how are you able to establish a coherent and consistent voice for your work while engaging with diverse problems and interests?

I have no concern about establishing a consistent voice or aesthetic for my work. I'm consistently inconsistent! I never take the smart decision [*sighs*].

I'm not taking decisions that are driven by the notion of what one *should* be doing. I came to realize that my definition of success is very different than the standard definition of success. I can make a list of all the smart and safe things that I've avoided doing. Two things that we tend not to question are popularity and profit. A consistent voice is necessary for these two things to exist. Profit is always nice, but if it's the sole driver, that's problematic. It's never something that I pursued just for the sake of it. It's a dangerous game. While it is important to be able to pay rent, it needs to be a collateral and not the endgame in itself. When it comes to popularity, that's something that I think about a lot. I was lucky or privileged to work with some famous, popular characters, and the offices where I've worked were also coincidentally quite high profile. I came to realize that it's a very misleading game. Popularity is fleeting. It also doesn't really take me anywhere I'd want to be in the long run. I've learned to focus less on the exterior perception, less on the superficiality that some of those things come with.

I'm not interested in selling anything… I have nothing to sell. After dissolving Family, I was technically starting on my own and wasn't quite sure where to go. I wasn't eager to take on new projects right away. Yet I had all these projects. I was anxious, because I was trying to make sure people know that I exist, but wasn't quite sure how. I knew I needed to build a website, but I hate websites. I'm not interested in putting my time into designing the way others perceive me. The work and who I work with is what matters to me.

Plus Pool has been in the spotlight for some time now. How has this project been a learning process about publicly funding architectural work, as well as dealing with bureaucracy associated with the nonprofit founded for the pool?

It's been ten years of Plus Pool, and such a significant learning process. The project began just after the financial crisis. We were four young architects and designers just trying to find ways to put this concept in the world. At the time, none of us thought it would stick. Sometimes you just do things and don't always question where they will go and what will happen with them. Ultimately, that project opened so many doors for us as young practitioners. It enabled us to have conversations with people we normally would have never been able to talk to. This was in spite of not having experience and in spite of being young and so on. This is a great example of assuming certain risks and just putting things out there, without knowing where they might take you. The fact that the project ended up where it is today is a testament to the power of an image and people's visceral reaction to design. Everyone had such a positive reaction to the project. Such a unanimous reaction is rare in architecture. Another reason why I love the project is that we never really talked to other architects about it. It's one of those projects that immediately involved politicians, the general public, the community. We learned that so much of getting things built is being on the ground and dealing with the general public and users. In the end, the theoretical side of architecture is such a small component of realizing a project. It's really about what people want and how you can be of service to the community. Working on Plus Pool and learning this was a very sobering experience.

Another aspect of the project was the challenge of doing something that hasn't been done before. It's extremely difficult for a good reason—there is no road map for how to build a project like that. It's not a boat, it's not a building… what is it? This uncertainty means that you have to deal with every single department in New York City, from the Department of Health to Transportation and beyond. It's in those conversations that you see the value of doing something that hasn't been done before, because projects like that reveal the limitations of the regulations that we're dealing with. In the end, it was a wonderful choose-your-own-adventure type of project because there was no singular or right way of going about getting it permitted and built. To understand the intricacy of something as simple as putting a swimming pool in the river is really fascinating because it shows you how interconnected everything is.

What has been your most rewarding or fulfilling moment in your career?

You're probably not going to believe me, but actually, it's doing this. It's being able to sit with friends and colleagues and have conversations about the world at large and how one designs and thinks through things. Having these moments as part of making a living, part of my job… that's privilege in its finest form. That's as good as it gets.

Fig. 89

Only If: Karolina Czeczek and Adam Frampton

What does it mean to practice architecture?

Adam Frampton: Practice, by definition, is related to the implementation of ideas or methods, not just their theorization, and is performed regularly and repetitively, hopefully toward greater skill and proficiency. In this sense, we really appreciate "practice" as a description of our own work that is hands-on, ongoing, open-ended, and hopefully always getting better.

Was starting an office something that you always planned to do?

Karolina Czeczek: Yes, I've always wanted to run a practice. Adam and I were working together at OMA when we decided to leave and start our own practice. Without the opportunity to have a partner, I don't know that starting a practice at that moment would have happened.

Adam: I worked for about seven years after school before we started this practice. There was a real advantage to working in one place during that time and having the opportunity to make meaningful contributions to multiple projects. The experience built some confidence in my ability to start and run a practice, but nothing really prepares you for the challenges of having your own office.

Does your experience working at OMA influence your work today?

Karolina: Definitely. In particular, how we approach projects is something that is inspired by our time at OMA. We try to understand the broader issues of each project. We're not always able to solve that issue solely through building, but our position is embedded in our design. What was also impactful about spending time at OMA was the opportunity to take on a lot of responsibility really quickly. We weren't just executing sketches by more experienced architects. It was an office environment that encouraged the newest and youngest employees to insert themselves from the start. This collaborative, relatively nonhierarchical environment is something we try to maintain in our office today. We're not simply handing off sketches to our employees, but are promoting a collaborative effort.

Who would you consider to be the primary audience for your work? Is it colleagues and other professionals, the general public, or someone else?

Karolina: Other architects, no! Of course, they are an audience by default, but we're not designing for architects—we're designing for a much broader audience. It's important to keep that in mind, because we have to understand the issues and needs of the general public. We have to understand the economic and political context in which we work to respond more appropriately through design.

Adam: An architect's obligation is to the public. Even with projects for private clients, there is a responsibility to imagine how a project engages society and an audience beyond who commissioned it. I agree with Karolina. We do not explicitly design for other architects, but we take pleasure in working on disciplinary issues through drawings, collages, and models … everything that precedes the building.

How does the location of your practice affect your work?

Karolina: We're based in New York, and this requires us to focus on New York right now. We're dealing with issues that are specific to this context—such as housing—and it takes a lot of time, effort, and expertise to understand and navigate building in New York. We don't want to pretend we know everything about everywhere, but at the same time, some specific issues we're working on now in New York could also apply to other areas. Expanding where we practice is on the horizon.

Adam: Having an office in New York as young architects almost seems to entail working on local projects in a very hands-on way. It's very different from what we experienced previously, where large projects or budgets enable global collaboration: everybody in the office was from a different country, traveling constantly, and working on projects scattered around the globe. But starting an office requires commitment to the place where the office exists. Eventually, we'd like to take on much larger projects, and projects outside New York, but we're enjoying working on smaller projects in New York right now. We can be on construction sites, work directly with contractors, and watch projects evolve on a daily basis.

Is your built work more meaningful to you than your unbuilt work, or vice versa, or do they hold equal value?

Karolina: We're definitely interested in building and executing buildings. That being said, we also find tremendous value in working in a more speculative manner on urban-scale projects. We understand that you have to engage projects at a variety of scales and with vastly different objectives in order to execute one project. For example, Narrow House came out of research on overlooked and irregularly shaped narrow lots in New York City. The research at an urban scale was ultimately realized as Narrow House at an architectural scale.

Adam: We know there is value in research and in developing master plans and working the scale of the city and even the region, but these types of projects can take a long time to be implemented. They afford us space to think and design in a more speculative manner, but, in the end, they often get passed to others to execute or become smaller-scale projects related only slightly to the initial conception. We enjoy the smaller-scale projects right now because they can be executed and have an impact quickly.

You've said that you view Narrow House as a prototype for confronting unused narrow lots in the city. What are the qualities of Narrow House that transcend its site?

Karolina: Of course, we do not imagine this to be a copy-paste prototype, because every narrow lot is slightly different, with different zoning regulations and different existing conditions and contexts. The notion of "prototype" corresponds more to a development approach that challenges existing models of building in the city. We are thinking in terms of strategies young architects can employ to be more proactive when it comes to development and construction. We mapped over 3,400 of these narrow lots scattered throughout the city. Six hundred of these lots are city-owned and not suitable for development relative to existing financial models. But they are suitable for development if other priorities take the place of simply earning profit, such as helping to ameliorate the housing crisis or inventing new forms of housing. In that sense, we're thinking about methods and policies that will enable us and others to work with these types of sites.

Adam: Working on Narrow House has allowed us to think about a broader approach to designing for other narrow lots. What's critical for these sites is not the outward expression or form of the building, but interior circulation and how to deliver light into a very deep floor plan. The strategies we've developed in Narrow House to solve these issues can certainly transfer from lot to lot. We're also excited to be working with New York City to help develop twenty-three of these city-owned lots for affordable housing.

What have been the biggest highlights and challenges that you've faced during the design and construction of Narrow House?

Adam: Those are two different things, right? Well, the biggest highlight will be getting it done!

Karolina: It's going to be our first completed ground-up project as Only If—definitely

Fig. 90

Fig. 91

a highlight on its own. When we conceived the project, we didn't even know if it was legally or logistically possible. I'm not going to go into detail, but we had to prove certain things to show that it's possible to build on the site within the existing zoning. Receiving the permit was a highlight! With construction, the biggest challenge was getting out of the ground. The specific conditions of the site constrained the staging area as well as space for construction.

Adam: There are hundreds of challenges. The zero-lot condition, where you're building one structure right up against another one, requires layers of legal agreements, seismographs for construction, vibration monitoring, surveys for optical deflection of movements… I'll share one specific challenge. In New York City, all of the natural gas comes from the Marcellus Shale. It comes through pipelines in an area where it's becoming more and more challenging to build pipelines. There's actually a pipeline that the utility company is trying to build right now under Rockaway Beach, but they can't build it, and there's no more natural gas in Long Island. I was on the phone recently with a gas company asking them where to put the meter when I learned about this. All of a sudden, we have to redesign the building without natural gas, which is a good thing because we'll be able to transition the building off fossil fuels. It's a challenge that will ultimately have a positive impact in the design. All things considered, it's been a very long and challenging process.

Do you approach smaller projects differently than larger projects?

Adam: Our approach is different at different scales. Each scale has its own degrees of indeterminacy or looseness. When you put dimensions on the drawing, there are some dimensions you omit because there are always deviations in construction. In small projects, there might be tolerances of an eighth of an inch. In urbanism, there are other degrees of indeterminacy that need to be built into the project, but the techniques for doing so are very different. Every scale has its own techniques and approaches. We're also interested in developing ideas for one scale and applying them to another. For example, in a competition for a temporary installation, we thought about urbanism playing out within a very small interior. We developed an idea about how a city grid hosts events and activities that unfold over time. The architect or planner cannot choreograph or script everything happening in the space of the city, but they can set up a system or structure in which activities take place. This scenario became the basis for our entry.

How do you allocate resources for research? Does your research generate revenue, or are you using revenue from other projects to fund your research?

Adam: To be honest, we're not terribly successful in managing time or money in the office. It's difficult. We both teach and are very fortunate to be supported by academic institutions. We're not an office that has bread-and-butter work that we don't publish and that we're just doing to make money. A lot of offices do that. Our time is very valuable, and we can't imagine working on something that we're not invested in simply for financial gain.

Karolina: Research also has potential to create other projects for us. We don't see it as research for the sake of research. It's always combined with something that we're teaching or that we're personally interested in.

How have recent global events related to social justice and public health affected your approach to practice?

Karolina: Our practice has always been concerned with larger social and political questions through its multi-scalar approach. This interest also seems to be shared by the younger generation that we teach, in contrast to a previous generation preoccupied by the autonomy of the discipline. The past year has brought focus on architecture's capacity to play a socially engaged role. During this period, we've become more connected to and involved with our community in Bed-Stuy, and have designed, pro bono, two outdoor dining structures for Black-owned businesses. That being said, we don't want to label ourselves explicitly as "social" or "activist" architects. Similarly, in the face of the ongoing climate crisis, we feel that our work on the environmental impact and performance of our projects should not define or label us as "sustainable" or "green" architects. Rather, we see these elements of our approach as ethical obligations and technical competencies that should be an integral part of what all architects do.

What types of projects do you hope to work on in the future? What do you see as the trajectory of your firm going forward?

Karolina: Housing is definitely on our minds, and we want to work on housing at a variety of scales...single- and multi-family, affordable, senior. It's something that we're planning on working on for a long time. But, of course, we have other interests. We understand that housing is not the only component of the city. We've been looking at public amenities and infrastructures that also constitute the city.

Adam: Working on public and cultural projects is an ambition. But we'd be happy to do parking garages, too. We're not thinking of the future of the office solely in terms of types. We want to work with really enlightened, ambitious clients who see the value of design. Maybe this is not connected to your question, but looking at all the practices that are being interviewed as part of this seminar—everyone is teaching. We have mixed feelings about the role of teaching and academia in our practice. On one hand, teaching and being connected to and supported by an academic environment facilitates and enables research. But on the other hand, teaching takes a lot of time. It's rewarding on many levels, but it sometimes feels difficult to devote enough time to both ends, as a teacher and scholar in the academic world and as architect striving to make significant contributions to the built environment.

What has been the most rewarding moment in your practice thus far?

Adam: Architecture is a very difficult profession. We find pleasure in the act of design, as simple or complex as it may be. Having an opportunity to work on projects is incredibly rewarding in and of itself. We are not motivated by the outward accomplishments. It's simply the ability to work on complex design problems, struggle through them, find a resolution... When everything clicks, it's very rewarding.

Fig. 92

Fig. 93

Outside Development: Elisa Iturbe

What does it mean to practice architecture?

Elisa Iturbe: Practicing architecture has meant different things across time and is coming to mean something different as we develop a stronger understanding of our own complicity in the climate crisis. Architecture is waking up to an ugly picture of the past few centuries and to what building has been doing to our ecosystems, and there are practices that are waking up to those kinds of issues and are starting to encompass many things beyond building. Of course, architecture has always had the capacity to address things beyond building. Architecture is a mode of knowledge—it's a way of seeing the world. It has a cultural and a symbolic power. There are modes of architectural production that are fully embedded in a capitalist system where practice means serving that system and creating value for it, but there are also modes of practice that engage with the broader history of the discipline of architecture. I am resistant to the idea that practice is necessarily divorced from theory and I am reluctant to say that practice is just about the profession and not the discipline. The multiplicity of possibilities of what practice means is something that all practitioners have to navigate today.

How did Outside Development come into being, and how does it operate differently than what we might understand to be a more conventional architectural practice?

Outside Development started with me and my partner, Stanley, having a beer at a bar in New Haven. We had just graduated from Yale, and we were lamenting the nature of practice today. We asked ourselves, "What if you and I work together to initiate projects that embody our ideas?" The first few projects we did together were simply drawings we made in response to what we were seeing around us, and the riots in Ferguson were happening at that time. We started to think about the spatial nature of protest. We asked, "How can our spatial thinking contribute something in this moment?" We knew that segregation is spatial, and that architects have a hand in the spatial distribution of people. We began with the basic premise that Outside Development would be a practice where we would use architecture as a mode of knowledge to see the world and take responsibility for what architecture is capable of, which can be both positive and negative. It was important that Outside Development would not become a conventional practice. In a situation where most acts of construction are so embedded in the things that we see as problematic, we had to find new modes of production. Our project Casa Familiar is a perfect example of how we want to work *with*, rather than *for*, clients—carefully, and by asking questions rather than only giving answers.

A term you use often, "carbon form," puts form at the forefront. Why do you feel this is important, and why do you think so many architects who work with ideas of social and environmental sustainability shy away from form—or even think of it as an unethical focus?

No matter what kind of architecture you make, it will have form. To think about form as unethical is perhaps the wrong understanding of what form is, or at least extremely limited. All architecture has form. All architecture gives form. There's a reciprocity between architectural form, urban form, and social form. To ignore form is to blind yourself to one of the major

Fig. 94

intersections between architecture and the sociopolitical landscape about which we are concerned. Architecture, if built, or even if not, has a suggestion of construction. It organizes materials and energy flows. Architects have to be able to understand that environmental questions are not separate from understanding how architecture acquires form and gives form. I believe it's our responsibility as architects to take on the question of spatial organization and of form. I don't believe that attention to form requires a siloed discipline. Architecture just has medium specificity that encourages a specific way of seeing the world. It does not mean it's separate from the world. To accept the specific characteristics of architecture—the specific characteristics of the medium—gives us more agency.

Do you think your project for Casa Familiar in San Ysidro can act as a model for projects elsewhere, or is it specific to that place? And if it's a model, what would make the idea of a community land trust (CLT) attractive to other places and communities?

There are many things about the proposal for San Ysidro that are super specific to that context. For example, there are a fair amount of rental properties in the neighborhood. The people who do own their houses would be unlikely to just hand them over to a community land trust, because it's not a very wealthy neighborhood. If they own a home, they probably see it as an asset, and they probably see it as an opportunity for intergenerational wealth, which has not been common in that area. Other places that have tried community land trusts have high rates of vacancy, dilapidated properties, vacant lots. San Yisidro has a high rate of occupation. The model that we developed around forms of cooperative labor that can be organized through the CLT was a reaction to the fact that people were probably not going to give up their property, but also an opportunity to question the basic tenets of private property by imagining that the work that community does crosses lot lines. Also, Casa Familiar is a nonprofit organization that's many decades old. As far as nonprofits go, they would be more likely than many others to be able to organize something like this.

The aspects of the project that I think can serve as a model include questioning the isolation of a person or a family to a particular parcel and plot of land, which is at odds with what Georges Bataille would call the general economy, or the larger flows of energy and materials that exceed all of these fictional lines that we draw on the ground. Our system of private property assumes the ecological isolation of residents and landowners, which is basically farcical if we think about the broader material basis of our lives. The basic tenet of how we organize ourselves into the system of private property has to be questioned. We believe the CLT model can be pushed to take on questions of larger forms of cooperation and networks of relationships. This enables us to address how we are made vulnerable by our dependence on global supply chains. We've seen it perfectly in the pandemic. When supply chains break down, we're extremely vulnerable. Our capacity to live in and through these disasters will require different forms of local production. Part of the model is to help communities visualize what cooperative labor might look like in order to produce new relationships of production and become less dependent on a consumer economy. Of course, I don't think any community can really become fully self-sufficient. It's not about a back-to-the-land movement It's about trying to invent new hybrid models, where there is some level of self-sufficiency and where it's possible to loosen the grip of the consumer economy and global supply chains. That's the model, but how it plays out in any particular location could be wildly different.

Who do you envision as your primary audience in a project like Casa Familiar? What do you envision your role as the architect to be as the project continues to develop?

We imagine multiple audiences throughout the life of the project. There is the nonprofit, the people of the neighborhood, and the architectural community. Ultimately, we imagine that the audience would be evolving depending on the state of the project. Aside from making renderings of what a housing project might look like in a particular site, we proposed a long-term relationship that we might have with both the non-profit and the residents. We imagined we would eventually produce open-source design kits for the community, the planting cooperative, and the building cooperative. We proposed an open-source design kit for how to build a hydroponic system and an open-source design kit for how to build with rammed earth. Overall, our role as architects would be to share knowledge and to assist the community in establishing building as a cultural practice.

How do you think about the role of representation in your work?

It's really important, especially when working with a community in which you're proposing a major change in their relationship to their property. One of the representation strategies we developed was to create "portraits" of the place, imagining it in its process of transformation. It was really important to include people, to suggest that the architecture was a scenographic element, a set piece for the community. We looked at medieval painting because it often used architecture as a framing device. One of the things that we in architecture always struggle with is the idea that a design is an imposition. But we were imagining that the architecture is actually something through which people can connect. In the work of thinking about how architecture comes into being, there's a reciprocity between the life lived and the building itself. That wasn't something that we were going to communicate with diagrams and arrows.

It's clear you feel that architecture has a responsibility to engage political, social, and environmental issues. Where does this value system come from?

When I was studying as an undergraduate student at Yale, I drove across the country with a friend. We went hiking in Utah one night and got stuck in the desert... We were lost and had to spend the night outside, totally unprotected—we didn't even have a flashlight. In some ways, it was terrifying, but in other ways, it was totally transformative. It was a moment of reckoning for me—I was just this creature in an immensity. We were in Arches National Park, and there was no moon. It was the deepest darkness I've ever experienced. Even the sun coming up was not a reduction of that infinity. That experience really made me think about environmental questions. I began to read a lot about the climate crisis. When I went back to school, I knew that I had to do more than just architecture. That's why I decided to return to Yale—because it offered a dual degree in architecture and environmental management. I felt that if I didn't include environmental questions in my education, then I would come to realize that the thing that I loved the most—architecture—was compromised. Maybe eventually I wouldn't even want to practice anymore. I'm sometimes surprised that I realized that then because my knowledge of the climate crisis was much more limited than it is now.

How have our contemporary global challenges such as the pandemic and racial injustice altered the way that you've operated or encouraged you to think differently about practice?

Because I've been studying climate change for roughly ten years, I knew it was just a matter of time before we encountered some kind of global emergency. One of the things that made the beginning of the pandemic particularly emotional for me was the feeling that the thing I had been fearing my whole adult life—a future of global crises, displacement, political and economic upheaval—was finally starting in earnest. At the same time, I felt affirmed in my decision not to go into conventional practice. I am more convinced than ever that building buildings as often as possible is not the answer.

What has been the most rewarding moment of your professional career thus far?

One of the things that has been most incredible for me is seeing how the idea of carbon form has been a useful device for thinking about the ecological crisis. I use it in my classes, and I've seen it on many occasions, where something clicks for students in their understanding of where we are... not only what our complicity is, but also what our agency is. Whenever that happens, that means a lot to me and is extremely gratifying.

Fig. 95

Fig. 96

SCHAUM/SHIEH: Troy Schaum and Rosalyne Shieh

What does it mean to practice architecture?

Troy Schaum: Practice is a process of continual reflection on the entanglements that produce the built environment. Those entanglements can be engaged in real and meaningful ways, but any practice is formulated with a necessarily incomplete set of tools. Sensitively confronting the gaps between your tools and the world is something that starts to generate a unique kind of knowledge—built up over time.

Rosalyne Shieh: To practice implies a pragmatism or a concern for outcomes of real conditions that are beyond representation. We can debate what those outcomes need to be or what is addressed, but increasingly we are realizing, as a profession or discipline, the urgency for us to address and positively affect lived and material conditions at whatever scale we are working. As we continue to grow and awaken to the world, as we continually reposition ourselves—this pursuit of growth or becoming is, for me, what characterizes a critical practice—we set and move toward new limits or goals.

You've been in practice for more than ten years. Did starting out in 2009, in the midst of a recession, limit your growth?

Troy: Both of us were teaching when the recession hit. Rosalyne was a Taubman Fellow at the University of Michigan and I was a Wortham Fellow at Rice. What we anticipated would be a brief foray into the academy was extended as a result of the macroeconomic situation in this country. We had to figure out how to work as architects without being hired to work as architects. So, we started making our own projects—competition submissions and university-sponsored independent research projects and installations. It was only after we were invited to participate in the Venice Biennale in 2012, which was curated by David Chipperfield, that we started to get commissioned work. I don't know if those two things were related, but we started to pick up projects in both New York and Texas, and we very quickly had four additional employees. Our office size hasn't grown a lot since then, but when we look at the numbers every year, it's been relatively steady, which is its own form of success.

In response to the challenges of starting a practice at that time, have you used unconventional methods to promote your firm or to attract potential clients?

Rosalyne: We began our practice in an academic setting with little opportunity to practice in a conventional manner. In 2009, by starting in the midst of the recession, there was little momentum to be lost and the work we made was unsolicited. I don't mention this to bemoan how it happened—rather, I want to state the conditions in which we set out and to explain why, in the beginning, most of our work was speculative, invested in an alternate economy of ideas and discourse, one partially insulated from the macroeconomic situation of professional practice. We may have had a small audience tied to the academy, but we didn't have clients. We started by thinking about what it meant to make work that nobody was asking for, about what questions could be posed or offerings made through the framework of an architectural project. The parameters and conceptual territory of this early work were partly self-defined, but also defined by our educations, conversations with our peers and collaborators, and things we were reading and looking at. This was an important incubation period for us, but it didn't necessarily transition seamlessly into attracting clients and working on commissioned projects.

Troy: What encouraged that transition for us was a desire to work at a certain scale. We were conducting design research and building temporary installations, but we were interested in engaging building at a much larger scale. When we received opportunities to work on larger projects, we realized that the two of us couldn't do it alone anymore. We had to build an ecosystem of people to support us. All of a sudden, we had to develop an economy around the work in order to support the people who were supporting us. At that point, we found ourselves running a business. We didn't say no to a lot of requests, because you never know where certain journeys are going to take you. In 2012 or 2013, we were asked by some relatively young people in Houston if we were interested in designing a music venue. We made some sketches and renderings for a very small amount of money. We just assumed these people would go away and we'd never hear from them again. What actually happened was that they took those renderings all over town and raised significant capital to build the music venue. What also happened was that lots of people who build things in Houston saw the renderings. They didn't necessarily want to invest in a music venue, but were very curious about us as architects. Developers would contact us and request a portfolio of built work. The problem was that we hadn't actually built anything! It's a common and unfortunate catch-twenty-two, especially for a US-based practice in its earliest stages. That said, some of them hired us anyway.

Not entirely unrelated to self-promotion… How do you mediate between presenting your work to a broader public audience versus an audience of architecture students, colleagues, and other professionals?

Troy: This is a huge issue for us, especially as we oscillate between our audiences. We're both teachers and we both have conversations with very erudite students and colleagues, and with people who work out of the back of their truck and know a lot about building things, but not so much about architectural discourse. The importance of communication and the ability to articulate ideas to many different audiences is primary to our understanding of architecture. You mentioned two audiences, but there are probably twenty audiences we communicate with throughout the day, from the people who are sending us metal samples to the lawyers helping us draft contracts for our clients.

Rosalyne: Also, communication is a very personal thing. You have to respond to whom you're talking to. Depending on what each person is able to receive or wants to talk about, you have to meet each other somewhere, and you both need to arrive from where you're coming. I like to speak with my own voice across different conversations, but communicate differently given the situation or who I'm talking to.

Troy: It's become very apparent to me that when we talk about audiences in school, we're talking about collectives. And we're very interested in creating projects for collectives. There's a democratizing idea that architecture is for everyone. It is. But one of the things that I underestimated was how powerful architecture can be for individuals—our individual clients and the contractors who build our projects.

What do you understand to be your responsibility as an architect?

Troy: Wow—that's a difficult question! Our practice is named after both of us for a reason. SCHAUM/SHIEH wasn't just a default. That decision makes the practice a very personal thing for us. I imagine there's a certain ethics in our work. I believe we have a responsibility to use these professional tools and our ways of seeing the world to be as careful and reflective and deliberate about our decisions and our work, especially in cities and in public spaces. To be stewards of the resources that we're given, to be stewards of opportunities that we're given to shape cities—these are very important responsibilities.

Rosalyne: I agree and would add that we hope our projects enrich the world and make more connections possible. We hope our efforts lead to building more complexity into the world. One of the quotes that we come back to a lot is one that Jane Jacobs included at the beginning of *Death and Life of Great American Cities,* from Oliver Wendell Holmes Jr.: "Life is an end in itself, and the only question as to whether it is worth living is whether you have enough of it." He's talking about the vibrant complexity of civilization, and Jacobs sees cities as an engine of that. There's an interest in the pursuit of what we do as architects, but also as people, to contribute to more life for more people.

Some architects believe that there should be a separation between being a citizen and being an architect, specifically in relation to political issues. With your office, it seems to be the inverse. How much effort do you put into making a project political? Does it come naturally from its inception?

Rosalyne: That's a good question, and it's one that comes up again and again in architecture: what is the relationship between architecture and politics? If being political means seeing and engaging structural inequality, I can't live in a world where those two things can be separated, because it would mean willfully denying a part of reality—if not my own, then the reality of someone else with whom I share this world. There could be different reasons why people feel the need to separate these roles. It could be because the very act or idea of the work—its property—requires that its limits are circumscribed. One way to work on something is to isolate or bracket it from other things. Or it might be a matter of survival: the world can be difficult; maybe you're at capacity with what you can handle, and creative work is a kind of expression that feeds you. Some might have the choice to separate the two where others don't. Broadly speaking, people undertake creative work for so many different reasons. I would just ask whether your position to proceed in any certain way is predicated upon an invalidation of someone else's, and if it does, I would find it hard to support. I do not require you to not be in order for me to be. That said, work that is explicitly political is not the only way to be political as an architect or artist. Jean-Luc Godard said, "The problem is not to make political films but to make films politically." That might mean simply expressing or applying yourself without explanation. There's no way to escape this question. It's not fair, actually, to say that those worlds should be separate. I can't say that every project we do is political; we're not a political practice per se, but I am who I am, who I am, who I am... whether that's an architect, an educator, a person in the world, a cis woman, a Taiwanese person, visibly Asian a daughter of immigrants in the United States, today. The tension of trying to hold all these things together is at the heart of my humanity.

Troy: There's a certain disciplinary agenda in the work of some practices, and a legacy of a particular kind of formalism. That way of approaching architecture is very different from how we understand practice. One important role of the architect is to construct agreement. The explicitly political aspects of practice necessitate engagement with a broad audience and a range of issues well beyond the purview of the discipline of architecture. I don't know how you practice any other way. It's beautiful that buildings have the ability to engage political issues, and that architects have the ability to engage political issues.

How have recent global events related to social justice and public health affected your approach to practice?

Troy: This is really two questions that overlap but manifest differently in the work. The murder of George Floyd and reckoning with systemic racism affected me deeply on both a personal and professional level. It is hard to reflect on the outrage surrounding these deaths at the hands of police and offer an immediate reflection that escapes cliché. That said, there are many steps and many responses underway simultaneously—listening, organizing, and acting. The isolation brought on by COVID-19 has created space for our staff to have more independence. It has forced us to be more deliberate in our interactions with everyone. We have become quite close with some of our remote clients because we "see" them as much as we see anyone else in our lives. This has made the development of projects with them much more collaborative and intimate than in the past. It is hard to lean on formalities when you are talking to someone from their child's bedroom.

Rosalyne: Practice keeps me concerned with real conditions or lived realities, and one question that is urgent, pressing, and unavoidable is, what is the relevance in what we do? How is it meaningful? And most importantly—for whom? Not just meaningful, but how does it make an impact or have an outcome that affects lived, material reality for those who are in need of it? It is a conversation I find myself having with my closest architect friends these days. How does what we do connect to larger questions of systemic inequality and oppression on one hand, and affect the smaller realities of everyday life on the other hand? Is it even possible given our current processes, concerns, values, ways of operating? How do we get out of a comfy middle zone—where the middle is the status quo, the space of equilibrium, the matrix of existing systems. Perhaps we can say it's the operations and values of the academy or the systems of prestige-making of professional practice as they exist. Striking out beyond the middle zone is risky, but no good change will come without it. We need to work with our frustrations, harness our anger, listen to our own discontent, and operate from those places of disquiet. That's my way of identifying an impulse without yet defining an approach.

What's been the most rewarding moment in your professional careers thus far?

Troy: We recently had the opportunity to observe how powerful work can be for an individual. This positive impact is not something you can encounter until you build something. White Oak Music Hall was embedded in a lot of politics around how music is booked in this country. We made a lot of sacrifices in order to complete that project. We were criticized by a portion of the local community, but also supported by many diverse groups within the community. Recently, after finding out that we designed White Oak Music Hall, a local musician said to us, "That space you've created—we didn't have a space like that. That's my temple." There's an entire ecosystem of creative people who can now work in this space we designed.

Rosalyne: I agree with that, and I'll give you pretty much the same answer, but in a more abstract sense. We've had that experience a few times with the projects that are out in the world, with both White Oak Music Hall and Transart, a home in Houston that we designed for an artist and curator. You talk to people, and you might not know them well, and they're like, "I know that project," and they share some story that gives you an understanding that the project somehow belongs to them. These are the moments when we realize that projects, once they are out there, belong to the world and not just to us. It can come back to us through clients, contractors, or anyone really. When they share a sense of belonging to this thing that we helped create, that's a really special moment.

Fig. 97

Fig. 98

Fig. 99

Fig. 100

Shumi Bose

What does it mean to practice architecture, and do you consider what you do to be a form of practicing architecture?

Shumi Bose: As much as I understand the need or desire to clarify what the discipline of architecture is, I'm reluctant to make a statement that claims to be definitive. It's constraining and exclusive. I identify with a modernist organizing principle or enlightenment principle: "Tell me what it is, and then I can figure out how to make use of it."

Do I consider what I do to be a form of architectural practice? Yes. Having cheekily denied a definition for practice, I still claim to contribute to it. If we accept that the discourse, culture, ethics, and intellectual work of architecture is part of the practice of architecture, then yes, undoubtedly… I practice architecture.

In the interview you gave to *Scaffold* in 2019, you made the claim that curation is the idea of "taking care of conversation." What do you mean by that?

In my role as a curator, one of my responsibilities is to manage conversations between authors, exhibitors, gallery managers, contractors, budget holders, sponsors, and so on. Exhibitions can be showcases; they can be commercially motivated; they can be critical; they can be all sorts of different things. So my job as a curator is not necessarily to impose anything on my collaborators, but to discern what in the conversation is necessary and fulfilling for the institution, for the exhibitors, for the sponsors, and for those we understand to be our audience. Ultimately, the conversation that I care most about is between the exhibition and the audience.

As a curator, how do you balance your curiosities and interests against things that might be in high demand, or come with a built-in audience?

My job as a curator is to determine the tone of the activity. I don't think I've ever been in a situation where I've had to accept a predetermined angle or perspective. My job is to find it. My creative work is in discerning and determining the conceptual ambitions of an exhibition. I see that as a creative practice. I don't see it as a case of bringing my personal research or personal perspective to an exhibition, because I'm not on display. But there are things that I gravitate toward more than others. For instance, a lot of my exhibition work has been on housing and domestic architecture, which is a research interest of mine—and those opportunities have often come to me. In the case of working for RIBA… It was after Home Economics at the Venice Biennale that RIBA wanted to do an exhibition on social housing. Through these kinds of opportunities, I've been able to position myself in architectural discourse where I feel like I have expertise or some critical perspective that I can add. It's not necessarily that I'm bringing my own research to the topic, but I'm bringing my own position. I wouldn't expect to pursue my personal agenda through an institution. Beyond this general approach, though, there's still plenty of critical negotiation. There have been situations that I've walked away from because there was an ethical disagreement. In all the activities I participate in, there are lots of negotiations, with the goal being to arrive at a position where everyone is fulfilled and satisfied. That's simply part of the job.

You've spoken about how you're much more excited to talk and write about things than you are to make them. What are your motivations when it comes to talking and writing about the work of others?

I believe speaking and writing about architecture is the most direct form of engagement with the culture of architecture, because I'm using my words and representing myself. In the early part of my career, I had a chip on my shoulder, and anxiety about not practicing architecture in a traditional sense. I am a second-generation immigrant and a minority, and my upbringing and culture revolved around seeking professional validation in order to become financially secure. Traditional practice may have provided that, but I'm not so motivated to seek that kind of validation anymore.

I am still scared of making definitive statements when I speak or write. What I'm most interested in is opening critical conversations around topics that are relevant in architecture today. I want people to be able to talk openly about topics they are interested in, to actively engage in discourse in architecture and put some skin in the game. If I relate this to teaching, I can tell you that I'm thrilled when my students feel comfortable taking over the discussion in class. I often have to stop lecturing because they're arguing between themselves. I love those moments. I enjoy enabling and facilitating others. I don't mean to sound like I'm denying my own position or my own voice. I'm not… In fact, I'm very strong-willed and opinionated, and I get equally angry and excited about all sorts of different things. When I'm writing, I'm not approaching it with the attitude that I have something you need to hear. It's not really like that. I'm interested in sponsoring new conversations and clarifying positions held by others. This may be why I enjoy editing more than I enjoy writing. Editing is about diagnosing what is at stake. I find joy in returning text to an author and hearing them say, "Exactly—that's what I was trying to say!" Whether it's in editing, speaking, teaching, or writing, I really find delight in the richness of discourse in architecture.

What's your relationship to people that you collaborate with and to other architects? Do you adjust relative to the person you're working with or writing about, or do you always take a consistent approach?

That's a complex question, but a really good one. While I've been conscious of the parallels across collaborations, I don't know how conscious I've been about the unique roles I may take on in each situation, whether I'm acting as a copilot or a sounding board or a therapist. In many collaborations, I'm getting better at acknowledging that I want to play a primary role rather than being a support structure. Although if I'm required to be a support structure, I'm okay with that. For me, it's about noting what a collaboration needs and trying to adapt to that need. As I gain experience, I'm gaining confidence. I'm able to acknowledge what I bring to a collaboration rather than simply following someone else's lead. With each collaboration, I'll ask myself: To what extent can I help this person do what they're trying to do? Do I agree with what they're trying to do? How much can I get behind it, and in what way?

You use social media to amplify certain narratives and support certain causes. We're thinking about the conflict in Palestine, aid for COVID, support for Office Hours… How have our current global challenges redirected your interests or inspired your work in unexpected ways?

Another day, we should set up an hour just to discuss this topic! It's been a lot. Where to begin? Let me begin with the academic strike that happened at the beginning of 2020, which was a demonstration of solidarity with respect to issues of labor, gender, and race. This moment was necessary and pivotal. And then immediately after the lockdown happened, George Floyd was murdered, and that changed a lot of things. I found that responses to the pandemic and to the murder of George Floyd from many institutions were fairly managerial and had less to do with politics of care. It's not possible to ignore racial politics in America right now. In contrast, our government published a paper this year claiming that racism is not an issue in the UK—rather, it's an exemplary country for the rest of the world. Such an outrageous claim provides motivation to address these issues publicly. Additionally, the inadequacies of the institutions where I have given my time and energy motivate me to fill some of those gaps. Being outspoken on social media is a cumulative thing—we're witnessing a collective response and cumulative confidence to make positive change. I've always been a participant in discussions around identity, labor, gender, and race, but during the last years these issues became even more urgent to discuss. My friends and I were very aware that our students need a safe space for conversation, and we were very aware of the cost of not acknowledging these issues. Office Hours, which is organized by Esther Choi, was, in part, born from this acknowledgment.

How do you imagine your career evolving from here?

I've always been a strong believer in systemic change over optics or optical change. I don't care about the black square on your Instagram feed—show me what actions you are taking to make a difference. But through conversations with my students, I came to slowly realize that optics do matter to the people I'm talking to whether I want them to matter or not. That took a bit of time to digest. I get it, but no one likes being instrumentalized. No one likes being tokenized. No one likes knowing they're on a panel because of the color of their skin. But optics do matter. It's been a difficult pill to swallow. Overall, the events of the last year and the limits of optical change have reinforced my desire for systemic change.

I'm in the process of registering a charity because the thing that I want to do needs to be funded outside of an institution. I do believe in the institution—I don't want to abandon it completely. However, I have recognized over the last year that there ought to be other spaces where certain discussions can happen that don't fit into the academic institution. I'm in the process of building an organization called HoldSpace. The tagline for it is "for the stuff that doesn't fit in architecture school." I've never done something like this on my own before. It's quite scary for me. Well, it's not really on my own ... we have a group of what will be trustees when this is more official, and I have a panel of student advisors as well. The conversations that I want to have require generosity that institutional bureaucracy oftentimes does not allow. Something that changed in the last year is that we can be generous with our time. So, yeah, HoldSpace—it's a therapy term for holding space for somebody to share their experience. I want to hold that space for others, rather than take it up. I don't know if I will ever be financially remunerated, but the value to me is in having that space to do what I think is a critical component of practice.

What has been the most rewarding moment of your professional career?

When my collaborators and I can deliver our message with clarity, or when a student has a breakthrough because of my support, when they have direction and confidence to go forward … those are the most rewarding moments.

Somatic Collaborative: Anthony Acciavatti, Felipe Correa, and Devin Dobrowolski

What does it mean to practice architecture?

Felipe Correa: This is an extremely loaded question that defies a precise answer. The answer is going to be unique for every office and dependent upon the background of each office. One of the greatest things about architecture as a discipline is the instrumental and methodological diversity that comes from the very inability to answer this question. There is no singular definition of architecture, nor is there a singular approach to practicing architecture.

How does this view inform the way that the three of you work together? Is your collaboration something that was conceived in a deliberate manner, or did your working relationship emerge naturally?

Anthony Acciavatti: It's a great question. To begin, the name that we gave ourselves—Somatic Collaborative—was intentionally selected to reveal our interest in working collaboratively. We work collaboratively among ourselves as well as with people outside the office and people outside the field of architecture. Internally, there's a certain amount of triage that we're always performing and a strategy to always be conscious of where we are going, within each project and as an office. As Felipe mentioned, we embrace the variety of ways in which architecture can be practiced, and even within the office we are always working together to develop new methods and techniques for research and design.

Devin Dobrowolski: One of the things that makes our practice productive is having a set of shared affinities, but coming at those affinities from very different places, with very different references and backgrounds. Each of us brings a unique perspective to the work. The process of coming to a consensus is an incredibly important aspect of how we work. The fact that we are three is very helpful when resolving internal debates!

Felipe: Another aspect of the way that we practice is that writing, drawing, and talking about architecture have equal value. Our work is very iterative across these three outputs. There are certain questions that get asked in writing and answered in drawing. There are certain questions that a drawing might pose that get explained in text. There are issues we write about that have to be explained to clients or to larger constituencies verbally. How we write, how we speak about architecture, and how we draw are very entangled.

What do you imagine is the impact of your research? What happens after the books and the exhibitions? How does your research get picked up and used by others?

Felipe: We imagine our work casts a net across multiple audiences and constituencies. For example, in the case of *A Line in the Andes*…yes, it is published as a book, but it is also one of the eleven official reports that a municipality used to secure funding from the Inter-American Development Bank, World Bank, and CAF development bank. It's the first project in the world to be financed by these multilateral organizations. It was also one of the official reports that was then used to convince the citizens of Quito that a metro was worth the investment.

Your projects address formal organization, environmental performance, local culture, and domestic ritual, to name a few issues. In the design development of your housing projects, is there a hierarchy among these concerns?

Devin: Every one of our design projects is an invitation to speculate. When we take on a new project, our first act is to establish an ethic that informs our design decisions and structures considerations of form, environment, culture, and ritual. What's also interesting is that many of those factors—environmental performance, social organization, domestic ritual, and so on—cannot be easily separated. When we look closely at a place where we are designing, we try to understand the context and assemble the design project through the observations that we have made about that place. After that, it's a process of active negotiation and calibration, working on how each of those issues begins to inform the design.

You design objects as small as tables and as large as master plans. What are the advantages and disadvantages of working at such different scales? Do you imagine the practice continuing to be involved in projects at a variety of scales?

Felipe: One of the things that defines us and interests us is this idea of being amateurs across scales. We like the idea that we are able not only to work across a wide variety of scales, but also to understand that an analytical framework we develop, or a way of describing and understanding a particular condition, might be deployed at a variety of scales and in multiple projects. Bringing those things together is an act of synthesis for us—a way of defining architecture. For example, I can be fascinated with the dynamics of inhabiting a forest and come away with the realization that the best design projec to be able to inhabit a forest is a survivor backpack. So, th scale of analysis might be the forest, but the scale of desig might be the backpack. The relationship between forest and backpack is what drives the practice. Another aspect of working across scales is the dialogue between analysis, description, and speculation. Analysis alone will never yield speculation. Speculation alone will never allow you t understand the particular conditions of a place. It's really about the way that all of these things come together that begins to define how we work.

Anthony: Going back to what Felipe said about the forest and the backpack: our task is as much about trying to tease out narratives of a place as much as it is about projecting design onto a particular site. To that extent, our design proposals can range not just across scales, but across mediums and methods as well. Something that runs through the three of us is our diverse backgrounds—architecture, landscape architecture, history of science, technology, and fine arts. There is a persistent and collective desire to move across different mediums and methods when it comes to design and not just focus on or limit ourselves to practicing architecture through designing buildings.

We know from your research on the Amazon and the Ganges that you've long been focused on issues of climate change, environmental degradation, and ecological infrastructures. We're curious about social justice and public health issues—have recent events redirected your interests at all or inspired you to work in in new or unexpected ways?

Felipe: These issues are inherently linked. You cannot separate environmental degradation and climate change from issues of social, racial, and economic injustice. In most cases, one is directly tied to the other. A lot of the work that we've done looks at a larger set of parameters and frames many of those issues through the perspective of urban and environmental form. Throughout the pandemic, and because of the restrictions that prohibited us from using the city in the ways we've used it previously, the three of us have been looking at notions of publicness and what it actually means to rethink the role of architecture in advocating for new forms of publicness in the contemporary city. If we look carefully at the last twenty or thirty years, public-private partnerships have eroded many different forms of publicness. When COVID-19 hit New York City, privately owned public spaces were the first to be shut down. It was only public parks that remained open. Rethinking notions of publicness in the twenty-first century is an extremely important question for us.

Anthony: Because I've continued to research areas outside of North America for more than fifteen years, I have a clear idea about what makes the United States unique in these situations. The debates that are happening in the United States amplify American exceptionalism in a way that is really problematic. In India, for example, the pandemic exposed how strong the welfare state was in terms of dealing with agricultural India, but not with urban India. Because of the history of India as an agrarian society, there has been a safety net in rural places for many decades. This is a very different condition compared to what we are seeing in this country. There is something to be learned from the different effects of the pandemic in different places. Questions about environmental degradation have much more to do with environmental uncertainty. One of the wonderful things about studying the Ganges was understanding how the monsoon has been such a precarious condition for so many centuries. It is a microcosm of what so many other places are going to face in terms of climate change with climate uncertainty. In the case of the Ganges, it's been very helpful for me to study it in terms of exportable analytics. A lot of architectural practices have struggled to engage in the temporality of space, but I believe we have something to contribute to that discussion.

Devin: Something that I believe is important is the idea of ecologies. The present environmental crises and events surrounding racial injustice have made us aware of the importance of relationships between everything in our physical surroundings. As designers, being able to use our skill sets to evaluate different ecologies in order to provide a sophisticated response through design is very important.

Anthony: This reminds me of the notion of expertise, and of recognizing that there are limits to what we can do as architects and, more generally, as designers. Part of trying to cultivate expertise is recognizing what you bring to a discussion and that you need other experts around you to work on a problem in a meaningful way, through collaboration.

What has been the most rewarding moment of your professional careers?

Anthony: The work that we did in Manaus was incredibly rewarding simply because it was a project in which so many of our individual interests and areas of expertise aligned and were synthesized. We addressed issues of housing, public and private infrastructure, dwelling spaces… It all came together in a really exciting way. Developing projects for Manaus together in the office and with collaborators elsewhere was something I really enjoyed.

Devin: Professional accolades are wonderful, and they reinforce some of the things that you're hoping to achieve through the work. But for me, spreading enthusiasm and positivity for architecture through teaching is very rewarding. In our professional work, we've been able to build a wide network of collaborators across the world, and with every project that we do we're able to expand our network of partners and friends. Working with students in the courses we teach and practicing collaboratively with others is incredibly rewarding.

Felipe: Devin stole my answer, but I'll say it anyway! The most rewarding thing is the everyday work. Having the opportunity to wake up and do something that doesn't feel like a job is truly amazing. The incredible cohort of collaborators we've been able to work with for over a decade now—it's really special. We have an incredible team working with us. At the end of the day, an important aspect of how we approach architectural practice is in setting the table for ideas from a much larger set of collaborators to flourish. For me, that's extremely important.

Fig. 101

Fig. 102

Fig. 103

Spinagu: Maxi Spina and Jia Gu

You established your practice in 2016. What were your individual goals, and what led to your collaboration?

Jia Yi Gu: At the time, I was trying to figure out how to be involved in architecture across multiple modes of production. I had a desire to practice in the conventional sense and at the same time contribute to architectural culture more broadly, through scholarship and curatorial practice.

Maxi Spina: Prior to Jia and I deciding to practice together, I was running my own architecture office and teaching. I was engaged in advanced digital design, the organization and representation of complex form, and the production of meaning beyond the discipline of architecture. I had worked for Neil Denari in Los Angeles and studied with Jesse Reiser at Princeton University, and some of the initial ambitions and interests that surrounded the formation of my own practice were extensions of what I encountered and participated in during these two experiences. In 2015, Jia and I began having discussions about practicing together and what would constitute the basis of our collaborative practice.

We were, and still are, very interested in working on the medium of exhibition and revisiting modes of display for architecture. Jia's background working on exhibitions provided a foundation for our first collaborative endeavors.

How do your distinct backgrounds and interests inform your collaboration, and how do practicing, teaching, and conducting research either converge or remain independent?

Jia: I like to think of practicing, teaching, and research not as separate activities, but as different modes of production that engage with similar sets of issues in architecture. So, some activities, like teaching, are opportunities to provide, share, and reflect on certain forms of foundational knowledge—however that is defined within a pedagogical practice. Other activities, like curating, are about bringing architecture and public audiences closer together. Both are opportunities to reframe what we think we know in architecture.

Maxi: Exactly—and every endeavor has a different set of conceptual and logistical requirements. Our different backgrounds allow us to divide and share responsibilities in each of the unique contexts in which we seek to make contributions, whether that's practice, research, or curation.

Can you be more specific about how your academic research and teaching inform the way you practice?

Jia: On my end, there is a broader interest in labor and in what architects "do." This is related to the status of architectural education today, where there are quite a few discrepancies between what students do in an educational environment and what is being asked of them in professional and nonprofessional practice. Our research into these issues informs the way that we, as a practice, understand the conditions and agency of architecture today, but also, for example, the conditions of financing that allow architecture to be produced. We're trying to be reflective and proactive in the way we engage with realities of professional practice, and we're also trying to develop new values around which we can operate. I want students to understand their place in architecture and in broader society in terms of the content they produce, but also the container or conditions that they operate within—to redesign the very conditions by which architecture comes into being.

Maxi: The content of the classes we teach and the work we do in our office are not easily separated, but we try to keep them distinct for a few reasons. We don't believe in the apprenticeship model that asks students to replicate our techniques and adopt our aesthetic sensibilities. We prefer to teach in a way that opens up questions about design and representation, and more specifically the status of software with regard to representation. We prefer to give students agency in developing a trajectory for their projects that is more personal, but still within the scope of the broader topic that we introduce. We also do not want to pretend that practice and teaching are entirely separate. They intersect from time to time, but are unique in ways that allow for continuous exchange and evolution.

You've engaged architecture's relationship with finance as one of the critical conditions within which architecture operates. In your practice, how do you engage traditional models of producing architecture? Do you pursue alternatives?

Jia: I feel anxiety about hyperfinancialization. In the United States, ninety-five percent of housing is financed and constructed by developers. Unless architects seriously rethink the financial system by which architecture comes into being, we are basically going to lose out to high-return developers, who have very different often problematic value systems. Yet these ways of working have become so naturalized that we fail to remember they are ideologically and economically constructed. We can reconstruct this. Our field's livelihood is directly tied to our society's equity distribution and wealth accumulation. No one in the middle class can afford an architect these days. The field's response to the livelihood question—and it's a response shared by many of our peers—is to teach as a way to sustain ourselves and enable a form of practice that can operate slightly outside of the service model. I believe architects don't think enough about generating new, more equitable economic models for practice. There are entire sectors of the economy, like nonprofit and community development organizations, for example, that have access to funding and that are also values-based. So there are other ways to practice… other economic models for practice. We are more aggressively pursuing these other ways of practicing right now. But this is not only about financing our work—I also want to know how we can redesign equity models in order to become an equitable field, and how we can rethink property and asset ownership in ways where stakeholders and core values are in alignment. We made a decision that rather than spend the next ten years building up a client base, we'd rather spend that time engaging with alternative development and financing models, essentially to become developers, in order to learn and test new processes of development that align with our core values.

How have recent global events related to social justice and public health affected your approach to practice?

Jia: Prestige, pedigree, and recognition are not and should not be the most important aspects of practice. BLM and the anti-racist movements in architecture show us that the system of awards and rewards in architecture is highly problematic, circular, and self-fulfilling. We know architecture to be a highly privileged profession constituted by white actors, but I think to change it, it is not enough to merely bring people of color into the system. And our system of rewards, from access to Ivy League universities to individual "genius" awards and scholarships, are in many ways just that—inviting different people to a toxic table. I often repeat three mantras that are borrowed from the principles of mutual aid via Dean Spade's writings, which have crystallized for me in 2020: (1) identify harmful systems; (2) redistribute resources; and (3) model alternatives. There are a lot of harmful systems in architecture and not enough alternative models to practice. We are a factory reproducing the same model of architect: young recent graduate with high student debt enters into commercial and transactional practice for a client-driven project in order to survive. Very little chance for establishing your own independent practice, almost zero chances to experiment and explore, and absolutely no chance of working for low- or middle-income families, or on public and civic projects, which are often bestowed to large corporate offices with decades of portfolio experience.

Fig. 104

Fig. 105

Speaking of the larger context of a project, can you tell us a bit about some of the critical contextual factors that informed the design of Piaggio House?

Maxi: One of the issues that played a critical role in the development of the design was security and layers of defense. I mention it first because it inspired a conceptual investigation into registering thickness through movement. Because of issues of security and the need to incorporate certain features native to the type of single-family homes in the neighborhood, things like thresholds between significant spaces became important as a series of checkpoints or layers in relation to physical access. So, the house has an incredible range of spaces, from fully enclosed and private to open and very visually accessible. The urban condition of that particular neighborhood, in Rosario, Argentina, also dictated certain qualities. For example—and again, this was tied to security concerns—the house could not be freestanding, as a way to limit the accessible perimeter. The threshold between interior and exterior, which could have potentially been rather banal, became the most interesting aspect of the design. Every house in Rosario has about five layers of security. It's not just a gate and a front door that separate public from private. Multiple layers need to be incorporated to properly address this issue. In this way, the practical and pragmatic aspects of security became important to us in the overall conceptualization of the house—its form, interior organization, and even materiality.

Beyond your sensitivity to context, your design work investigates issues of perception through the manipulation of profiles. Where does this interest come from and how has it evolved from project to project?

Maxi: The work on profiles was developed in installations and conceptual projects completed across a two-year period. It started when we were invited to participate in an exhibition at Jai & Jai Gallery, in Los Angeles, in 2015 that asked architects to produce objects inspired by chess pieces. This opened up an avenue of investigation for us that engaged ideas of perception and the posture of an architectural object. Profile as a topic in architectural form is very different from the topics of surface and volume, which I had been working on previously. Working on profiles enabled us to expand our engagement with form beyond more familiar topics.

Jia: The invitation to produce artifacts for the chess exhibition also provided an opportunity to study the physical production of chess pieces. And it turns out that chess pieces have strong profiles because each profile is the result of rotating the wood around the lathe, which allows for carving of the piece—a figural condition that is distinct from a machine's toolpath, let's say. So, from the start, there was an interest in the relationship between profile manipulation in the digital, immaterial environment compared to profile creation in a physical, material environment. This relationship, along with issues of corners, offsets, and thickness, was explored in a variety of ways across two additional projects.

What are some of the most rewarding aspects of being architects and educators?

Jia: Teaching is incredibly rewarding. I learn so much from students and I'm inspired by the ways in which they prepare for practice. Every generation will proceed in architecture differently, and I'm keen to observe the shifting landscape of expectations that each generation, each cohort of students, embodies. By the time someone has entered the profession, they are a formed subject, and it's in working with students where I see formation in real time, and where change can occur as one prepares to practice and engage the world more critically.

Maxi: I can point to two things. The first is that we've been given and have earned opportunities to create projects that make genuine contributions to contemporary discourse. We're thankful to have peers with similar ambitions whom we can talk to, exchange ideas with, be inspired by, and hopefully inspire. The second thing is very simple: it's just an afternoon in the office working on projects. That's probably the most rewarding time for me. We're so busy, so I really try to appreciate the time I have in the office to work and be productive.

Fig. 106

Fig. 107

T+E+A+M: Thom Moran, Ellie Abrons, Adam Fure, and Meredith Miller

We're really interested in how the four of you came together. What is it like for four architects who previously practiced individually to form a collaborative practice?

Thom Moran: The answer to how we started working together is pretty prosaic, and also a bit humorous. We started a reading group to learn more about the architect Emilio Ambasz, whose work resonated with each of us, but in different ways. It was during the time of this reading group that the opportunity arose to apply to represent the United States at the 2016 Venice Biennale. We decided to turn our reading group conversations into the basis for our application. Our application was successful, and we exhibited Detroit Reassembly Plant in Venice in 2016, but it still wasn't clear to us whether or not we were going to continue as a practice. Given that we enjoyed working together and acknowledged that we did something together that we never would have done independently, we decided to keep collaborating.

Meredith Miller: Detroit Reassembly Plant threaded so many themes together that we had developed individually. It was very exciting for us to see how the work came together. But regarding the mechanics of how we operate as a four-principal office—there are things that are hugely inefficient in terms of time management. We all like to be involved in the conceptual phase of our projects. It's what we enjoy the most, and we're at our best when we're sitting around a table, sketching and talking. With four of us, there's a lot of input. For the sake of efficiency, as a project moves forward, we divide tasks and responsibilities, but most of the work cycles through all four of us.

As a collaborative, what does it mean to practice architecture?

Meredith: There are so many models for what an architecture practice can be—which makes it both exciting and daunting to forge our own approach. For us, practice is synonymous with relationships. We each have our own history and thinking when it comes to design, but to practice architecture as T+E+A+M is to interact with other T+E+A+M members and the people with whom we do projects. Projects unfold incrementally as different groupings of people interact at different intervals with specific aims all organized under a larger purpose. Structuring those incremental efforts and interactions in a way that makes room for the core ideas and values that run through our collaboration is its own design challenge.

Thom: This characterization of practice as a kind of accumulation of small actions takes cues from Dana Cuff, who diagnosed a common dissonance between what design professionals—from partners to interns—believe the practice of architecture to entail and the professional activities they routinely perform. The premium that architectural education places on individual authorship and design, she argues, leads to disappointment in the managerial reality of nurturing projects to completion. We came to the task of managing a building practice with eyes wide open. After years of working more in the academic realm of exhibitions, research, and installations, we made a deliberate shift toward a more client-driven model of practice in order to begin translating those ideas into physical buildings that would have a life outside the speculative realm of representation. We've found that the collaborative nature of

T+E+A+M that made those early projects fun and surprising has enabled us to extend those channels of collaboration to clients and others involved.

What is the responsibility of the architect, and how do you think it has changed throughout your career?

Thom: There are a couple of different ways you could frame responsibility, and there are many ways in which this has changed in the last twenty years. There's the issue of sustainability, but I don't think there's much disagreement that it's an important part of what we do and should always be considered. More recently, there's the responsibility to be inclusive and consider how architecture intersects with social justice. But I have a more romantic view about the architect's role in society, as a visionary or as a critic or as someone who offers a different worldview compared to dominant ideologies. We have an opportunity and responsibility to offer a critique of the world through buildings we design.

Meredith: I agree and would also add that critique is much more collaborative today. There's an awareness and a willingness to work across different fields, acknowledging that executing a building design isn't the work of a singular author. There are so many people involved, and the responsibilities associated with building are distributed across an ecology of different disciplines. A successful architect can assert a vision while acknowledging the different roles and contributions of many other individuals.

Thom: Right, and I'll put a fine point on that. An architect can positively affect the world through design. You know, there are all kinds of ways an architect can be ethical, but if it doesn't show up in the building, we're not doing our part. There are lots of different hats you can put on. You can go out and be an activist. But we have a responsibility to make our beliefs and provocations manifest in the buildings that we design in addition to the ways we conduct ourselves as professionals and as citizens.

How have recent global events related to racial injustice and public health affected your approach to practice?

Meredith: In different ways, the recent reckoning with racial injustice and need for physical distancing have absolutely affected our practice and the relationships that compose our work as architects and educators. Putting buildings in the world is not the only, or most immediate, way that architects contribute to social and racial justice. It's important to pay attention to how we conduct ourselves as professionals—hiring, giving, forming collaborations, taking clients—and as teachers within an institution. So much of what sets the expectations of our profession begins in school, and each of us feels committed to shifting the culture away from what we experienced as students, where architecture was presented to us as an exclusive domain of the initiated, toward a pedagogical environment that elevates BIPOC and other marginalized voices and prioritizes anti-racist approaches to the built environment.

Thom: Regarding the COVID-19 pandemic, the repercussions are still rippling through vulnerable populations and the economy. Supply-chain problems are driving up building material costs, housing insecurity is on the rise, school-aged kids have lost a lot of ground, and despite the slowdown in travel in 2020, atmospheric carbon continues to increase at cataclysmic levels—these are some of the issues that our discipline will be contending with in years to come.

Where does your aesthetic sensibility come from? What are your sources of inspiration?

Meredith: It's a process of discovery. We begin by sorting out shared intuitions and values for a project. Our different approaches often lead us to certain aesthetics that surprise us.

Thom: And in some projects, we begin with a particular provocation that directs this process of discovery. For example, in Living Picture, we were really interested in the instantiation of a rendering in physical space. It's a really complicated thing to unpack. We all make renderings to represent buildings. But just making a building that looks like the rendering you made isn't going to deliver the experience of inhabiting a rendering. We were interested in building something that makes legible rendering techniques and rendering as a design tool. Throughout the development of this project,

Fig. 108

Fig. 109

we expanded our understanding of rendering and texture mapping. To that point, the aesthetic result of our work is often dependent on a critical inquiry into the tools and technologies we use to design and construct buildings.

Meredith: Exactly. There are often traces of digital processes in the products. There's a way in which the outcomes that are material or spatial are evidence of the particular tools we use and the way we use them. We're compelled by the ability of these specific interests to inform the aesthetic result and the experience of the environments we create.

Thom: We also really love early Frank Gehry, but we don't just want to do early Gehry. We're trying to figure out what early Gehry is in another context, using different technologies and responding to different economic forces. We're interested in architectural authorship that has an affinity for the inexpensive, the cheap—but it's an authorship that belongs to 2019, and it looks different and feels different than a Gehry project from the late seventies or the eighties.

The images you've created through these various tools are really compelling, especially to students, and especially viewed on social media. Who do you identify as your audience? Who is your work for?

Meredith: To begin, we think of students as a portion of our audience, but also architecture schools and architectural culture in general. It's one audience that we're definitely in dialogue with and aware of. But there are other audiences that are important to us as well. Currently, a lot of our work ends in representation, in images. That's not the endgame for us. The endgame for us is building, where the audience is more varied. Our hope is that our research into digital design procedures and material effects adds up to something that can be experienced by broader audiences and becomes part of architectural backgrounds that augment day-to-day activities.

Thom: We're really interested in the reality of our digital lives showing up in physical space. We are committed to not just participating in the role of digital media in contemporary culture, but also translating that into a spatial experience in a consequential way. We remain committed to the reality of buildings. We will not be satisfied with a fantastically popular Instagram page that circulates digital images everywhere. That would be fun, but we're more committed to what we can achieve through building. And we've been pleasantly surprised by the fact that potential clients have not been averse to our admittedly challenging aesthetic predilections yet. We've started to believe that if we get something built that is experimental aesthetically, it will be easier to get potential clients on board because they'll see not only what we can achieve, but also the added value of our approach.

Meredith: Also, it's important not only that our work is economically and environmentally conscious, but that we use each opportunity to experiment with off-the-shelf materials, conventional assembly systems, and familiar construction techniques. Even when operating in these territories, there's a lot of design authorship that's available to us while also being mindful of cost. Again, we want to demonstrate this added value to potential clients through built work. We are pursuing sophisticated material and aesthetic results without compromising affordability.

How do you select your source images? We see a lot of rocks and trees. Why rocks and why trees? What other types of images do you start with?

Meredith: Something we discuss a lot is how images we create interact with the context in which they are placed. For example, in Living Picture, we digitally modeled a historic theater that no longer exists. We also created renderings from that digital model in the context, and those renderings eventually became printed on vinyl in the final, full-scale construction. Living Picture was made of digital trees in dialogue with physical trees. There was a logic there regarding image selection. For us, it was a new kind of contextualism.

We are developing similar ideas in the Northwood ADU project, where the site of the existing house backs up to a wooded park. There is a scheme being developed that includes wrapping the exterior of the building with imagery that would visually merge the house with its context. For the inhabitants, there would be a blending of the real trees and the digital trees, of real sky and digital sky. On the interior, we are selecting images that would expand the sense of space. It's a very small apartment—750 square feet—and we are working on visually expanding the space through introducing an artificial horizon through imagery. There are ideas about

Fig. 110

Fig. 111

ground and sky acting as interior elements. We're working on blurring physical boundaries of space. Overall, it's about not just the content of images, but also the qualities that they can lend to the space. It all contributes to our larger interest in being playful and experimental with image production, material manipulation, and a combination of the two.

Thom: It's a great question. It's something we struggle with. We're drawn to the fact that there's simply a lot more content in a project when you saturate it with imagery. So, you probably wouldn't be asking us how we figure out where to put the bedroom. Those answers are almost evident, and far more objective than image selection. In general, we're primarily interested in what effects get produced as a result of our decisions, whether it's a rock or a tree or something else.

How does the location of each project affect the design strategy?

Thom: It's different for every project. For Detroit Reassembly Plant, we started with the initial observation that the Packard Plant wasn't really a building anymore. It was a pile of materials, and it was an image circulating in the media. It no longer functioned as a building. This describes two ways we look at almost every context. Whether we're engaging a vacant mall or an abandoned big-box or a factory that's falling apart, we often question the material reality of the object and locate the images the object produces that circulate.

Meredith: Your question also makes me think of the fact that Michigan is one context for our practice. It's not just the location for projects we've done, but the location for us—where we work and live, and also the location of the kinds of projects we hope to get to work on in the future. We're really interested in working locally. We're actively trying to get work in the area, and especially in Detroit, where there's an incredible building boom right now, some of it great and some of it not so great for the city. That's something that we want to participate in and help shape.

What has been the most rewarding moment in your professional careers thus far?

Thom: This is a silly one, but I have to say it tickles me. At the 2016 Venice Biennale, MOS made lenticular drawings. Michael Meredith was proud of making a drawing that made people move around in order to understand it. We were just sitting there, laughing, as people rocked back and forth. With Living Picture, we made a project where people had to traipse around in order to get things to visually align. We were watching people strain their necks and meander around our installation to figure out what we had done. We actually did what we set out to do with the project, which was to build a rendering in which people could walk around.

Meredith: I had a text exchange with James Wines recently.

The LADG: Claus Benjamin Freyinger and Andrew Holder

How and when did your practice start?

Andrew Holder: We started our practice when we were still students. Ben and I were in graduate school at UCLA from 2002 to 2005, and we began working on our first project together at the end of 2004. If you look at the older projects in our portfolio, you'll see stores for a ski-boot retailer called Surefoot. Surefoot in Vail, Colorado, was our first project. I don't think we intended to form a durable corporate entity at that time, and it wasn't our intention to be a practice forever. The Surefoot store was our first opportunity and was followed very quickly by a residential remodel in downtown Los Angeles and a loft building across the street from SCI-Arc. But to the original question, "How did it start?"—we were raised on a myth of how architecture firms start. You sit down and write to clarify your position in the world. After that is absolutely clear to yourself and others, you begin to work. Our experience was almost exactly the opposite—the work came first.

What does it mean to practice architecture?

Andrew: Practicing architecture means spending your time doing the things that architects do. You draw, you build models, you spin around in Rhino. This isn't a passive retreat into craft. It's a way of thinking and engaging the world. When you draw, you digest what you're seeing and you respond with any artifact that allows others to crystallize their own views.

What is the identity of your practice, and how has it changed over the years?

Andrew: We started our practice during boom years for construction in Los Angeles. It was a good time to be an architect. For the first four years we were totally consumed with work and executing projects commissioned by various clients. During the financial crisis of 2008, it became clear to us that architecture purely as a service for the market was not enough. We weren't making money anymore. The thinness of market-based incentives that we had thought would stick around forever was revealed. We needed new reasons to get out of bed in the morning, which led us back to the idea that we needed an operating theory of what architecture wants to be in the world. We asked ourselves why we do this on a very personal level, but also how architecture can engage a broader audience. It was in 2009, 2010, and 2011 when we first started thinking through architecture's relation to audience. In those years, you see the emergence of animal figures and biomorphic forms in our work. These things were essentially the most direct answer that we could imagine to the question of how architecture interfaces with a mass audience. Our answer to that was architecture sheds its status as an object, and it becomes a subject. I know how to participate in a crowd if I'm a living thing. We were doing everything we could think to do to turn architecture into a subject that could participate like other people. We reached a limit of this first set of thoughts on subjecthood with 48 Characters. That was an installation, at the University of Michigan, where we created plaster versions of balloon animals. They were beautiful, but also complex and technically tricky to make and install. We started to realize that there would need to be an alternate route to get to architecture as a subject other than formal complication.

We would have to come up with different ideas about how to make habitable space while retaining our interest in having inanimate things join audiences. It's a very simple initiating problem. And that question essentially initiated a string of investigations up to the present day where we are thinking about assemblies of objects that produce rooms.

Who exactly are you referring to when you talk about audience? Who is the audience for your work?

Andrew: We always want to have a couple of different conversations simultaneously. We are hoping that the balloon-animal projects are immediately legible with no specialized knowledge in architecture. Stuffed animals have a mode of communication that requires little to no expertise. It just requires enculturation. You have to have been a person on the planet for a while. At the same time, balloon animals have a kind of second life. They're plugged into issues in architecture that are for sophisticated audiences. That longer tale has to do with the history of complex form and architecture, and the history of the use of digital tools and a long conversation about character. What exactly that term means… It looks like Ben is joining us now.

Ben Freyinger: Hello. Sorry—I'm super late. This might be a bit tricky, given my reception and where I am.

We were talking about how your work resonates differently with different audiences. But now that we have both of you here—how do you maintain the identity of your practice considering both of you are in different locations?

Ben: Case in point.

Andrew: It'll be interesting if we have different answers to this question. Ben, what is that noise? Is that an airplane? I can assure you there is no airplane inside my office in Cambridge. Okay, so first, the geographic distance for us is profoundly clarifying. So, to revisit the history of how we started… Ben, there's incredible background noise.

Ben: I know. Hang on a second.

Andrew: Please go inside.

Ben: I'm on a job site. I'll mute my microphone when I'm not speaking.

Andrew: Great. Thank you. So, bear in mind, we started as students, which means that we didn't yet have formalized understandings of our roles. What we had was a desire to work together. It was when we started living on different coasts that we had conversations about who does what. It was that moment of specialization that also required us to have conversations about the operating theory of the practice. All of a sudden, in order to be efficient in schematic design, we needed to be constantly referring back to ideas we had about how to make space and how to use assemblies of objects loosely fit together to produce things like rooms and interior order. Those were as much theories of architecture and how it should work as they were a series of conversations regarding how to distribute labor between the two coasts, and how to clarify what Andrew does and what Ben does.

Ben: I agree. To be blunt about it, having two people with either similar ideas or productively conflicting ideas in the same room is not always productive. There's the personal growth that you need to go through in order to expand in your career and move forward and learn new things that tends to get stunted when there is someone else in the room. Independently, we've discovered that the practice can grow and that there is a need for specialization. In the end, we wear a lot of the same hats but take turns wearing them. I do a model, then you critique it; you do a model, then I respond…

Andrew: Here is an example of how, for instance, something we produce has multiple lives and becomes useful for the office. When I wrote "Notes on More," the Log piece about density, I was interested in an academic audience. But I was also writing it as a letter to our office. It was how I was structuring thoughts about design, and was asking, "Can this help give us a common understanding of how to sit down to work?" We're always growing and shrinking, so it means anywhere from two to six people are participating in schematic design. Everyone has to be extraordinarily coordinated in their work output. The essays help hold that together.

Can you talk more about the way in which the preference for using everyday objects informs your aesthetic sensibility? Also, how does this approach impact constructability and construction?

Andrew: Interesting. We haven't used the word "sensibility" a lot in our conversations with one another. But maybe we should more often, because we have definite ideas about where we want to end up in terms of how things look. We want a kind of casualness, as though materials could come together in a variety of orientations and we simply picked one of those possibilities. We want a sense that our material palette is not elevated and expensive, but is common to the point of being retrievable from a junkyard if funds are limited. We also want for the fits between things to produce an occasion for design. If things fit together too perfectly, design is discouraged. One way that we create opportunities for design is by subjecting our work to physics by frequently positioning things with respect to one another so that all of the energy and intensity is in an interface or point of contact.

Ben: We are using materials that are readily available and in some cases kind of ugly. And yes, the interface between the materials and how they respond to one another or how they coexist—that's where the invention is. The reality is that we have contractors who are looking at what we are producing. What they see is complicated or complex. We can break it down very logically, piece by piece, and explain why it isn't. But the reception of it is often "Oh, this is unusual. This is too complex to build." We can get somewhere by showing them that the parts are all familiar and we've just made small modifications to the way things are assembled, and these small adjustments add up to a big difference in appearance.

Andrew: I also want to say that the casualness and looseness is not just for its own sake. Actually, let me go back. I'm totally fine if it's casualness for its own sake. I have no need to justify it further. But maybe we have an additional possibility. One thing that starts to happen as things are loosely arrayed against one another is the production of crenellated edges, which makes it difficult to assign things to the inside or outside. Elements often fall outside of the proper territory of the house or building. This means more engagement in the surrounding context. If you can't figure out where the envelope is, you're always questioning what's around you. What belongs? What's the limit? Where are the physical lines of inclusion and exclusion? For us, that's good politics. We're trying to resort to things that have a democratic availability and low barriers to intellectual engagement. Then we arrange these things casually in arrays that don't have definite claims about what belongs where.

Given this attitude toward being democratic and inclusive, what kinds of projects do you hope to work on in the future?

Andrew: In the very immediate future, we're really interested in the suburbs and in the single-family home, which may seem a weird answer to your question. We're trying to think of ways in which the form of the house can open up and start to create shared regions with neighbors. So, imagine many versions of our project House in Los Angeles I next to one another. We'd have to imagine a different way of describing what constitutes a yard or private ownership.

Ben: We're looking at the fringe areas of Los Angeles, specifically hillside areas, which encourage invention with regard to what Andrew was saying about the concept of yard or the concept of private ownership. We want to challenge and reconsider these things.

Andrew: If you look at the larger context for House in Los Angeles I, you'll see that it's part of a series of suburbs that stretch between downtown Los Angeles and Pasadena. They're all super irregular, hillside lots. House in Los Angeles I looks kind of flat, but it's at the edge of a pretty steep hillside. What that means is that buildable area is tightly circumscribed, even though there's a lot of land per house. You can put houses only in certain spots, which leaves huge portions of the hillside unbuilt, but also given up for shared uses. The hill is covered with informal hiking trails. There are places where a publicly accessible staircase goes right over the roof of a garage. There are things like empty patches of private property that function like pocket parks for six houses. We want to be deliberate about how built form can preserve collective spaces that have already emerged and start to encourage the emergence of new collective spaces.

'ou spoke earlier of your dissatisfaction with conceptualizing architecture as eing subservient to the market. How would you position your practice in relaion to the market now? Is the market something you engage with critically?

Fig. 112

Fig. 113

Fig. 114

Fig. 115

Andrew: What the market asked of us in 2009 did not overlap with how we wanted to spend our time. We wanted personal and intellectual satisfaction that the task given to us by the open market did not demand. We wanted to do more thinking and more drawing and more model-building… and we weren't doing a lot of those things. When we talk about a reaction against an exclusively service-based practice, it's not that we were withdrawing from the market or the structure of how business works in Los Angeles. It's that we were trying to construct a viable business model with habits of life and thought and work that we found to be more humane and of interest to us in terms of the ways we wanted to live our lives. I would love to be a soldier of resistance against late capitalism, but my tools for thinking through that problem are more effective when I examine it at the scale of what I do when I get up in the morning. We're encouraged that the market is now telling us that it has niches that support our habits.

How have recent global events related to social justice and public health affected your approach to practice?

Andrew: We've doubled down on our ideas about using arrays of objects to loosen the private sphere and give room for more ambiguous collective arrangements. For us this means finding a layer of interaction underneath ideology, or maybe before it. We want a kind of low-level accommodation and interdependence among neighbors… and by neighbors, I mean things and people that are physically close to one another. Social justice needs the kinds of top-down mandate for reform that we're seeing now, but alongside this we want to develop a physical substrate for mutual dependence and shared activity. Ultimately this is about offering new models, made of physical stuff, that give the city a way to imagine itself differently.

What's been the most fulfilling moment in your professional careers thus far?

Andrew: I had a very fulfilling experience on my last site walk at House in Los Angeles I. It had been a while since I'd been out there. It was just after a heavy rain, but before the landscaping went in, so it was super muddy. My foot got stuck in one of the courtyards. I was stuck in an idea we'd only been kicking around on paper.

Ben: I'm going to play a similar card, but I'll zoom out a bit. For me, it's the physical evidence of the work. I can relate this back to Andrew's comment about how we choose to lead our lives in the office. If there's physical evidence of that work in the world, that is also the litmus test of our success in trying to bring a desire to operate, practice, and live a certain way into the market productively and reconcile those two things. I can look at it, I can touch it, and I can see it. That never gets old.

WeShouldDoItAll: Jonathan Jackson and Sarah Nelson Jackson

How did WeShouldDoItAll begin?

Jonathan Jackson: I was working at Lindy Roy's office in 2003. At that time, I was the impatient, hard-headed type—I kind of still am. I was just a junior designer, but I thought I should be leading design projects and didn't understand this idea of paying dues. I got a project with Jill Stuart, the fashion designer, on the side. She asked me to design her store in China. Working on that project occupied my nights and weekends… and eventually ended up taking a lot of weekday hours, too. I would call in sick to Lindy Roy's office so I could work on the project for Jill Stuart. I came in one day and said, "I'm feeling better from that food poisoning. What can I help out with today?" Her response was, "I'm letting you go." I was fine with this—I was ready to work on my own. I had some graphic design projects on the side and I had enough money in my pocket to the point where I was comfortable not looking for another studio to work for. I felt like I was talented enough to make it work. In the beginning there were a lot of small graphic design projects. Over time, the three-dimensional, more spatial projects came in. Slowly but surely, it worked out.

You design books, posters, storefront displays, and exhibitions. Do you imagine what you do is a form of architectural practice?

We do not see ourselves as an architecture practice. I've worked at a couple of architecture studios, and I know what an architecture practice looks like. We're different, but we borrow methodologies from architecture. For example, the idea of iteration is important, as well as open dialogue around design.

With different types of designers in the office with different areas of expertise, how do you all work together?

Sarah, my partner and wife, and I constantly look for what we call "chameleons," people who can move between different modes of design, whether that's graphics or spatial or product design. We feel that the best way to create this bridge of dialogue and procedure is to give opportunities to all of our employees to work outside of their comfort zones. And when a new project comes in, we sit with everyone in the office to discuss possible conceptual trajectories. Everyone has a say. It's a democratic environment in that way.

How have global events related to public health and widespread racial injustice affected your practice?

We're really anxious and excited to begin to tackle what it means to design spatially again. All of our spatial work was wiped out by the pandemic. The studio has been surviving off of graphic work. We have some long-term exhibitions that have been put on hold. From a sociopolitical point of view, our goal in the studio is to tell stories of cultures and people who are underrepresented and don't always have opportunities to be heard. That goal existed before the racial reckoning of 2020 and it's something that will continue beyond this moment.

We know you frequently work with Nike. How did that collaboration come about?

Fig. 116

Fig. 117

It was sheer luck. I was in their store in SoHo, in New York, one day, playing with the interactive display that lets visitors design their own shoes. These shoes I made were supposed to be ready in about a month and a half. A few weeks go by and suddenly I get a call from Nike. I pick up and say, "Wow, my shoes are done already?" The person on the other end was very confused and asked to speak to someone in the design department. Then I realized the call was from the 503 area code, which is Portland, Oregon, and I got really professional right away. It turned out to be the creative director of Nike North America. He saw our work on a design blog and thought we would be a good fit for a small graphic design project. I was completely embarrassed, but the call went really well. From graphic to exhibition design, we've done the full gamut with Nike in the twelve years we've worked with them.

We've read that you were disappointed with the vagueness of Nike's statement on Black Lives Matter. Is it important to you to reveal your political views? What gave you the confidence to speak out against Nike?

At age twenty-seven, I wouldn't have made that comment. Now, at forty-one, after having some success, I am more comfortable speaking out. Also, of those forty-one years, twelve were spent working with Nike as a consultant, as I just mentioned. Beyond that, I grew up in the eighties. Athletes like Michael Jordan and Bo Jackson, and other Black male and female athletes who are associated with Nike—they were superheroes in my eyes. Nike was so embedded in Black culture. For them to release the statement that they did was a total slap in the face, and hugely disappointing. If I didn't say anything, I would have been disappointed in myself. As someone who thought the company understood Black people, culture, street culture… It was clear to me that no one of color worked on that piece. It turned out to be true. In general, I don't feel like it's necessary for everyone and every studio to be socially and politically active, but it's a burden that Sarah and I are more than willing to take on. In the long run, people will know where we stand. If you want to work with us, great! If you don't, that's okay, too.

Fig. 118

Fig. 119

Your statement calling out Nike pointed to their lack of specificity in their response to the death of George Floyd. We're curious about your own awareness of language. How is language situated both in your work and your interactions with clients? How do you see this approach or awareness of language changing?

In order for us to be the studio that I hope for us to be, it's on Sarah and I to be flexible and adjust, and understand that language changes. Our culture is changing, and on the leading edge is where we want to be. It's important that we recognize that, in our work, we are really trying to embed ourselves in many different cultures. For example, if we're designing an exhibition about past events, we have to understand our role as storytellers. It's important to get things right. We're working on a project right now centered around immigration. The idea of a "legal" or "illegal" immigrant is totally offensive. This political way of confronting immigration is embedded in American culture, and we're constantly looking for cues within dialogue and delivery of messaging and content to make sure that how we speak, whether we are neutral or taking a stance, is appropriate, contextual, and progressive.

John Lewis introduced the concept of "living as if": "Live as if you're already there, that you're already in that community, part of that sense of one family, one house. If you visualize it, if you can even have faith that it's there, for you it is already there." What is your "as if" within the work of WeShouldDoItAll?

I would like our studio to operate as if white supremacy was eliminated. White people are not the only people who carry out white supremacy, from what I now understand. It's carried out by everyone because it is institutionalized—it's what we're taught. In a recent interview, I was asked, "What advice would you give to someone who's interested in starting their own studio?" I answered that another studio isn't needed if it's going to continue to operate under the ideals of white supremacy. There's enough of it in the world. I want to operate as if we can see the end of younger studios accepting white supremacy in the workplace.

How did what you were exposed to as a student influence your path as a designer? Does the lack of representation of the Global South in architectural school relate to your desires and goals in WeShouldDoItAll? Do you feel a responsibility to speak out about the lack of representation?

Modernism and postmodernism in Western architecture is great, amazing stuff, but to not understand what's happening in Asia, Africa, and South America is hugely problematic. What you study in architecture school is the foundation for everything. Most students are not going to have the fortitude to call out the lack of representation during their education. It just doesn't happen. We've done a disservice to everyone who has graduated from architecture school in the United States. It's shocking and sad to recognize that everything I know about design is through a white lens. There's so much more to celebrate.

Who have been the most influential figures throughout your life and career, and how has their influence affected the work you do today?

Number one is my mother, easily. She saw me drawing all the time when I was young and encouraged me to take a look at architecture. She introduced me to Frank Lloyd Wright at the tender age of eleven. I was blown away! Archea Associati in Florence was another huge influence. I did my first internship there. I found it really exciting that they were producing two magazines as an architecture studio. One was called *Audio*, which was like *Frame* magazine. The other was *Materia*. It was like *Detail*. To see that they had writers, editors, graphic designers, and architects all in house was really influential.

How much do you owe your success to luck and opportunity? How much do you owe to hard work?

This might be the toughest question of the day. I believe in luck. I believe in things that are beyond our control, that fall into our laps. Let's say sixty/forty... hard work sixty percent and luck forty percent. We've worked our asses off, so maybe I should say seventy-five percent hard work and twenty-five percent luck. We didn't have a mentor to leverage projects off of or guide us. It was hard work and a lot of trial and error and faking it until you make it.

WOJR Organization for Architecture: William O'Brien Jr.

Your undergraduate degree was in music theory, and we can see that influence in some of your work. Can you tell us about how music and music theory inspire your design work?

William (Liam) O'Brien: The relationship between music and architecture is tricky. There are easy and superficial ways to make comparisons. You often hear metaphors about music being used to describe architecture … "architecture is frozen music," for example. Most of the time, those metaphors are not so useful. Where architecture and music can benefit from being thought about concurrently is in thinking about form and formats. When I studied music theory, I was looking at Bach to understand rules he followed to organize sound. There's a lot of overlap between the way that compositions are created in terms of broad-stroke forms and repetition. Interestingly, I find a lot of corollaries between spatial composition and music theory, between the ways we think about organization of space and organization of sound. More recently, questions of symmetry and asymmetry have been coming into our architectural designs, which has me thinking about earlier work of mine as a student manipulating classical forms in music.

There's another layer to music that is not about form, but about atmosphere. When we're producing visualizations of our designs, we think a lot about trying to conjure atmospheres through referencing music. In each project, when we're doing art direction for the visualizations, there is usually a particular score that we're referencing, or a film that has a unique score we are inspired by. That's another way we're thinking about the impact of music on our work. There are qualitative aspects of music we are interested in that can have a direct corollary to the atmosphere of the architecture we create. To give an example … Melancholy or mournfulness in some of our visualizations might be attributed to a certain score. Philip Glass is somebody who comes up a lot in our conversations, as someone who produces beautiful ambient work. We attempt to produce visualizations that convey the same quiet, meditative ambiance.

We love the image of the Mask House—the one from the bridge. It's a beautiful image. It's also very melancholy. What was the score for that image?

In visualizations for the Mask House, we weren't talking about a score, but about the film *The Revenant*. It's dark, but in a different way—not so much because of the narrative, but because of the tonality. The mournfulness, something about the way that it's lit … Apparently no artificial lights were used in most if not all of that film. It likely made for a cinematographer's nightmare, but the lighting effects are really distinct from other films that try to do something similar. We were trying to capture something like that in the Mask House visualizations.

There's a backstory to that project and why we were seeking these particular effects. The house is not built, but it's a project that was supposed to be built in Ithaca. The client is a filmmaker, and his younger brother died in the lake that the house was to overlook. The project aimed to produce a threshold—a mask between the real world and another world. That other world is connected to the lake. One of the apertures in the house looks in the direction of where his brother was last seen on the lake. The project necessarily took a mournful tone, which is something conveyed in the visualizations.

Fig. 120

How do you use visualization and language to communicate not only to other architects, but also to the general public? How does your communication change when talking to people who aren't as familiar with architectural concepts and terminology?

The question of audience is so important. One of the things that any young architect learns quickly is that in order to get what you think is a deserving idea out into the world, there needs to be the ability to talk about it in many different ways. There's a necessary empathy that is required in trying to explain design work. The most difficult situations involve communicating with somebody who's cynical about architecture or sees architecture as a vanity practice. In a case like that, there are ways of speaking about the concept that make an appeal to logic—aspects like functionality or contribution to context. Whether it's functional or contextual issues, or material, social, political, cultural, formal, environmental…there are many registers that an architect needs to hit in order to communicate with the right people at the right time about the most critical aspects of a project. A built thing in the world is inherently a political act. It is a social act. It is an active form. It engages construction systems. You can go through the whole list.

We've been interviewing a lot of practices that are partnerships. The principals often cite the friction between them as a productive part of their practice—debate often spurs new ideas. We're curious how you maintain dialogue and productive friction when there's only one person leading the practice.

Just to undo that a bit… The name WOJR is not a great name for the office for a number of reasons. It is an awkward grouping of four letters, and people often think it's a radio station. Also, WOJR, which corresponds to my initials, does not accurately convey the collaborative nature of the office. I am the main principal, but there are an additional five team members right now, and they are amazing contributors. Any "productive friction" is coming through great discussions with each of them. We're trying to produce a nonhierarchical discussion that enables everyone to contribute equally. John [David Todd], who is the team member who has been here the longest amount of time—over six years now—is somebody I can have conversations with that produce what you're calling productive friction. I wouldn't even call it friction…maybe synergy, or simply great conversations that push the work forward. There's another answer to the question. We're constantly communicating with other architects and the architectural discipline at large. These conversations and debates are really helpful.

We have a question about House of Horns. We understand that it's being built atop an existing foundation, and that this condition ended up dictating, in part, the shape and size of the house. How did you work with these existing conditions when trying to design and construct the house, and what other factors informed the design and construction?

As you mentioned, there was a partially built house on the site. It was a Spanish-style mansion, with all the details that you would expect—like terra-cotta tiles, and there was about to be a lot of work on crown moldings—but these things were not reflective of the new client's values. Despite its size, the client is somebody who is quite interested in the diminutive aspects of the house, and trying to make the house as small and humble as possible. I say that while acknowledging that it's a very large house—but their aspirations are in line with ours. One of our challenges was to take the very odd, really bizarre shape of the foundation and imbue it with a different order. To do this, we created a series of different environments that were varied by the way that light might shine or be reflected within each domestic space. The "horns" that you see enable us to modulate daylighting and become the ordering device that negotiates symmetries and asymmetries in plan.

's this your first built work?

It is. We're going through an exciting transition right now. We currently have two projects that are under construction and two more that begin construction really soon. In the office we used to talk about a path toward legitimacy. As a young architect, you're always trying to become more and more legitimate, and there are all kinds of clues that it's happening. We rented an office space seven years ago. We have health insurance now. We have a payroll. We published a book of our work. There are many things that help us believe that we're becoming a legitimate office. Most recently, the clues are tied to construction of buildings we've designed. Some of our

Fig. 121

Fig. 122

more speculative ideas are finally being tested in the built environment, and we're learning a lot. Architecture is very humbling in that way. You think you are a smart architect and then you try to build something… and you realize you still have a lot to learn.

Now that you're nearing the completion of your first built work, what part of the concept to construction process have you reveled in the most?

I love the question, especially given that I was on-site last week. There are two major takeaways from my site visit that will help me answer this. One is the degree to which construction is a messy process. Despite the planning and precision that has gone into a really comprehensive set of drawings, there is an immense amount of in-the-field decision-making. You think you have everything worked out and then comes the humbling realization that there are many issues unresolved and questions left unanswered when construction begins. Whether it's a modest house or something more experimental, each act of architecture… each building is a single iteration. Everything is unique, and every aspect of the building is being figured out by a group of people in real time. The reality of building and the distance between a precise drawing set and the messiness of construction is something I quite enjoy. And the second takeaway, or another way to answer the question—in House of Horns, we have a very large marble egg that is a column in the project. I don't want to get overly romantic or poetic about it, but simply seeing something in the real that we had imagined for such a long time in the abstract was incredible. We had the luxury of going to the quarry and picking out the exact marble block that would be carved and put into the house. To be a part of the process and to be able to touch the thing that we had imagined for so long was more impactful than I could have imagined. It was really, really rewarding.

We recently read that you're now collaborating with Airbnb and Samara. Can you tell us about this new job?

Samara is a design start-up that is branched off Airbnb. It's a company with many team members who are really interested in critiquing the tech world, and who are cultural critics in general. The way that it started was that WOJR won a competition to be involved with defining the architectural design direction. It began as a consultative role. More recently, I've started in a full-time position with them and have started to build an architecture design team around me. Our current project has the ambition to offer new forms of living through architectural design, and our first offering is an architectural design system that has the capacity to be deployed in a variety of contexts. That's all I can say at the moment, but it's a project that's really reliant on architecture. It's been fascinating to brush up against engineers, storytellers, filmmakers, industrial designers, interaction designers, and lawyers ... all represented in our forty-five-person group. Samara is an interdisciplinary project, and it's getting us to think about architecture from many different approaches, which is thrilling and humbling at the same time.

Great. Thank you so much for joining us bright and early from San Francisco. We scheduled this interview thinking you'd be in Cambridge.

You're welcome—I enjoyed it! And I'm a morning person, so the timing was perfect.

Young & Ayata: Michael Young and Kutan Ayata

What does it mean to practice architecture?

Kutan Ayata: Do we have three hours? Actually, this is something I recently discussed at length in a lecture that I called "Practicing-Teaching." These two modes of operation are inseparable for us, as well as for many of our colleagues who established their offices after the recession in 2008. We actually started our office three months before the recession … we timed it perfectly! We quickly realized that traditional practice was not going to be viable for us. Our practice includes teaching, and our teaching includes practice. They're inseparable. Practicing architecture is pedagogical. It's about an exchange of ideas. Because we are primarily supported by teaching salaries, we can be very selective when it comes to our practice. Our office is a space where we actively explore our evolving curiosities about architectural potentials without too much compromise.

Was starting an office something that you always wanted to do or something that happened unexpectedly or circumstantially?

Both. I always knew I wanted to have a practice of my own. Michael would say the same thing. We worked for others for about eight years before starting our practice. The way we started was incredibly casual. Michael and I lived on 14th Street in Manhattan after we graduated. We met up one night for drinks and had an unplanned discussion about starting a firm. We had studied at Princeton at the same time, and we worked together at Reiser + Umemoto. We got along. At that time, forming a partnership was almost more of a social decision than a professional decision. We have been able to maintain the spirit of that moment—we enjoy working together, which helps us stay motivated. The answer is yes to both parts of the question: the practice came about rather unexpectedly, but it was also very intentional.

You mentioned the 2008 financial crisis. How did it affect the way you and your peers' practice?

That was a defining moment. In hindsight, it was the best thing that could have happened to us. We had real projects, real contracts, projects going into construction... and all that basically disappeared overnight. All of a sudden, no job, no income. It was obviously a moment to freak out. But we found ways to deal with the situation. That's when I started teaching, which changed the way I look at the world. The crises gave us an opportunity to slow down and contemplate our position in the discourse of capital-A Architecture. We began developing self-generated speculative projects, which to this day serve as the conceptual basis for much of our work.

Do you attribute the successes you've had—as an architect and as an office—to fortunate circumstances, or to skill and perseverance?

Again, both. Nothing happens without hard work. In the last ten years, both of us have started families, had kids... Our lives have become more and more hectic. We have less time to work. Additionally, we often teach every day of the week, at multiple schools each year, which is not common, nor easy. Before Michael earned the tenure-track position at Cooper Union, he was jumping around quite a bit, sometimes teaching at three schools in three different states in one semester. We figured out a way to make our work time more efficient in the face of all those scheduled pressures. But success doesn't happen without luck, either. We've had some luck. I still believe that in this country you're rewarded for hard work. That's what strikes me about living and working in the United States—value is assigned to sustained effort. Persistence is recognized here, and that's quite amazing.

What was the experience of starting a firm in a country where you didn't grow up?

When we started the firm, I had already been in the US for fourteen years. I came right after high school. The US was my home at that point. Now I'm quite removed from the place I come from, in the sense of customs and business … it's all very unfamiliar. I know my Turkish high school lingo, but I don't know how to operate there as an adult.

Do you think growing up in Turkey has an influence on your work, or have you been removed from where you grew up for so long that it does not affect the work?

It's hard to say. I'm sure there is an effect on some deep psychological level. It's been twenty-five years, and I've lived most of my life in the US now. But let's unpack this. When I was in Turkey, I was a die-hard skateboarder, and I always wanted to go to California. I didn't quite make it that far, but I found a partner who's from California. I tried to come to the US during high school as well. I ended up in a really small town, which was very depressing. At that moment, I didn't want to stay, but it was very clear to me that my future would be in the US. But where I come from certainly influences me. Exposure to certain conditions present in Turkey during the time I lived there definitely influence how I look at the world today.

Do architects have a responsibility to engage global issues?

You can't escape them. But I don't think architecture as a discipline is responsible for solving the world's problems. There are other issues that we are immediately engaged with, which are more disciplinary and, to us, more important, at least from the perspective of an architect. I'd like to draw the line between citizen and architect. We have our politics, we have our interests, we know where we stand. There are always voices within the discipline who claim a broader reach and express an urgency to deal with political issues. We're more interested in central disciplinary questions that operate through aesthetics, which has its own political agency.

Your answer reminds me of something you said in a 2014 talk at the Architectural League of New York, where you claimed that architecture should be separate from politics: "Architecture is not contingent; it develops its logic internally and grows from disciplinary concerns." How does this belief affect your work?

The relationship between architecture and politics is intensifying, but we have remained focused on issues internal to our discipline as a way to ensure its continual evolution. For us, it's most interesting to talk to other architects about architecture, to have deep discussions and debates about the pertinent and persistent architectural topics. Of course, architecture performs on a broader cultural platform once it's out in the world, but we believe that we have a responsibility to imagine that we can use our knowledge and tools to create new worlds rather than simply reflect and accommodate the one in which we live.

Keeping in mind this balance between disciplinary concerns and contingent considerations, how have recent global events related to social justice and public health affected your approach to practice?

Our practice, teaching, and lives are entwined with the events of our environments, and these are aesthetic, social, political, and ecological. There is a tendency to treat these as separate categories, but if any clarity has come from this year of living online, it is that these are always crossing through each other. To ignore their relations, or to act as if they can be treated in isolation, is not an option. One of the results in our daily lives of the interrelations between public health and issues of social justice has been an increase in what we should identify as bureaucracy. There have been meetings … meetings about meetings, written agreements and assurances, committees, subcommittees, and so on. The content of these meetings is not the problem—the intentions are good, and to listen, learn, discuss, and change is crucial. However, many of the issues that we are dealing with as a society, from racially biased police violence to climate emergencies to the COVID vaccine response, are exacerbated by bureaucratic structures. That we are responding to these with more bureaucracy is problematic. That architects believe that we should increase the number of bureaucratic responsibilities architecture is beholden to is problematic. Our responsibility as architects is to expose biased values within the discipline and profession and to offer, through design, alternative potentials for the built environment. We need more speculation, more creative provocation, more discursive invention, more challenges to assumed values and conventions, not more bureaucracy.

In many of your projects, there is a continuous translation between objects, drawings, and buildings. Where does this interest come from and how does it play into your work?

Michael and I are stuck in between architectural generations, which is simply a result of what was happening in architectural culture when we graduated from Princeton. We're close friends and colleagues with the generation of architects just older than us—let's call them digital formalists, or the affect and sensation generation, who focused on digital modeling, digital fabrication, and rendering—and the generation of architects younger than us, who are interested in things like figure, graphic expediency, and engagement, and who more commonly use physical models and collage. We're interested in the routines and techniques of both cohorts. When we completed graduate school, the digital project was winding down as it pertains to experimentation in an academic environment. Michael and I were never directly a part of the authorship of that project. We never rejected it, and we weren't looking to dismantle it. But we quickly realized that we were interested in engaging multiple contemporary mediums and modes of representation. We were operating through sketching, physical modeling, digital fabrication, lecturing, teaching, and writing. Our projects are intellectual pursuits as much as they are design speculations, and they are developed through and across each of those modes of operation. The combination of and translation between drawings, objects, and buildings is a way for us to combine unique mediums through which our aesthetic ideas mature.

Can you talk about this approach to design in relation to your project DL 1310? How does the building embody conceptual studies that may have first appeared in drawings or objects?

It's important to recognize that we evaluate all mediums individually. Throughout the development of DL 1310, drawings did things for us that objects could not, and vice versa. Equally important to note is that a drawing of the project by itself doesn't necessarily capture the entire idea of a project, nor does a model, nor does the building. Cumulatively, these three outputs are the project. In fact, I would argue that as much as we love to build, the building is the form of representation with the least amount of freedom in terms of articulating the architectural idea. This is because the building must account for more than a drawing or a model can—cost concerns, financing institutions, contractors, subcontractors. These aspects add more complexity. We don't think about these complexities as compromises. Rather, we recognize the addition of necessary forces beyond our control that claim partial authorship over the project. In DL 1310, the building is inspired by a range of drawings and objects we've produced over the years in addition to the ones produced for that project. All of our projects, including DL 1310, are part of a body of work with an interconnected and evolving aesthetic sensibility.

Who commissioned DL 1310? How did your relationship with the client influence the result?

The project is a collaboration between our office and Michan Architecture, an office based in Mexico City that is led by a former student of mine, Isaac Michan Daniel. We kept in touch after he graduated and moved back to Mexico, where his father owns a development company and serves as a collaborator. He called us one day a few years ago and asked us if we'd like to collaborate on a small housing project. That's how it all started. It's a relationship that developed

Fig. 123

Fig. 124

Fig. 125

through teaching that became a friendship and now a collaboration.

What has been the most rewarding moment in your practice thus far?

The office is a place where I can explore ideas freely without the pressure of economic performance. Teaching affords us the opportunity to approach practice in this way. The space academia has created for the practice is thrilling. It's an incredible luxury. To have time to think about issues that interest us and to speculate on the ways in which they become architectural … that's the biggest reward. It's incredible for Michael and me to have time to spend working on things that we love. For architecture, that's incredibly important. If you're working on a project that you're not interested in, you're not likely to do a good job. We really enjoy the day-to-day activities of the office. Because of the way we are able to practice, we remain excited and optimistic about the future and our ability to make meaningful contributions to the world through design.

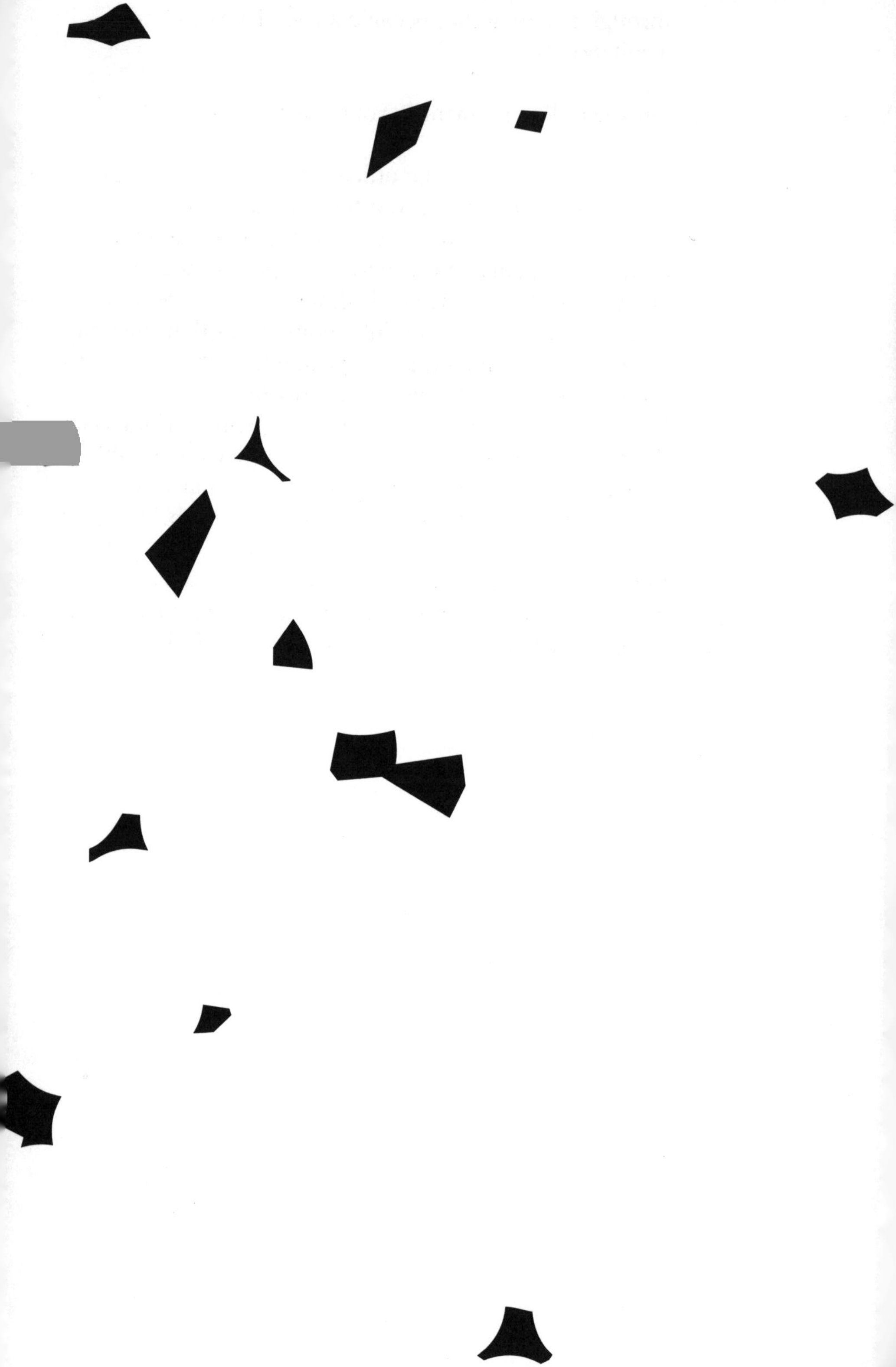

Index

Biographies

Authors and Editors:

Molly Hunker is Co-Captain of SPORTS and an Assistant Professor at Syracuse University School of Architecture.

Kyle Miller is Associate Dean and an Associate Professor at Syracuse University School of Architecture.

Contributors:

Ellie Abrons is Principal of T+E+A+M and an Associate Professor at the University of Michigan Taubman College of Architecture and Urban Planning.

Anthony Acciavatti is Principal of Somatic Collaborative and Daniel Rose (1951) Visiting Assistant Professor in Urban Studies at Yale University.

Emanuel Admassu is Partner at AD–WO and an Assistant Professor at Columbia GSAPP.

Paul Andersen is Director of Independent Architecture and a Clinical Associate Professor at the UIC School of Architecture.

Kutan Ayata is Partner at Young & Ayata and an Associate Professor and Vice Chair at UCLA AUD.

Jennifer Bonner is Director of MALL and an Associate Professor at Harvard GSD.

Shumi Bose is a Senior Lecturer at UAL Central Saint Martins and Founder of Holdspace Architecture.

Brennan Buck is Principal at FreelandBuck and a Senior Critic at Yale School of Architecture.

Tei Carpenter is Founder and Director at Agency—Agency.

Tom Carruthers is Partner at Dream The Combine and an Assistant Professor of Practice at Cornell University AAP.

Mollie Claypool is Co-Founder and CEO at AUAR Ltd and an Associate Professor at Bartlett UCL.

Felipe Correa is Principal at Somatic Collaborative and the Shea Professor at the University of Virginia.

Karolina Czeczek is a Principal at Only If and a Critic at Yale School of Architecture.

Devin Dobrowolski is Director of Applied Research Projects at Somatic Collaborative and an Assistant Professor at the University of Virginia School of Architecture.

Ivi Diamantopoulou is Principal of New Affiliates and Visiting Faculty and Princeton University Schoo of Architecture.

Iben Falconer is Global Marketing and Business Development Leader at SOM.

Benjamin Freyinger is Co-Principal at The LADG and a Lecturer at UCLA AUD.

Adam Fure is Principal of T+E+A+M and an Associa Professor at the University of Michigan Taubman College of Architecture an Urban Planning.

Adam Frampton is a Principal at Only If and an Adjunct Assistant Professor at Columbia GSAPP.

David Freeland is a Principal at FreelandBuck and Studio Faculty at SCI-Arc.

Anda French is a Principal at French2D and Visiting Faculty at the Princeton University School of Architecture.

Jenny French is a Principal at French2D and an Assistant Professor of Practice at Harvard GSD.

Beatrice Galilee is Founder and Executive Director at The World Around.

Julia Gamolina is Founder and Editor-in-Chief at *Madame Architect* and an Associate Principal and Business Development Director at Ennead Architects.

Jia Yi Gu is Co-Director of Spinagu and Director and Curator of MAK Center for Art and Architecture.

Andrew Holder is Co-Principal at The LADG and Associate Professor and MArch I Program Director at Harvard GSD.

Elisa Iturbe is Principal at Outside Development and an Assistant Professor at The Cooper Union.

Jonathan Jackson is Partner at WeShouldDoItAll.

Jaffer Kolb is a Principal at New Affiliates and an Adjunct Assistant Professor at Columbia GSAPP.

Wei-Han Vivian Lee is a Principal at LAMAS and an Assistant Professor at University of Toronto Daniels Faculty.

Helen Leung is Executive Director at LA Más.

James Macgillivray is a Principal at LAMAS and a Lecturer at University of Toronto Daniels Faculty.

Ajay Manthripragada directs an independent office and is Design Critic in Architecture at Harvard GSD.

Meredith Miller is a Principal of T+E+A+M and an Associate Professor at the University of Michigan Taubman College of Architecture and Urban Planning.

Thom Moran is a Principal of T+E+A+M and Associate Professor at the University of Michigan Taubman College of Architecture and Urban Planning.

Jess Myers is an Assistant Professor of Architecture at RISD and the creator of the *Here There Be Dragons* podcast.

Sarah Nelson Jackson is Partner at WeShouldDoItAll.

Jennifer Newsom is Partner at Dream The Combine and an Assistant Professor at Cornell University AAP.

William O'Brien Jr. is Principal at WOJR – Organization for Architecture and an Associate Professor at MIT Architecture.

Anna Puigjaner Baberà is Co-Founder at MAIO and an Assistant Professor of Practice at Columbia GSAPP.

Gilles Retsin is Co-Founder and CTO at AUAR Ltd and an Associate Professor at Bartlett UCL.

Justin Rice is a Partner at Knowhow Shop.

Bryony Roberts is Principal at Bryony Roberts Studio and an Adjunct Assistant Professor at Columbia GSAPP.

Troy Schaum is Partner at SCHAUM/SHIEH and an Associate Professor at Rice University School of Architecture.

Jack Self is Director at REAL and Editor-in-Chief at *Real Review*.

Rosalyne Shieh is Partner at SCHAUM/SHIEH and an Assistant Professor at MIT Architecture.

Maxi Spina is Co-Director of Spinagu and Studio Faculty at SCI-Arc.

Oana Stănescu is founder of Oana Stănescu Studio and a Design Critic at Harvard GSD. Kagan Taylor is a Partner at Knowhow Shop.

Elizabeth Timme is Director of Development and Design at Office of: Office.

Jen Wood is Partner at AD–WO.

Michael Young is Partner at Young & Ayata and an Assistant Professor at The Cooper Union.

Graphic Designer:

Cat Wentworth is a graphic designer at the Yale University School of Art.

Copyeditor:

Jayne Kelley is an editor and writer as well as a Clinical Assistant Professor at the UIC School of Architecture.

Image Credits

AD–WO:

13. Two Markets: Isuzu, Addis Ababa, Ethiopia, 2019. Courtesy AD–WO.
14. Two Markets: Ritual, Addis Ababa, Ethiopia, 2019. Courtesy AD–WO.
15. Two Markets: Perimeter, Addis Ababa, Ethiopia, 2019. Courtesy AD–WO.
16. Two Markets: Gap, Dar es Salaam, Tanzania, 2019. Courtesy AD–WO.
17. Immeasurability: ATL Bricks. Reconstructions: Architecture and Blackness in America, MoMA. New York, New York, 2021. Photograph by Naho Kubota. Courtesy AD–WO.
18. Immeasurability: ATL Bricks (Detail). Reconstructions: Architecture and Blackness in America, MoMA. New York, New York, 2021. Photograph by Naho Kubota. Courtesy AD–WO.
19. Immeasurability (Collage). Reconstructions: Architecture and Blackness in America, MoMA. New York, New York, 2021. Photograph by Naho Kubota. Courtesy AD–WO.

Agency—Agency:

20. New Public Hydrant (Hydrant on Tap, Hydrants for All, Hydration Space), New York, New York, 2018. Collaboration with Chris Woebken. Courtesy Agency—Agency and Chris Woebken.
21. New Public Hydrant (Axonometric Drawings), New York, New York, 2018. Collaboration with Chris Woebken. Courtesy Agency—Agency and Chris Woebken.
22. Street Remodel (with Hydrant on Tap; Green Escapes; Operable Transitions), 2021. Courtesy Agency—Agency.
23. Street Remodel, 2021. Courtesy Agency—Agency.

Ajay Manthripragada:

24. On Off-squares, 2019. Courtesy Ajay Manthripragada.
25. Page House, Berkeley, California, 2017. Photograph by Naho Kubota. Courtesy Ajay Manthripragada.
26. Page House, Berkeley, California, 2017. Photograph by Naho Kubota. Courtesy Ajay Manthripragada.

AUAR:

27. Block West, Bristol, United Kingdom, 2020. Photograph by NAARO. Courtesy AUAR.
28. Block West, Bristol, United Kingdom, 2020. Photograph by NAARO. Courtesy AUAR.
29. Block West, Bristol, United Kingdom, 2020. Photograph by NAARO. Courtesy AUAR.
30. House Block, London, United Kingdom, 2021. Courtesy AUAR.
31. House Block, London, United Kingdom, 2021. Courtesy AUAR.

Beatrice Galilee:

32. The World Around, The Times Center, New York, New York, 2020. Photo by Noam Galai/ Getty Images for The World Around.

Bryony Roberts Studio:

33. Corpeo Estraneo (with Melissa Lohman), Piazza del Campidoglio, Rome, Italy, 2016. Photograph by Claudia Pajewski. Courtesy Bryony Roberts Studio.
34. Corpeo Estraneo (with Melissa Lohman), Piazza del Campidoglio, Rome, Italy, 2016. Photograph by Antonio Convisto. Courtesy Bryony Roberts Studio.
35. Soft Civic, Exhibit Columbus, Columbus, Indiana, 2019. Photograph by Hadley Fruits. Courtesy Bryony Roberts Studio.
36. Soft Civic, Exhibit Columbus, Columbus, Indiana, 2019. Photograph by Hadley Fruits. Courtesy Bryony Roberts Studio.
37. Restorative Ground (with WIP Collaborative), Hudson Square, New York, New York, 2021. Photograph by Sam Lahoz. Courtesy WIP Collaborative.
38. Restorative Ground (with WIP Collaborative), Hudson Square, New York, New York, 2021. Courtesy WIP Collaborative.

Dream The Combine:

39. Columbus Columbia Colombo Colón, Exhibit Columbus, Columbus, Indiana, 2021. Photograph by Hadley Fruits. Courtesy Dream the Combine.
40. Columbus Columbia Colombo Colón, Exhibit Columbus, Columbus, Indiana, 2021. Photograph by Hadley Fruits. Courtesy Dream the Combine.
41. Hide & Seek, MoMA PS1 2018 Young Architects Program, Long Island City, New York, 2018. Photography by Pablo Enriquez. Courtesy MoMA PS1 and Dream the Combine.
42. Hide & Seek, MoMA PS1 2018 Young Architects Program, Long Island City, New York, 2018. Photography by Pablo Enriquez. Courtesy MoMA PS1 and Dream the Combine.

FreelandBuck:

43. Second House (Image Object), 2018. Courtesy FreelandBuck.
44. Parallax Gap, Renwick Gallery, Smithsonian American Art Museum, Washington, DC, 2017. Photography by Kevin Kunstadt. Courtesy FreelandBuck.
45. Second House, Los Angeles, California, 2018. Photography by Eric Staudenmaier. Courtesy FreelandBuck.
46. Second House, Los Angeles, California, 2018. Photography by Eric Staudenmaier. Courtesy FreelandBuck.

French 2D:

47. Kendall Square Garage Screens, Boston, Massachusetts, 2019. Photograph by John Horner. Courtesy French 2D.
48. Outlier Lofts, Boston, Massachusetts, 2018. Photograph by John Horner. Courtesy French 2D.
49. Outlier Lofts, Boston, Massachusetts, 2018. Photograph by John Horner. Courtesy French 2D.
50. Outlier Lofts, Boston, Massachusetts, 2018. Photograph by John Horner, virtual staging by Spotless Agency. Courtesy French 2D.

Independent Architecture:

51. Motherhouse, Denver, Colorado, 2020. Photography by James Florio. Courtesy Independent Architecture.
52. Motherhouse (Plan), 2020. Courtesy Independent Architecture.
53. Motherhouse (Section). 2020. Courtesy Independent Architecture.
54. Motherhouse, Denver, Colorado, 2020. Photography by James Florio. Courtesy Independent Architecture.
55. Motherhouse, Denver, Colorado, 2020. Photography by James Florio. Courtesy Independent Architecture.
56. Motherhouse, Denver, Colorado, 2020. Photography by James Florio. Courtesy Independent Architecture.

Jack Self:

57. *Real Review* (Cover Images). Courtesy Jack Self.
58. Acid House (Rendering), Milan Triennale, Milan, Italy, 2020. Courtesy Jack Self.
59. Acid House (Rendering). Courtesy Jack Self.
60. Exceptional House (Rendering), 2020. Courtesy Jack Self.
61. Exceptional House (Rendering), 2020. Courtesy Jack Self.

Knowhow Shop:

62. Lighthouse Office, Los Angeles, California, 2018. Photograph by Stephen Schauer. Courtesy Knowhow Shop.
63. Altadena Listening Studio, Altadena, California, 2019. Photograph by Stephen Schauer. Courtesy Knowhow Shop.
64. Altadena Listening Studio, Altadena, California, 2019. Photograph by Stephen Schauer. Courtesy Knowhow Shop.

LA Más and Office of: Office:

65. The Backyard Homes Project (Illustration), Los Angeles, California, 2017. Courtesy LA Más.
66. The Backyard Homes Project (Illustration), Los Angeles, California, 2017. Courtesy LA Más.
67. Storefronts, LA (Santa Luna), Los Angeles, California. Courtesy LA Más.
68. Storefronts, LA (Maya), Los Angeles, California. Courtesy LA Más.

LAMAS:

69. Eat Food, The Stop Night Market, Oyster Boy, Toronto, Ontario, 2015. Courtesy LAMAS.
70. Townships Farmhouse, 2017, North Hatley, Quebec. Photograph by Stéphane Groleau and Laetitia Boudaud. Courtesy LAMAS.
71. Townships Farmhouse, 2017, North Hatley, Quebec. Photograph by Stéphane Groleau and Laetitia Boudaud. Courtesy LAMAS.
72. Townships Farmhouse, 2017, North Hatley, Quebec. Photograph by Stéphane Groleau and Laetitia Boudaud. Courtesy LAMAS.

MAIO:

73. 110 Rooms, Barcelona, Spain, 2016. Courtesy MAIO.
74. 110 Rooms, Barcelona, Spain, 2016. Courtesy MAIO.
75. 110 Rooms (Plan), Barcelona, Spain, 2016. Courtesy MAIO.
76. 110 Rooms, Barcelona, Spain, 2016. Courtesy MAIO.

MALL:

77. Haus Gables, Atlanta, Georgia, 2018. Photography by NAARO. Courtesy MALL.
78. Haus Gables (Material Palette). Courtesy MALL.
79. Haus Gables, Atlanta, Georgia, 2018. Photography by NAARO. Courtesy MALL.
80. Haus Gables, Atlanta, Georgia, 2018. Photography by NAARO. Courtesy MALL.
81. Haus Gables, Atlanta, Georgia, 2018. Photography by NAARO. Courtesy MALL.

New Affiliates:

82. Tunbridge Winter Cabin, Tunbridge, Vermont, 2017. Photograph by Michael Vahrenwald / Esto. Courtesy New Affiliates.
83. Tunbridge Winter Cabin, Tunbridge, Vermont, 2017. Photograph by Michael Vahrenwald / Esto. Courtesy New Affiliates.
84. Tunbridge Winter Cabin, Tunbridge, Vermont, 2017. Photograph by Michael Vahrenwald / Esto. Courtesy New Affiliates.
85. Tunbridge Winter Cabin, Tunbridge, Vermont, 2017. Photograph by Michael Vahrenwald / Esto. Courtesy New Affiliates.

Oana Stănescu:

86. Yeezus Stage (by Family New York with Kanye West, Vanessa Beecroft), 2014. Courtesy Family New York. Credit: We believe that Virgil Abloh took this photograph, but cannot confirm as a result of his passing in 2021.
87. Off-WhiteTM HK (by Family New York), Hong Kong, 2014. Courtesy Family New York.
88. Off-WhiteTM HK (by Family New York), Hong Kong, 2014. Courtesy Family New York.
89. PLUS Pool (Rendering), New York, New York. Courtesy Friends of Plus Pool.

Only If:

90. Narrow House, Brooklyn, New York, 2021. Photograph by Iwan Baan. Courtesy Only If.
91. Narrow House, Brooklyn, New York, 2021. Photograph by Iwan Baan. Courtesy Only If.
92. Narrow House, Brooklyn, New York, 2021. Photograph by Naho Kubota. Courtesy Only If.
93. Narrow House, Brooklyn, New York, 2021. Photograph by Naho Kubota. Courtesy Only If.

Outside Development:

94. Meeting Room (Illustration), San Ysidro, California, 2018. Courtesy Outside Development.
95. Laundry Garden (Illustration), San Ysidro, California, 2018. Courtesy Outside Development.
96. Tree Planting (Illustration), San Ysidro, California, 2018. Courtesy Outside Development.

SCHAUM/SHIEH:

97. White Oak Music Hall, Houston, Texas, 2016. Photograph by Peter Molick. Courtesy SCHAUM/SHIEH.
98. Shenandoah House, Lexington, VA, 2022. Photograph by Naho Kubota. Courtesy SCHAUM/SHIEH.
99. Shenandoah House, Lexington, VA, 2022. Photograph by Naho Kubota. Courtesy SCHAUM/SHIEH.
100. Shenandoah House, Lexington, VA, 2022. Photograph by Naho Kubota. Courtesy SCHAUM/SHIEH.

Somatic Collaborative:

101. Proposed intermodal hub connecting small watercraft with the Manaus Central Station (Rendering), Venice Biennale of Architecture, Venice, Italy, 2021. Courtesy Somatic Collaborative.
102. The Switchback Housing Typology seen from the Mindu River in Manaus (Rendering), Venice Biennale of Architecture, Venice, Italy, 2021. Courtesy Somatic Collaborative.
103. Cultural Center and Observation Deck along the Mindu River in Manaus (Rendering), Venice Biennale of Architecture, Venice, Italy, 2021. Courtesy Somatic Collaborative.

Spinagu:

104. Thick, SCI-Arc Gallery, Los Angeles, California, 2017. Photograph by Joshua White. Courtesy Spinagu.
105. Thick, SCI-Arc Gallery, Los Angeles, California, 2017. Photograph by Joshua White. Courtesy Spinagu.
106. Piaggio House, Rosario, Argentina, 2019. Photograph by Javier Agustin Rojas. Courtesy Spinagu.
107. Piaggio House, Rosario, Argentina, 2019. Photograph by Javier Agustin Rojas. Courtesy Spinagu.

T+E+A+M:

108. Living Picture, Ragdale Foundation, Lake Forest, Illinois, 2017. Courtesy T+E+A+M.
109. Living Picture, Ragdale Foundation, Lake Forest, Illinois, 2017. Courtesy T+E+A+M.
110. Additional Address (Model Photograph), Adjacencies, New Haven, Connecticut, 2018. Courtesy T+E+A+M.
111. Additional Address (Model Photograph), Adjacencies, New Haven, Connecticut, 2018. Courtesy T+E+A+M.

The LADG:

112. House in Los Angeles I, Los Angeles, California, 2017. Photograph by Saam Gabbay and Injinash Unshin. Courtesy The LADG.
113. House in Los Angeles I, Los Angeles, California, 2017. Photograph by Saam Gabbay and Injinash Unshin. Courtesy The LADG.
114. House in Los Angeles I, Los Angeles, California, 2017. Photograph by Saam Gabbay and Injinash Unshin. Courtesy The LADG.

WeShouldDoItAll:

115. Nike Tech Pack, NYC, NY, 2015. Photograph by Floto+Warner. Courtesy WeShouldDoItAll.
116. Nike Tech Pack, NYC, NY, 2015. Photograph by Floto+Warner. Courtesy WeShouldDoItAll.
117. Nike Kevin Durant 8, Nationwide, 2015. Courtesy WeShouldDoItAll.
118. Nike Kevin Durant 8, Nationwide, 2015. Courtesy WeShouldDoItAll.

WOJR: Organization for Architecture:

119. Mask House (Rendering), Ithaca, New York, 2017. Courtesy WOJR: Organization for Architecture.

120. House of Horns (Rendering), Los Altos, California, 2017. Courtesy WOJR: Organization for Architecture.
121. House of Horns (Rendering), Los Altos, California, 2017. Courtesy WOJR: Organization for Architecture.

Young & Ayata:

122. DL 1310 Apartments (with Michan Architecture), Mexico City, Mexico, 2020. Photograph by Rafael Gomez. Courtesy Young & Ayata.
123. DL 1310 Apartments (with Michan Architecture), Mexico City, Mexico, 2020. Photograph by Rafael Gomez. Courtesy Young & Ayata.
124. DL 1310 Apartments (with Michan Architecture), Mexico City, Mexico, 2020. Photograph by Rafael Gomez. Courtesy Young & Ayata.

Interview Credits

Biyun Zhang and Hao Zhou interviewed Brennan Buck and David Freeland on September 19, 2019.

Tianyi Hang and Yifei Luo interviewed Paul Andersen on September 19, 2019.

Genevieve Dominiak and Hannah Michaelson interviewed Ivi Diamantopoulou and Jaffer Kolb on September 26, 2019.

Aditya Jain and Stewart Tillyer interviewed Karolina Czeczek and Adam Frampton on September 26, 2019.

Sanat Dangol and Peter Maffei interviewed Meredith Miller and Thom Moran on October 3, 2019.

Ella Arne and Eliza Williamson interviewed Claus Benjamin Freyinger and Andrew Holder on October 3, 2019.

Rachael Gaydos and Kate Kini interviewed Troy Schaum and Rosalyne Shieh on October 10, 2019.

Félix Samó and Tirta Teguh interviewed Kutan Ayata on October 10, 2019.

Alise Lamothe and Hanneke van Deursen interviewed William O'Brien Jr. on October 17, 2019.

Isabella Calidonio and Tanvi Rao interviewed Jennifer Bonner on October 17, 2019.

Anna Korneeva and Irmak Turanli interviewed Wei-Han Vivian Lee and James Macgillivray on October 31, 2019.

Maria Daniela Andino Donoso and Demitri Gadzios interviewed Jia Yi Gu and Maxi Spina on October 31, 2019.

Jessica Libby and Hao Zheng interviewed Anda French and Jenny French on November 7, 2019.

Sachio Badham and Tommy Wang interviewed Anna Puigjaner on November 7, 2019.

Zain Elwakil and Brittany Leung interviewed Jack Self on September 16, 2020.

Kristabel Chung and Mary Kate Krege interviewed Jonathan Jackson on September 23, 2020.

Jamely Ramos and Eryn Young interviewed Helen Leung and Elizabeth Timme on September 30, 2020.

Dylan Crean and Jesse Valgora interviewed Oana Stănescu on October 7, 2020.

Coumba Kanté and Janani Suriyanarayanan interviewed Iben Falconer on October 14, 2020.

Coumba Kanté and Janani Suriyanarayanan interviewed Julia Gamolin on October 14, 2020.

undhra Aggarwal and c Rovensky interviewed in Rice and Kagan lor on October 21, 20.

vani Doshi and Aaron ss interviewed Bryony berts on October 28, 20.

nessa Poe and Oswal ez interviewed Beatrice ilee on November 4, 20.

lly Hunker and Kyle ler interviewed Shumi se on June 17, 2021.

lly Hunker and Kyle ler interviewed Elisa rbe on June 17, 2021.

lly Hunker and Kyle ler interviewed Ajay nthripragada on June 2021.

lly Hunker and Kyle ler interviewed Tom ruthers and Jennifer wsom on June 24, 2021.

lly Hunker and Kyle ler interviewed Tei rpenter on July 1, 2021.

lly Hunker and Kyle ller interviewed Anthony ciavatti, Felipe Correa, d Devin Dobrolowski on y 1, 2021.

lly Hunker and Kyle ller interviewed Mollie aypool and Gilles Retsin July 8, 2021.

lly Hunker and Kyle ller interviewed Jess vers on July 15, 2021

lly Hunker and Kyle ller interviewed nanuel Admassu and Jen ood on July 15, 2021.

Notes:

Interviews conducted between September 2019 and November 2020 were conducted by Syracuse University School of Architecture students enrolled in ARC 500: Building Practice, a professional elective taught by Molly Hunker and Kyle Miller.

With the exception of the interview with Brennan Buck and David Freeland on September 19, 2019, which took place in Slocum Hall at Syracuse University, all interviews were conducted using Zoom.

In 2021, the 2019 interviewees were presented two additional questions to answer; 1) What does it mean to practice architecture? and 2) How have recent global events tied to public health and social justice affected your approach to practice?

All interviews were edited by Molly Hunker and Kyle Miller for clarity.

All interviews were copyedited by Jayne Kelley.

Published by
Applied Research and Design Publishing
An Imprint of ORO Editions
Gordon Goff, Publisher

www.appliedresearchanddesign.com
info@appliedresearchanddesign.com

Project Manager
Jake Anderson

Authors and Editors
Molly Hunker
Kyle Miller

Associate Editor
Jayne Kelley

Design
Cat Wentworth

10 9 8 7 6 5 4 3 2 First Edition

ISBN 978-1-957183-49-7

Color Separations and Printing
ORO Group Ltd.

Printed in China.

International Distribution:
www.appliedresearchanddesign.com/distribution

AR+D Publishing makes a continuous effort to minimize the overall carbon footprint of its publications. As part of this goal, AR+D, in association with Global ReLeaf, arranges to plant trees to replace those used in the manufacturing of the paper produced for its books. Global ReLeaf is an international campaign run by American Forests, one of the world's oldest nonprofit conservation organizations. Global ReLeaf is American Forests' education and action program that helps individuals, organizations, agencies, and corporations improve the local and global environment by planting and caring for trees.